JOHN TIPLER

CHARTWELL
BOOKS, INC.

TRUCKS

Published by

CHARTWELL BOOKS, INC.

A Division of BOOK SALES, INC.

114 Northfield Avenue
Edison, New Jersey 08837

ISBN: 0-7858-1090-0

Editorial and design by
Amber Books Ltd
Bradley's Close
74-77 White Lion Street
London N1 9PF

Printed in Italy

ACKNOWLEDGEMENTS

Thanks are due to all who helped with the compilation of this book. They are: Nigel Andrews, Workshop Manager of Duffield Volvo of Norwich, who briefed me on the evolution of truck mechanicals and let me borrow some of his personal archives; truck industry specialist Dr Paul Nieuwenhuis of Cardiff University Business School for help with reference material; Dominique Brun of Fondation Marius Berliet; Amber Rowe and Mike Schram for photography of US trucks – his thanks go to: Red Erwin and Blain Bennett of Can-Win Truck Sales, Rexdale ON; George English, Don Hope, Peter McGill, Dale Billington and Bob Trimble for help with the antique trucks; Mike McDonald and Cheri Colgan of Starship Transportation Ltd, Mississauga ON; Bob Meilleur of Polymer Distribution Inc., Milton ON; Hino Truck Centre, Missisauga ON; Premier Peterbilt, Brampton ON. And representing the truck industry: Les Bishop of MAN Truck and Bus UK; Malcolm Little of Eddie Stobart Ltd; Lisbeth Andersson of Volvo Truck Corporation, Gothenburg; Jason Metcalf of Dennis Specialist Vehicles; Bill Brookes of ERF Ltd; Bob Hoare of Fiat UK; Spencer Harrop of Foden Trucks; Simon Sproule of Ford Corporate Affairs, Detroit; Mrs Daelemans of Hino Motors Europe; Helen Tennant of Iveco Ford Truck Ltd; John Mies of Mack; Ian Norwell, Mercedes-Benz (UK) Ltd; Robin Dickeson of Renault V.I.; Phil Sampson; Jackie Burr of Scania GB Ltd; Ashley Proctor of Seddon Atkinson Vehicles Ltd and Dennis Robertson of Road Master Haulage, Sydney.

My old friend Paul Roseblade snapped the cover of the Commander Cody LP, and my eldest daughter Keri and her friends Jane and Joanne carried out a little background research into the trucking business. And not forgetting project editor Helen Wilson, picture researcher Samantha Nunn and copy-editor Chris McNab at Amber Books Ltd who put it all together.

CONTENTS

INTRODUCTION

Love them or hate them, trucks are a feature of everyday life, no matter where you live. In the city they transport every kind of product from depots to stores to people's front doors. In remote regions they can literally be a lifeline, bringing vital supplies across the wilderness to far-flung communities. They're also involved in construction work, used by the emergency services, utility companies and the military. So they come in all shapes and sizes and all the colours of the rainbow.

Perhaps nowhere is the romance of trucking kept alive more than in the USA, where the sight of huge classic trucks rolling into a truck-stop at sunset, one after another, is truly poignant, a vision intensified as their drivers lovingly polish up some chrome detail before heading off again after their break. It's an image that transcends all other freight hauling situations, although most truckers the world over take pride in their vehicle's appearance.

In the 1970s, the romance of trucking received a boost among the general public with the movie Convoy starring Kris Kristofferson accompanied by plenty of esoteric banter on CB radios. Trucking anthems boomed out from the hippest hi-fis – tunes like 'Willin'' by Little Feat, 'Breaker Breaker' by the Outlaws, and the memorable LP *Hot Licks Cold Steel and Truckers' Favourites*, featuring the unforgettable lament 'Mama Hated Diesels So Bad' by Commander Cody and the Lost Planet Airmen. Sounds a bit weird? There were plenty more where they came from. Trucks and trucking were hip, and were filtering into popular culture as

Trucks come in all shapes and sizes and are an everyday fact of life. Manufacturers produce models for a host of different tastes, like this RD Series Mack cement mixer.

the perception of truckers as swaggering highway desperadoes gained romantic cachet. The irony was that trucks themselves had just started to get boring: standardisation and regulation meant they were all starting to look pretty similar.

A decade on, classic trucks were starting to be revered and personified. And while GMC trucks were celebrated in the US *Cannonball* TV series, British viewers were treated to a series dedicated to classic models, presented by the ebullient pop personality, John Peel, demonstrating once and for all that trucks were well established in the public consciousness.

LIFELINE

On the world stage the truck – or in English 'old money', the lorry – takes a wide variety of forms. From lightweight pickups, which are a separate culture, to US class 8 heavyweights, trucks are an inescapable way of life, accessing goods and freight door-to-door, in a way that railways and water transport cannot match. The truck is a veritable lifeline in remoter areas, and is celebrated in Afghanistan and Pakistan with wild paint schemes on the cab.

India is blessed with a host of motor manufacturers, many of which produce designs based on presses and jigs acquired from other countries. The Hindustan J6 looks familiar? That's because it's based on a 1950s Bedford, and runs with a 5.4-litre (329-cubic inch) 112bhp diesel engine and four- or five-speed gearbox. Genoto in Turkey builds a similar vehicle, while another Indian truck maker, Tata, bases its products on Mercedes-Benz designs, of both cab-over-engine (COE) and conventional layouts. The Premier Company makes the Perkins-engined PFR 122SF Roadmaster, and other Indian truck makers are Ashok Leyland and Shakti, which has connections with the German MAN concern.

The evolution of the trucking industry has to an extent followed the fortunes of the prevailing global economy and the social upheavals of the twentieth century. It was not until well into the century's second decade that the horse and cart were gradually replaced by the motorised wagon, particularly in the USA. The first motor vehicles were only capable of carrying a couple of people, but it wasn't long before proper load carriers came along. It's fascinating to trace long and distinguished family trees, and a handful of the pioneers are still active today, although they may have been swallowed up within some giant corporation.

A typical truck producer that had its roots in steam power was the British company Thornycroft. Its first effort was made in 1896 and saw service in the Boer War. In 1902, Thornycroft switched to making petrol-engined trucks, of which the J-type was used by the British Army in the First World War.

FLATBED

Taking a capacity of 2 to 5 tonnes as the benchmark for trucks of around 1903 – that's very modest by comparison with today's big rigs – the first trucks worthy of the name were made by Diamond T, Rapid, Mack, Reo, Studebaker and Saurer. Their subsequent products would go on to become classics. In appearance they were nothing more than a flatbed wagon with an engine. The driver usually sat directly over the engine, perched on nothing more sophisticated than a wooden bench, and was totally unprotected from the elements. It used to be a common sight in the 1950s to see rolling chassis being delivered in this way, the exposed driver wearing goggles and clad in wet-weather gear, but this was the norm in the days when cabs and creature comforts were as yet unheard of.

The first US truck show was staged in Chicago in 1907. Many of the

The romance of trucking culture was manifest in popular music, such as this early 1970s US 'country rock' LP by Commander Cody and the Lost Planet Airmen, which featured a Peterbilt conventional model 359 'Little Gypsy' tanker on the album sleeve. The most memorable track was 'Mama Hated Diesels So Bad'.

customers were farmers, and in agricultural areas commercial wagons known as high wheelers were popular. International Harvester, followed by Brockway, Cortland, Riker and Winton, was the first company to introduce these light delivery wagons, characterised by tall spoke wheels and a rear cargo platform. Their ample ground clearance enabled them to take dirt roads and rutted tracks in their stride. Other manufacturers concentrated on a more basic concept that placed the engine under the driver's seat and, until roughly 1914, this configuration was standard. But almost overnight most truck makers adopted a new layout, placing the engine ahead of the cab. This became known as the conventional or normal-control configuration, and it would continue to be the recognised shape of trucks for the next 20 years.

In 1912, there were no fewer than 461 commercial motor manufacturers in the USA, and over the decades this number would rise even further, to well over 2000 in total.

It was Henry Ford's inception of an assembly line manufacturing system that gave the USA the lead in the truck production stakes. The first dedicated truck assembly line was set up at Ford's Dearborn plant, Michigan, in 1914.

GREAT WAR

The event that really gave a boost to production and influenced the design and general acceptance of motor trucks was the outbreak of the First World War. Between 1914 and 1918, notably in Europe, the demand for simple but reliable heavy-duty trucks of American manufacture increased dramatically and, as a consequence, both Mack and White shipped thousands of trucks to France and England. The war was also responsible for the introduction of the universal USA truck chassis, which was produced by a number of different truck manufacturers. The aesthetics of these US models may not have been very pleasing, but they proved honest workhorses and performed remarkably well for that time, even in the most gruelling circumstances. Before the war trucks had only ventured

Leyland is one of Britain's oldest makes, going back to 1907, and its products are to be found all over the world. When a new cab-over range appeared in 1948, conventional Super Beaver and Super Hippo models were made for export only.

occasionally beyond the boundaries of built-up areas. One reason for this was the lack of decent highways, and it was only after the war that the US national highway system took shape. With the help of surplus army trucks, which were donated to operators in various states by the Federal Government, road transport took a big leap forward in the early 1920s. Ex-army wagons, particularly with four-wheel drive, were put to good use. Equipped with scrapers and tipping bodies, they proved invaluable in the construction of new roads across the country.

Typical of established British makes around at the time were AEC and Albion and Commer. AEC was based at Southall, Middlesex, but started production in Walthamstow in 1912 with buses.

One of the oldest British makes was Albion, founded in Glasgow in 1899.

Commer – or Commercial Cars – started in 1905 with a 4-tonne truck with iron-shod wheels.

TRADITIONAL CONSTRUCTION

The production of civilian trucks had taken a back seat during the war, but by 1918 truck makers were offering new models again. Methods of construction were entirely traditional, with wooden-frame cabs mounted on the chassis. Manufacturers who built vehicles using solely their own parts were few. They accounted for only 11 per cent of the market, while about 23 per cent used various components from other suppliers. The majority of truck builders used as many standardised parts as possible in their assembly.

At this time more distinctive models with closed cabs began to appear on the road. Until then, completely open or very simple box-shaped structures were used as cabs. In the 1920s, the most popular cab fitted by various truck manufacturers was the so-called 'C' configuration which was used with or without a windscreen, and at last gave trucks a character of their own. The truck was maturing mechanically as well, and electric or steam power had all but disappeared in favour of four-cylinder petrol engines. These had remained popular for a long time because of their relatively simple construction and good power output.

Some six-cylinder petrol engines were in use before 1920, but it was another 10 years before they gained widespread acceptance in heavy-duty trucks. Chain drive began to be replaced by bevel, worm and double-reduction rear axles, and the first signs of multi-speed transmissions were evident. Some manufacturers retained chain drive for some time, and Sterling finally gave up on it in 1951.

LIGHT AND HEAVY

It didn't take long before there was a need to differentiate between light-duty and heavy-duty trucks. Because light trucks could be based on

Ford's first truck was the Model TT, introduced in 1917. This 1-ton stake-truck was adapted from the popular Model T passenger car.

passenger cars and used many standardised components, which facilitated large-volume production, they lacked both the capacity and sheer strength of heavy trucks. By contrast, heavy trucks were produced in smaller numbers and often needed more specialised design and manufacturing methods. Significant early models that paved the way forward in the two categories included the delicate-looking but useful Ford Model T in the light to medium sector, and the pugnacious and resilient AC Mack Bulldog in the heavy-duty segment. By the 1930s, this difference became less distinct and even in the lower-weight category the industry was becoming more specialised in order to satisfy customer demand. At the same time, in an effort to depart more markedly from car design, large-volume producers increased the capacity of their trucks from 1 to 1.5 tonnes or even more.

Not until the 1950s did the major manufacturers begin to offer genuine light truck models. By developing new presses and dies they were able to distance their commercial products from their car designs. But in the lowest weight categories, commercial vehicles continued to be based

on car-derived platforms. The independents concentrated mainly on heavier trucks and sometimes buses. It's here that some of America's best-known makes are to be found, including Autocar, Brockway, Diamond T, Federal, Mack, Reo, Sterling and White. They all produced high-quality vehicles and are known as the 'thoroughbreds' of the heavy truck segment. They manufactured bespoke vehicles exactly to customers' requirements, a facility that the mass-producers were unable to match. There was thus a distinct diversification as the mass producers went for standardisation and the specialists offered an increasingly personal service.

WEIGHT GAIN

Regulations governing the design and operation of heavy trucks led to many changes in the US industry that would endure for some time. While the carrying capacity of most trucks manufactured up to around 1930 was not a lot more than their unladen weight, vehicles made subsequently were much stronger and capable of carrying at least double their own weight, and more. This was in response to the common practice of hauliers overloading their trucks, and some makers such as Diamond T and International made a selling point of the fact, stating that their vehicles were capable of withstanding 50 per cent excess cargo.

A major contributory factor in the emergence of heavier and faster trucks was the availability of pneumatic tyres in the late 1920s. Previously, trucks shod with solid rubber tyres were restricted to 15mph (24km/h) in urban use, but with pneumatic covers, speeds shot up to 40mph. The new balloon tyres caused less damage to road surfaces as well.

These tyres were not designed for ultra-heavy loads however, and many operators fitted a third axle to increase carrying capacity and reduce tyre stress. This configuration became regularised in the 1930s when manufacturers began to offer six-wheeler models. Typically, the specification of the heaviest models included tandem-

drive rear axles, air-brakes all round, a big six-cylinder petrol engine and multi-speed transmission. The air-brakes were a great improvement on the hydraulic brakes common to most four-wheel trucks in the 1930s. Brake lights were fitted from about 1930, although direction indicators were not fitted as standard for another 10 years. US trucks have never relinquished the spoked wheel, and although they are generally made of cast metal today, the detachable rim predates motorised transport.

CAB COMFORT

During the 1920s and 1930s, truck cabs evolved to the point where they almost compared with the interiors of contemporary passenger cars. Instrumentation and cabin ergonomics gradually expanded to include speedometers, rear-view mirrors, hooters, sun visors, and adjustable padded seats. Vacuum-powered or electric windscreen wipers began to replace the hand-operated wipers that had first appeared in 1920. Electric headlights superseded the old acetylene gas headlamps, and on certain models a knob on the dashboard could adjust beam strength. Better illumination naturally meant improved nocturnal safety, and promoted through-the-night, long-distance services, aided by the introduction of cab heaters and windscreen defrosters in the late 1930s.

While car manufacturers wooed customers with styling evolutions, revising and updating their model ranges and designs on an annual basis, truck makers were less inclined to emulate them. This was mostly due to economic circumstances because development costs were substantially greater, although those in the light to medium segments pandered to fickle fashion to an extent. They were the products of passenger car manufacturers, able to absorb design and tooling costs due to larger volumes. It could be argued that there's little justification for restyled trucks every year in the quarry, the forest or the oilfield and while trucks are by definition functional vehicles, there's always been a stylistic distinction between varying uses.

Some of the stylistic changes to truck cabs had practical benefits, such as the increase in strength brought about by rounding off the corners of the roof, wings and headlight cowls. The adoption of front-opening, rear-hinged bonnets made for easier maintenance while the incorporation of radiator grilles didn't merely protect the radiator but helped establish the model's identity. Indeed, chromium plating wasn't simply applied for show — it prolonged component life too. Paint finishes had been applied in spray booths by some manufacturers from the mid-1920s, but specialist coachbuilders retained traditional brush painting techniques. And while some trucks left the dispatch bay with just a cursory sweep of the spray gun, others were lavished with a glossy enamel finish, bedecked with stripes and traditional gold leaf lettering.

It was regular practice for specialist truck makers to fit cabs and bodies sourced from the same coachbuilder, which accounts for similarities of style. On the other hand, the wealthier, major-volume producers, such as Ford, General Motors and Chrysler, capitalised on their automotive steel pressing resources to build their own truck cabs as well. While badge engineering created identical vehicles from ostensibly different manufacturers for domestic and export markets, it also threw up some dramatic designs from specialist coachbuilders that were as arresting as they were futuristic.

Some US manufacturers specialised in servicing the export markets. Many trucks were shipped in CKD-form – that's Completely Knocked Down – which meant that they were dispatched in crates and assembled in the destination country. Typical of these operations was the part played by Bedford in the UK. Now owned by GM, Bedford began assembling CKD Chevrolet and GMC trucks in Hendon, England, in 1930, switching to their own truck manufacture in 1931.

It wasn't just the large US manufacturers who had their vehicles assembled in overseas markets, as a number of smaller independent concerns, including Condor, Stewart and Willys also built trucks and buses abroad. But big league exports were really the province of the major players.

LENGTH AND WEIGHT

Truck developments in the USA were also motivated by new length and weight regulations for commercial vehicles imposed by the Federal Government in 1933, and streamlining and the use of lightweight aluminium were simply a means of legitimately circumventing the rules. Size regulations were augmented by the Motor Carrier Safety Act and the Interstate Commerce Commission in 1935, which brought about further changes in the trucking industry, and as interstate road freight transport increased, truck manufacturers were encouraged to improve their products. Other innovations included sleeper cabs and semi-trailers, while the reappearance of the cab-over-engine chassis lasted until revised federal overall length regulations brought about its decline in the USA in 1982. The payload capac-

Weight and length regulations played a part in cab design, especially in the USA, but by the 1970s interiors had become quite civilized (below), while by the time Renault introduced its Premium Single cab (right) in 1998 they had become positively palatial.

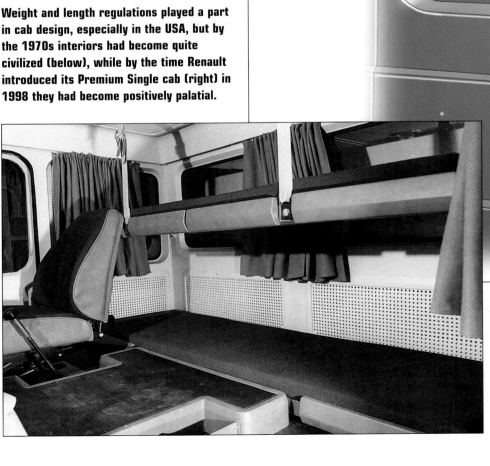

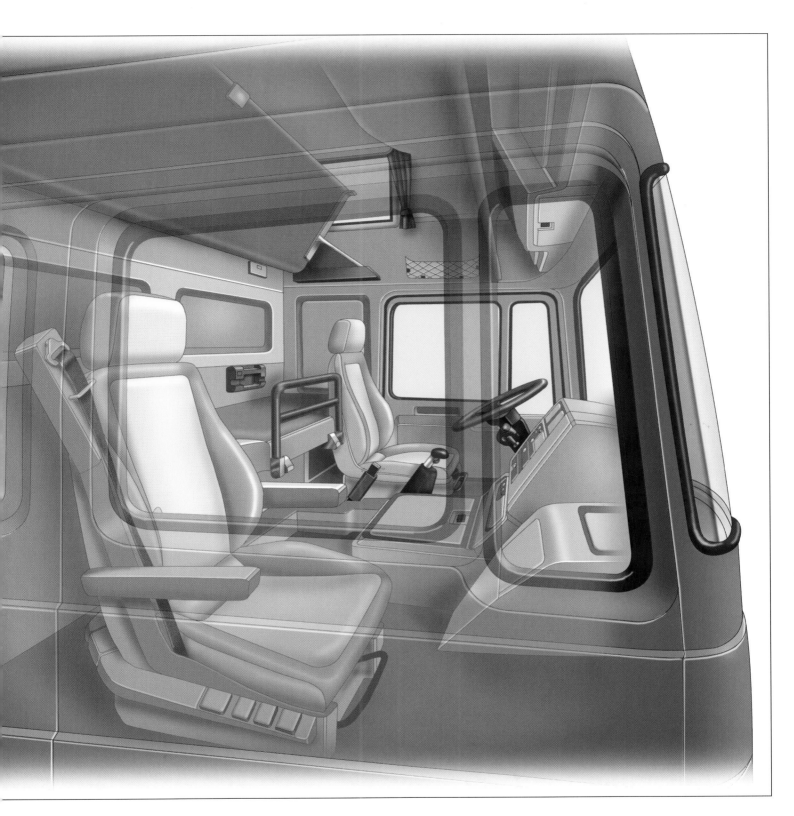

capacities of trucks are measured in Gross Vehicle Weight (GVW) and Gross Combination Weight (GCW), terms that were universally adopted in 1942.

Although the cab-over-engine chassis was around from the start, it's likely that the first tilt-cab truck dates back to Hartford, Connecticut, in 1912, and subsequently the format was wholeheartedly embraced by many US manufacturers. Clearly, its major benefit was that it provided unobstructed access to the engine and its ancillaries, and also, its weight distribution was better from a practical point of view in that it could carry more weight on its front axle. However, for many years the cab-over-engine configuration trucks were regularly outsold by the more common long bonnet variety where the driver sat behind the engine and front axle. But as the city streets of the mid-1930s became more and more congested, the cab-over-engine trucks with their shorter bodies proved a more attractive and practical proposition. Complying with the overall length regulations, the cab-over-engine truck could pull a much longer trailer, and if the vehicle was serving as a tractor unit, the shorter length of the cab-over design scored over a conventional bonneted tractor.

A lot of the early cab-over-engine vehicles were basically conventional chassis with flat-fronted cabs fitted, with the driver subjected to the intrusive bulk of the engine in his cab, and by the late 1930s this had given rise to heat insulation and noise-damping measures. In addition, advances in suspension damping, improved ergonomics and seating positions contrived a much better working environment for the cab-over-engine driver. To give some idea of how the dimension regulations

affected their popularity, US sales of cab-over trucks amounted to some 4500 units in 1936, but a quantum leap during the next four years took the figure to 32,000 by 1941. Another make that has military connotations is Scammell. It began building tractor and semi-trailer combinations at its Watford factory in England in 1922. Scammell was one of a handful of manufacturers to build trucks especially for fairground operators.

SEMI-TRAILERS

Another form of truck that was about to blossom was the semi-trailer. Trailers and semi-trailers had been around since the early 1920s, but when the new generation of more powerful trucks and tractors arrived a decade later, the day of the big articulated combinations had arrived. To an extent the configuration

was tempered by legislation governing overall length, but manufacturers responded by shortening the distance between the rear of the truck cab and the front of the trailer, which still gave greater interior load capacity. Even closer linkage was obtained by rounding off the front corners of the trailer, which brought with it better aerodynamics. The series of four White 'Streamliner' beer trucks designed by Count Alexis de Sakhnoffsky for Canadian brewers Labatt's between 1936 and 1947 is a case in point, as is Heil's streamlined 'Doodle-Bug' tanker of 1934, built on a 1934 Diamond T rear-engined chassis for Texaco to run at airports.

The trailer concept is almost as old as the truck itself. Daimler's UK operation was already on the case back in 1908 when it came out with the Road Train

The 1996 Ford AeroMax linehaul tractor cab featured an integral sleeper unit, which was tall enough for the driver to stand up and walk through to his cabin. Similar designs were typical of US and Australian long-distance semi-trailer rigs.

– a name that would come to be associated with Australian trucking much later on – which hauled a string of trailers. Another UK firm taken over by Jaguar, in 1961, was Guy, whose distinctive radiator cap was a red Indian chief's head. The sleeper cab that's taken for granted today first came into use about 1930, as long-distance trucking took off. There was normally a crew of two for such operations, and one drove while the other slept on an integral full-length bunk, located across the cab behind the driver's seat. Factory-built separate sleeping quarters mounted on the chassis behind the truck cab were introduced by Kenworth in 1939, but it's a fair bet that sleeping in a moving truck wasn't that restful until the later advent of sophisticated air-suspension systems. However, sleeper cabs were essential for long-distance operations and over the years they have developed into relatively salubrious quarters.

In 1932, the Indiana company became the first US truck manufacturer to fit a diesel – a Cummins unit – and they were followed by Sterling and Kenworth. Several manufacturers had experimented with diesel engines in the 1920s, but it never took off due to a number of factors, including high-weight penalty, complex construction, minimal fuel savings and significant exhaust pollutants. Even by 1937, a mere 2500 diesel engines were registered. But despite these tentative first steps, the diesel would supersede the petrol engine in the commercial world. Manufacturing quality improved, and the inherent torque factor and fuel economy of diesels made them an essential option in every truck manufacturer's catalogue. By 1940, almost all US truck manufacturers were offering vehicles with a full range of petrol and diesel engines, transmissions and rear-axle combinations, plus an extensive list of optional extras.

WARTIME OUTPUT

Some interesting statistics for the wartime period reveal that 4.8 million trucks were in use in the USA in 1941, and over half were run by single vehicle

operators. While 90 per cent of US output during the Second World War was conventional vehicles, the 2.5-ton 6x6 GMC 2 general cargo truck, powered by a 104bhp six-cylinder petrol engine, is a good example of a Second World War army lorry. More than 500,000 were made, some with steel cabs and some with soft tops, many of which saw service overseas, as did the bulk of the 2.6 million US trucks and half-a-million trailers produced for military service between 1940 and 1945.

My father, Don Tipler, drove medium- and heavy-duty Dodge, Chevrolet and Thornycroft trucks for the RAF in the war, supplying forward air bases deep in the Burmese jungle. Apart from coming under attack at Imphal, he said that the worst aspect of being in a convoy of trucks was the clouds of dust that permeated the cabs. Their windscreens were removed so the sun didn't glint on them and give their position away to the enemy. The articulated Queen Marys that he drove over poorly surfaced mountain roads were prone to jackknife in mud, and of course there was no jackknife prevention system in those days.

Post-war recovery in the truck market was slow, even in the USA. Despite the fact that military innovations had brought the engineering of heavy trucks and off-road vehicles on in leaps and bounds, the shortage of materials and new designs drove truck makers to resort to their pre-war pattern books. But any trucks that were available were

This ERF model EC11 is a 4x2 tractor with tipping trailer, operating at a gross combination weight (GCW) of 44 tonnes. It is powered by a Cummins M11 405 Euro 2 engine and is designed for heavy-duty construction site work.

allocated to private buyers on a very limited basis as very many were exported. According to the American Trucking Association almost a quarter of a million trucks operating in the USA in the post-war period were veterans from the 1920s, while many operators naturally capitalised on the vast reservoir of army surplus vehicles. Although more than 1.3 million trucks were produced in the USA in 1950, a third of all those then in operation were pre-war models.

In the UK, the story was much the same in the immediate post-war years. My father drove a Ford V8 'Woodie' after the war and spoke of deserted country roads, with few commercials and fewer cars. Trucks would normally be carrying agricultural products, and steam-driven vehicles were not uncommon. In spite of the war, road surfaces were well-maintained tarmac and granite chippings, but petrol was scarce – and pricey too at 1/- (a shilling) a gallon from hand-cranked pumps.

By the 1950s, labour disputes and materials shortages had largely been resolved, and truck manufacturers began to offer new vehicle ranges. In the medium-sized truck market the petrol engine was still supreme, but in the States, diesel-engined 18-wheelers now took precedence in the long-distance haulage game, and it was a time of intense new road building that included both inter-state highways and private toll-roads.

An extensive road-building programme bolstered truck production in the second half of the decade, with the 1956 Highway Act legislation authorising the construction of 41,000 miles (66,000 kilometres) of new Interstate Highway.

A number of factors influenced the growth of the European truck industry, including the Transport International Routiers (TIR) Customs Convention set up in 1957, which gave member

This 155bhp four-cylinder MAN diesel engine is typical of a modern, fuel-efficient, light-duty truck engine, built to satisfy Euro 2 emissions regulations in the late 1990s. The main components are annotated here.

vehicles access across frontiers without being opened up for inspection. Then the capacious roll-on, roll-off ferry services between Britain, Continental Europe and Scandinavia were starting to appear, which facilitated the freight container revolution of the mid-1960s.

As trucks grew in power and stature through the 1960s, conformity of appearance clouded vehicle design, and some individual makes could at best be identified only by their logos. Trucks in general, and cab-over models in particular, began to look the same because of legislation aimed at improving safety and enforcing noise and exhaust emissions regulations. By now, tilt-cabs had become the norm and, as alternative materials use increased with improved manufacturing techniques, they were often made of lightweight aluminium or GRP – glass-reinforced plastic.

While the excellent lugging capability

of the diesel engine made its position more and more entrenched, especially in the heavy truck sector, many operators still clung to big petrol engines like the Hall-Scott 400 and Buda and LPG – liquid petroleum gas – engines. And indeed, over half the trucks produced in the USA in 1969 were powered by V8 petrol engines. Some manufacturers also toyed with the gas turbine engine, but it was stymied by high production and fuel costs.

From 1976, the Soviet Union's Kamaz (Kamskiy Avtomobilniy Zavod) was a major player in central Asia, with no less than 19 factories including 14 on one site in Tatarstan, 800kms south east of Moscow. Potential capacity was a colossal 150,000 units a year. Using Deutz diesel engines made under licence, Kamaz made a range of cab-over heavy-duty models in 4x2, 6x4 and 6x6 configurations from 15 to

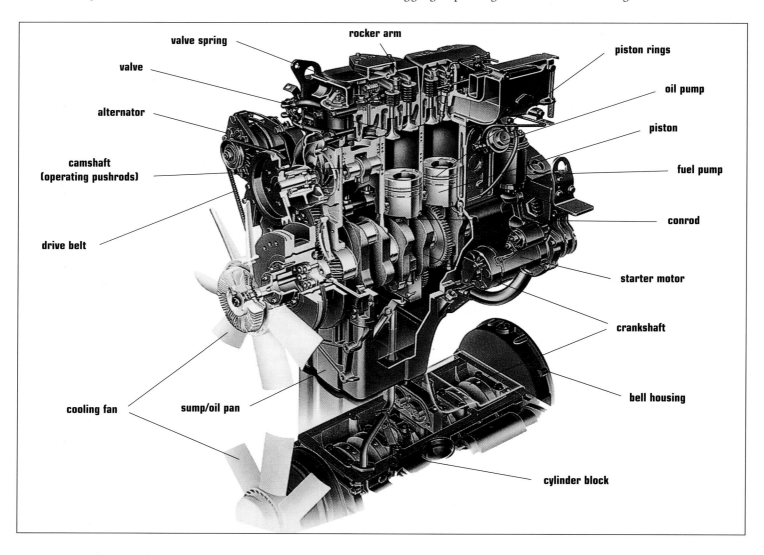

26 tonnes GVW. After a disastrous fire in 1993 that seriously reduced production, Kamaz entered into a joint venture with Cummins to make Kamdizel engines and Rockwell axles in 1996.

We're all familiar with the big independent names – Mack, Peterbilt, White and so on – but nearly 2000 small-time truck makers have gone to the wall in the first century of trucking. They failed because they weren't able to match production with design and manufacturing costs, even though quality and price was not a problem. Others endured by using standardised components that were either made in house or bought in. But while drivetrains could easily be sourced from outside suppliers, the cab was frequently the crucial design factor, which meant smaller manufacturers had difficulty keeping up with volume producers due to compromised creature comforts and ergonomic failings. Survivors adapted and built tailor-made trucks for niche

markets that were inaccessible or not viable for the mass producers. For example, of the myriad small independent producers, one of the most interesting, and certainly one of the longest survivors, was the Texas-based Marmon company, which was still making Class 8 trucks into the late 1990s on a virtually hand-built basis at the rate of three units a day. It rose from the ashes of the demised Marmon Herrington special equipment manufacturer and produced both conventional and cab-over models in sleeper and non-sleeper and truck and truck-tractor format. Cabs were custom-built all-aluminium, and the vehicles could be powered by Cummins, Caterpillar or Detroit Diesel engines, while transmissions were sourced from Fuller or Spicer, and axles were either Eaton or Rockwell. Many of the independents were taken over and absorbed into big corporations, and some still survive in that context.

Many European haulage contractors operate over large distances, travelling from the UK and Scandinavia to the Black Sea, for example. Here is an Eddie Stobart DAF 95XF with 38-tonne, high-cube drawbar trailer in Croatia.

There is the odd firm that hasn't had to undergo a merger or take-over to switch national allegiance. Tatra began production in 1897 in Nesselsdorf, Monrovia, which was part of the Austrian empire until 1918 when it seceded to Czechoslovakia, and the town was renamed Koprivuice. In 1900, Tatra produced a 15hp 2-tonne truck powered by a flat-twin cylinder engine mounted under the cargo deck at the rear of the truck. From 1923, Tatra produced trucks with a backbone chassis and independent suspension all round, and powered by air-cooled engines. In the late 1990s, when Tatra specialised in military and off-road heavy trucks, these basic features endured. For example, the 6x6 Tatra T815 was available with V8, V10 or V12 air-cooled diesel engines of up to 320bhp. Typically, the 15.8-litre (964-cubic inch) V10 produces 266bhp. Another Czech make was Skoda. Its 706 cab-over models became familiar throughout Europe in the 1970s, operated by the Czech State transport company. Another truck maker of the former Eastern bloc is Liaz, a Russian company building highway trucks, some of which were built in Bulgaria and badged as Madara trucks.

EASTERN PROMISE

The manufacturers of the Pacific Rim in Japan and Korea have not been slow to climb onto the truck-building ladder. Hino is noted for its heavy truck range, while Mitsubishi manufactures trucks under the brand name of Fuso. Nissan UD manufactures medium trucks in its CMA and CMD ranges, which are 150bhp six-cylinder diesel-powered cab-over trucks with tilt cabs.

Isuzu is another Tokyo-based concern with links to General Motors. Beginning with car production in 1916, it made CKD Wolseleys and trucks under licence. By 1941, Isuzu was building diesel-engined trucks for the Japanese Army, with peacetime production centred on off-road 4x4s and medium to light trucks, such as the 6x6 TWD20 general-purpose vehicle of 1979, powered by a 125bhp six-cylinder 6126cc diesel engine.

Distances are vast in Australia, a continent not dissimilar to the USA, yet conditions are equal to those of Africa, where a 24-hour journey can start in the south at 5 °C and end in the north

at 40 °C. Some terrain is equally tough on vehicles, and the country is split north–south by the Great Divide mountain range. To the east lies Sydney, Melbourne, Brisbane and Adelaide, and the Australian trucking business developed between these cities in pre-war days, with US Fords and Internationals and British AEC and

Leyland the most common trucks of the 1930s. Post war, the rail network was protected, but not substantially improved, so the trucking industry took on this role. Only single-trailer rigs were allowed to operate in the eastern seaboard states, while the celebrated road-train concept was developed to cover the enormous distances to the

The Australian road train services far-flung communities, and this six-trailer combination, hauled by a Western Star tractor, weighs in at 500 tonnes, making it the biggest road train in the world.

west of the Great Divide. In a move to standardise trucking regulations throughout the Continent, the Australian Road Transport Forum was set up in 1989, so that weight limits and driver hours were constant. One feature of the rules was that only single 49-ft (15-m) trailer combinations were normally permitted in the eastern seaboard states, while road-trains consisting of two or three 49-ft (15-m) trailers operated in the hinterland to the west. This rig was known as B-double (or B-train in Canada).

In some mining situations in the outback, four and five trailer combinations were not unknown. The typical configuration consisted of the 6-tonne truck-tractor, 16.5-tonne second trailer with tri-axle bogie including a semi trailer coupling at the rear, drawing two 20-tonne trailers, adding up to 62.5 tonnes GCW. It was anticipated that weights would increase in 1999.

The Australian environment favoured US makes, particularly those of the western manufacturers like Kenworth and Freightliner, whereas British makes were reckoned to be more comfortable

1857 ACTROS MEGASPACE

Make: *Mercedes-Benz*
Model: *1857 LSE/LSN*
Type: *4x2, cab-over*
Engine: *Mercedes-Benz OM 502 LA V8, 571bhp at 1800rpm*
Gearbox: *Mercedes-Benz G 360 with 16 speeds*
Suspension:
  front: parabolic leaf springs, shock absorbers and anti-roll bar
  rear: Telligent suspension, four pneumatic cushions, shock absorbers and anti-roll bar
Chassis: *parallel side frames with sheet-steel cross-members, assembled with bolts and rivets*
Trailer: *curtain-side, 23-tonne capacity, side-loading. Strapless facility available with air-powered tensioning system*

Truck designs have grown ever more sophisticated and high-tech, like this Volvo FL-series model. Truck sales are won or lost on their potential down-time. So servicing intervals of 70,000kms (43,500 miles) were normal for most Volvos by 1999.

but less reliable and suffered from cooling problems. Most manufacturers traditionally imported their products as 'glider-kits' – consisting of chassis and cab, and a choice of Cummins or Detroit Diesel power. By the 1990s, European makes had 'Australianised' their vehicles, and Volvo trucks were being made in Brisbane, while Scania and Mercedes-Benz also had a presence. Of the US makes, Kenworths were built in Bayswater, Victoria, and Macks were made in Brisbane. A typical Australian operator was Dennis Robertson's Roadmaster Haulage company, which operated chiefly in the eastern seaboard states, running 50 refrigerated artics. Dennis Robertson was also chairman of the Road Transport Forum, retiring in 1997. By the 1970s, joint ventures, partnerships and trade agreements contrived to unify the design and production of heavy trucks. Individuality was increasingly sup-

pressed, and escalating development and production costs brought truck makers to their knees.

PRACTICAL TRUCKING

But what of the practicalities of driving and servicing a truck? It wasn't until the 1960s that things began to get a bit more civilised, with advances in hydraulic and vacuum-assisted brakes and air-assisted clutches and power steering. These meant that drivers no longer had to be macho strong-men, which was certainly the case with unassisted steering and mechanical rod clutches and rod brakes. In US models, the lengthy gear lever and handbrake lever lingered on far longer than in European trucks, which were more like a car to drive, whereas the US truck builders seemed reluctant to relinquish the strong-man image. Creature comforts were probably better in the typical European truck cab. US interiors were

relatively crude, with chunky fittings and haphazard location of switchgear and no adjustment for seat or steering wheel. Again, matters improved in the 1960s, with the advent of heaters, and the more recently introduced night heater provides a thermostatically controlled environment for an early morning take-off. In technological terms, chassis development kept pace with the demand for systemised transport and interchangeable load carriers, and by 1977, Scania was offering pneumatic rear suspension as an alternative to the conventional leaf-spring type.

Lighting laws changed, and traffic indicators were a major step forward as they did away with the archaic mechanical system that consisted of semaphore arms activated by a rope that traversed from one side of the cab to the other. Heavy truck speed limits in the UK were raised from 20mph (32km/h) to 40mph (64km/h) on

A-roads only in the late 1960s, with a 56mph (90km/h) maximum on motorways. Follow a heavy truck in pouring rain on a motorway and you'd think he was travelling much faster than that just by the spray thrown off the wheels. But in fact wheel flaps were quite strictly specified by the late-1990s, and spray was certainly less of an issue than previously. Tyre evolutions point to super-wide single tyres as the coming thing for single-drive axles, pioneered in 1999 by Michelin which was also developing run-flat truck tyres.

The late 1960s was a transitional period for the truck mechanic as well, when a vehicle might be off the road for a fortnight having maintenance done to secure its annual MoT certificate of roadworthiness. By the late-1990s, truck sales were won or lost on their potential down-time, and it was normal for a vehicle to be in the workshop overnight just once a year, and be on the job the following morning, fully serviced. Servicing intervals were extended to 100,000km (62,000 miles) for the Mercedes-Benz Actros, (1999's Truck of the Year), and 70,000km was the norm for most Volvos. Most manufacturers relied on feedback from servicing depots to refine their products.

Probably the most innovative vehicle was the Volvo F-86, which pioneered hydraulic clutches and turbocharged engines in the early 1970s, and opened the door for technical innovations. Progressively stringent emissions legislation led to increasingly sophisticated, electronic, engine-management systems and electronically controlled brakes and suspension, and this equipment became particularly specialised in different makes and from model to model. As a consequence, there was less a general mechanic could do, and the truck fitter was born, replacing complete components instead of mending them.

LEGISLATIVE RESTRICTIONS

Trucking has always been governed by stringent legislation, varying in degrees from one country to another, and vehicle weights, dimensions, axle numbers and trailer combinations are extremely complex. The UK inherited the Tachograph – regarded as the Spy in the Cab – from Sweden, which governed the length of time a driver could remain at the wheel. In 1999, EC rules stated that a driver could only spend four-and-a-half hours at the wheel before taking a break of at least 45 minutes. UK domestic regulations were based on a daily limit of 10 hours driving. By the 1990s, legislation was a nightmarish gauntlet that the truck operator had to run, requiring him to have a licence, renewable every five years from a Licensing Authority, and pay a fee for each truck in his fleet. He would also need to be able to substantiate an ability to run the fleet from a fixed depot, and have an operable servicing contract. Factors such as MoT failures, roadside checks and other complaints go against the issuing of the licence. Annual road tax alone on an 8x4 rigid tipper of 31–32 tonnes GVW would be £4400, while a two-axle truck-tractor and two-axle trailer of 35 tonnes GVW would cost £5170 in road fund licence. By 1999, operators were looking at registration outside the UK, where licensing was cheaper.

Certain big European operators like Norbert Dentressangle and Giraud run huge fleets, jointly numbering 6000 vehicles, most of which are 4x2 tractor units. One of the UK's largest operators, James Irlam, ran a fleet of 300 trucks in 1999, centred on the Renault Premium 6x2 model. Another high profile operator was Eddie Stobart, a Carlisle firm that started off in 1970 and came to prominence in the 1990s by projecting a smart image and accommodating service. Stobart's 1998 fleet of 860 vehicles included a variety of 38-tonne MAN and Volvo curtainside semi-trailers and 4x2 Volvo drawbar rigids, together with some 17-tonne Scania tail-lift rigids. Its control and warehousing centres at Carlisle and Daventry were manned constantly in support of its trucks, which operate as far as the Black Sea. Many operators have contractual arrangements that enable them to part exchange their vehicles every two years, but this was a mixed blessing as, by 1999, some truck makers were beginning to suffer from increasing numbers of nearly new vehicles on the used-truck market. Scania in particular declined to get involved in the two-year cycle.

The trucking industry certainly has a fascinating subculture. Drive one, and you could be hooked. There could even be a job with it, as some manufacturers including Scania, Mercedes-Benz and Volvo were considering offering qualified drivers as part of their sales package.

DATA CONVERSION

Throughout the book, statistics such as engine size and payload capacity are given in whatever measurement is normal in the country of origin. For instance, European engine sizes are expressed in litres, while US makes are in cubic inches, with the appropriate conversion in brackets.

Weights are given in tons for US and older British vehicles, and in metric tonnes and kilogrammes for European makes.

Similarly, speed and distances are in miles or mph for the USA and UK, and in kilometres or km/h for Europe.

With regard to mechanical componentry, it would seem that most items have a transatlantic identity, although certain trucking jargon is unique to individual countries. Mention a 'truck' to anyone over 50 in the UK and they'll think of a pick-up. But refer to a 'lorry' in the US and no one will know what you mean.

John Tipler

DAIMLER-BENZ

The credit for producing the world's first truck goes to Daimler-Benz. It must have been clear from the outset that the internal combustion engine would provide the motive power for cargo-carrying vehicles, and both Gottlieb Daimler and Karl Benz, who built the first passenger vehicles in 1886, went on to make trucks, buses and fire appliances within the following decade. Over one hundred years later, the company had gone from strength to strength, merging with US giant Chrysler to become Daimler Chrysler, and taking over Ford's US heavy-truck division in 1998.

In September 1896, Daimler-Motoren Gesellschaft launched the world's first motorised trucks. They made a four model range with gross weights ranging from 1500kg and 2500kg, to 3750kg and 5000kg. Their two-cylinder engines increased progressively in power from 4, 6, and 8 to 10hp, and contemporary sales literature contained relevant technical statistics and advice on which power band would be the most suitable for certain applications.

Actros, the new heavy-duty truck class from Mercedes-Benz. The cabs are larger, better thought out and better equipped in comparison with their predecessors.

They had artillery-pattern, iron-rim, wood-spoked wheels, and the driver's accommodation consisted of a wooden bench on which he was completely exposed to the elements, just as on a stagecoach or horse-drawn wagon.

Steering was by a vertical column and horizontally mounted steering wheel, while brakes consisted of a foot pedal linked by rods to a transverse that carried the wooden brake shoes. When the pedal was depressed the shoes acted directly on the metal rims of the rear wheels. The front suspension was made up of transverse leaf springs, bolted to the beam axle, with a bearing that took account of oscillation and the steering. The rear suspension consisted of a single-coil spring on either side, attached directly to the beam axle and the underside of the load platform.

Early engine designs worked on the belt drive system that was eventually superseded by chain drive. Mechanical reliability was improved dramatically in 1898 when Daimler fitted Bosch magneto ignition.

Karl Benz built the first petrol-engined bus in 1894. It was called the Landau and carried eight passengers. Benz's first truck came out in 1898 and was sold to an American firm in New York for use as a delivery vehicle with a 600kg (1350lb) carrying capacity. Daimler, on the other hand, found an alternative market in Great Britain, and launched his first truck in 1898. The prowess of the vehicles was demonstrated to the public in field trials, and Daimler's products proved themselves more than a match for the then ubiquitous steam-engined trucks. Daimler's British agent was Frederick Simms, who also held the rights to the company's patents throughout the British Empire. Daimler's light delivery

An example of a car chassis being used for light-duty commercial purposes is this 1903 Mercedes kettenwagen, powered by a 9.0-litre four cylinder engine. Wheels are spoked artillery type with detachable rims.

trucks were bought by a number of London stores and in 1901 a Daimler became the first vehicle to be used by the British Postal Service. The following year, the Dunlop Tyre Company bought a Daimler and fitted it with pneumatic tyres, although it would be some time before pneumatic tyres became standard. In the USA, Daimlers were popular with shops, bakeries and breweries as delivery vehicles, and the first truck service centre was established in Philadelphia in 1902 and provided maintenance and breakdown services. However, a disastrous fire at Daimler's American factory in 1913 spelled the end for production there.

MERCEDES-BENZ

The origins of the Mercedes name are quite unusual. It came about in 1899, when Emil Jellinek won the Tour de Nice race in a Daimler Phoenix under the assumed name of Herr Mercedes, which was the Christian name of his ten-year-old daughter. Jellinek commissioned Daimler to build a run of long wheelbase cars with a lower centre of gravity, on the condition that he had the rights to sell them in Europe and the USA, under the name Mercedes. They proved a success, so the Mercedes name was registered as the trademark of Daimler Motoren-Gesellschaft in 1902. Gottlieb Daimler had died in 1900, so it was his successor, colleague and friend Wilhelm Maybach who authorised the adoption of the name.

In the decades before the First World War, the vast Austro-Hungarian Empire was hugely influential in European politics and trade, and consequently in 1899, Daimler Motoren Gesellschaft was set up at Wiener-Neustadt in Lower Austria. Gottlieb's son Paul was put in charge of Austro-Daimler, as it was known, in 1902. One of its first products was an all-wheel-drive off-roader, while another was a 3-tonne, 4x2 general cargo truck with a flat top and curtain sides. It was powered by a four-cylinder 12hp Daimler engine, with shaft drive to the rear axle. Both vehicles were snapped up by the Austrian military, which was clearly a significant market. Austro-Daimler also produced 4x4 truck-tractors powered by 80 and 90hp six-cylinder engines for hauling heavy equipment and field artillery. The all-wheel-drive vehicle led to Austro-Daimler's ammunition-carrying road train, which was equipped with a powerful six-cylinder unit producing 100hp. In 1911, the British Daimler Company built a similar road train, which used three-axle trailers with shaft drive to the centre axle, and these were exported to India.

Daimler bought the Marienfelde factory in Berlin from Motorfahrzeug und Motorenfabrik AG in 1901, and although Daimler was the first manufacturer to fit shaft drive, the most popular army trucks at the time were chain-drive products from the Marienfelde factory. They were 3.5-tonne 4x2 cargo trucks powered by two-cylinder 12hp petrol engines, and a number saw service with the Russian Army. The Marienfelde plant also made 1-tonne electric trucks that were sold locally, as well as fire engines.

Among the military vehicles produced at the Marienfelde plant were 60bhp 4x4 vehicles that were widely used during the First World War, including a 3-tonne chain-drive version with glass windscreen. Benz's equivalent Gaggenau-produced 37bhp 3-tonner was equally as popular with the troops.

POST-WAR DIFFICULTIES

Post-war economic conditions were nowhere so bad as in Germany. This was due in the main to reparation payments, and things only began to improve in the 1930s. However, it was not a period bereft of innovations, as both Daimler and Benz started to employ diesel engines. Daimler's Marienfelde plant had already been making industrial and marine diesels for some time, and the new truck engines used pressurised fuel injection. One of its six-cylinder units produced an amazing 380bhp at 1700rpm. At the other end of the scale, it also made small diesel units for agricultural machinery. In 1921, a bus was fitted with a supercharged 40bhp four-cylinder engine and these units were subsequently fitted in trucks.

In the meantime, Benz had been at work on a 30bhp pre-combustion diesel unit, and in 1922 the company's Stationary Engine Department became the Motor Works, subsequently known as MWN. After testing, 100 of these engines were built, one of which was fitted in the 5-tonne OB2 Benz truck that was shown at the 1924 Amsterdam Show. The Benz injection pumps and nozzles that were originally fitted were later replaced by Bosch units. Daimler and Benz had already been in active co-operation for a while, and in 1924, Daimler dropped its own combustion system in favour of the Benz method.

Mercedes-Benz was one of the pioneers of diesel-engine technology. The advantages of better torque, greater economy and less complicated construction, however, only began to be appreciated in the early 1930s.

In 1926, the two firms took the major step of amalgamating officially, and the new company was called Daimler-Benz AG. Its headquarters and new central design department was located at Stuttgart-Unterturkheim, and the joint company logo logically combined Daimler's three-pointed star with Benz's laurel wreath.

As the twenties' depression bit deeper, the Marienfelde plant was obliged to concentrate entirely on repair work, and production didn't get going again there until 1934 with the manufacture of all-terrain vehicles. At Gaggenau and Mannheim, production was limited to three designs, including a 1.5-tonner and a 3-tonner, with a 5-tonner which was also used for bus chassis.

Daimler-Benz production was running at 2000 units in 1932, rising to 10,000 by 1935. These included the L Series models, the standard German Army truck, the G3A all-terrain model, as well as heavy-duty tractor units, all of which were conventional bonneted

designs, and these vehicles saw the company through to the Second World War.

The Daimler-Benz plants suffered mixed fortunes during the war, and predictably, were targeted by Allied air raids. The Marienfelde factory survived, ironically, as it was seen as a potential truck repair base by the US Army. However, production there didn't resume until 1950, and that was simply the manufacture of marine and industrial diesels. The Gaggenau plant came on stream first in spite of the fact that it had been virtually obliterated in 1944. It began making 5-tonne trucks in

High wire act. Mountain cable was transported to a height of 2600m (8530ft) in the Swiss alps. An organisational plan involving a variety of Mercedes-Benz trucks got 53 tonnes of cable to its destination despite severe weather conditions.

small numbers, but by 1948 it was turning out the versatile new Unimog off-roader. The Mannheim plant was able to continue production of 3-tonners even in 1945, although the production rate varied from 37 to 271 units a month in 1946. The Unterturkheim and Sindelfingen factories were ordered

2x4 L-SERIES – 1931

The designation reflects the payload in kilograms

Engine	Cylinders	bhp
L 1500 diesel/petrol optional	4	45
L 3000 diesel/petrol optional	4	70
L 5000 diesel/petrol optional	6	110

to build a variety of small delivery vans, pickup trucks, personnel carriers and ambulances. Volumes were small at first, with 214 units built in 1946. Yet this figure rose to 1045 in 1947 and production more than quadrupled in 1948. The Daimler-Benz workforce too had almost doubled, standing at 22,548 in 1948. The occupying Allied Control Commission restricted all German manufacturers to the production of two-axle goods vehicles, and construction of multi-wheeled vehicles was banned. However, when you're up against the ropes, you generally find a way to spring back, and operators circumvented the rules by the simple expedient of hitching one or two trailers to trucks. This restriction gave rise to the principle of building vehicles with a good power-to-weight ratio, which characterised German trucks for some three decades. The axle restriction was eventually lifted in 1951, but at this point the state-owned railway attempted to restrict further road transport, and the Federal Government brought in rules to protect the railways by restricting the weight and size of commercial vehicles, a policy that hasn't entirely disappeared.

The setting up of the first Federal German Government in 1949 encouraged the post-war reconstruction of the German economy. Commercial vehicle production contributed significantly towards the resurgence, though the attractiveness of trucks as exports was tempered by the poor value of the DM against the Dollar.

Mercedes-Benz introduced its new models at Hanover in 1949, including a new 90bhp diesel engine fitted in the light-duty L 3250, which evolved into the L 3500 in 1950. The medium-duty 5-tonne L 5000 was powered by a 120bhp diesel, built at Gaggenau, while the Mannheim-built 6.6-tonne L 6600 heavy truck used a 145bhp diesel unit.

SILVER ANNIVERSARY

The 25th anniversary of the Daimler-Benz partnership in 1951 was marked appropriately with a brisk output of nearly 9000 4-tonne trucks and 900

buses leaving the Mannheim plant, and nearly 2500 5- and 6.6-tonne heavy trucks and 250 buses produced at Gaggenau. By 1955, production had risen to 19,000 units at Mannheim and over 10,000 heavy trucks and buses at Gaggenau. Nearly 5000 Unimog off-roaders were built there too.

Many developing countries were keen to set up their own truck industries, and a wide range of Mercedes models were exported on a Complete Knock Down (CKD) basis to more than 20 countries in Europe, Africa, Asia, Australasia and South America. Mercedes-Benz's overseas ventures took off in the early 1950s when it set up assembly and manufacturing plants at Buenos Aires and Sao Paulo. In addition, a joint venture with the Tata Locomotive Engineering Company in 1954, enabled Tata to assemble conventional-design Mercedes trucks for the Indian market at its Jamshedpur factory. During the 1950s, Mercedes-Benz Argentina SA assembled the

The Actros cab defines the modern long-distance truck and contributed to it winning the 1997 Truck of the Year accolade. High roof designs have become the benchmark of today's long distance cab specifications.

L 312 at the rate of 300 units a month, while Brazil's biggest truck plant was built at Sao Bernardo do Campo in the early 1950s.

The company changed its vehicle identification system in 1954, so that the vehicle's development number was used instead of its weight. First of the new models was the L 315, which with its 7-tonne payload would previously have been the L 7000. The mechanically similar LP 315 appeared in 1955, and this was the first cab-over model to be made since the war. The P stood for 'Pullman', which identified it as a forward-control vehicle, and it contrived to look far more up to date than its conventional, bonneted siblings. The corporate three-pointed star symbol was prominent in an ovoid grille, and the contours of the cab were pleasantly rounded. The LP 315 was also notable in that it was the first Mercedes-Benz truck to use an exhaust brake as standard. It was followed into production by the 1.75-tonne LP 319/319D light delivery truck, which was also a forward-control layout.

ADVENT OF CONTAINERISATION

The company's progress in the 1950s was in part due to demand from municipal authorities and the construction industry, but the European trucking industry was gathering momentum and now required bigger and more powerful vehicles to haul heavier loads across the continent. There's no doubt that containerisation also played a part. Major changes in West Germany's vehicle construction and weight regulations, including in 1956 a minimum power-to-weight ratio of 6bhp per tonne, brought about a switch to larger three-axle rigid trucks and lighter two-axle rigid models. Mercedes responded in 1958 with the LP 333, a twin-steer, three-axle truck of 16 tonnes GVW, powered by the 200bhp OM 326 diesel engine, which was also built as a truck-tractor for pulling articulated trailers up to 24 tonnes GVW. Semi-forward-control models, the L 323 and L 328, which had very short bonnets, later superseded these vehicles and were sought after particularly by the construction industry. The new LP/LPS 1620 and LP/LPS 1920 ranges had new cabs that were in fixed position at first instead of tilting, a facelift in 1969 reintroduced tilt cabs.

When Daimler-Benz became a major shareholder in Auto Union in 1958, it effectively gained control of the Düsseldorf-Derendorf plant, which produced some 60,000 DKW cars a year during the 1950s. From 1962, when Auto Union moved its operations to Ingolstadt prior to the Volkswagen take-over and reinstatement of the Audi name, Mercedes began the process of gearing up for light truck and van production there.

After a disappointing year in 1957, Mercedes-Benz fortunes looked up the

By the late 1990s, Mercedes-Benz's versatile Actros Distribution range provided options for most applications, from short-haul urban deliveries to long-distance operations where on-board accommodation was crucial.

following year as sales of the Mannheim-built, light-duty range rose by 10,000 units. As the company grew more prosperous, a 14-storey administration block was built at Unterturkheim in 1958. By 1960, volumes at Mannheim had topped the 40,000 mark, although almost a half of these were CKD vehicles for export.

By 1960, the Mannheim and Gaggenau plants were working at maximum capacity, and something like 130 medium- and heavy-duty trucks were rolling off the lines every day. Accordingly, a programme of rationalisation was drawn up, which included the building of a new plant on a 470-acre, green-field site at Wörth, close to the Rhine Harbour, where local incentives were on offer. This was to become Daimler-Benz's main medium- and heavy-duty, truck-assembly and cab-manufacturing plant, and the first vehicles – the LP 608 model – began to leave the factory in 1965. At this point, a new foundry and engine plant opened at Mannheim, and together with the Gaggenau factory, the old plants produced only the major drive-train componentry, including engines, gearboxes and axles. The Mannheim foundry cast all the commercial vehicle crankcases and cylinder-heads as well as certain items for the Unterturkheim car plant. Among its first commissions were the V-cylinder engines that powered the 400 Series of medium- and heavy-duty trucks and buses that came out in 1970.

NEW REGULATIONS

New legislation in the early 1960s brought about changes in the production of components. In 1964, Mercedes-Benz dropped the pre-combustion chamber, indirect-injection ignition system and went over to direct-injection diesel engines. The first trucks to use the

S CAB

The short cab is aimed at distribution transport. The cab interiors are among the widest in Europe.

Engine: *Mercedes OM 501LA*
Capacity: *12 litre (732 cubic inch)*
Power: *313bhp/354bhp*
Torque: *1129lb.ft/1276lb.ft*
Gearbox: *Mercedes 16 speed*

new power plant were the OM 352 and OM 346, launched at the Amsterdam Show in February 1964. The new engines were the 140bhp and 220bhp six-cylinder units. The new legislation meant that a 24-tonne payload became a practical proposition if an articulated semi-trailer was used. On the other hand, the maximum practical payload for a lorry and trailer combination was only 23 tonnes, and this led to the decline of draw-bar trailers in favour of articulated rigs, however, there were complications. Technicalities within the regulations meant operators had to link a three-axle tractor unit to a rear-steer, two-axle semi-trailer, or alternatively hitching a two-axle tractor up with a three-axle, rear-steer semi-trailer, because a two-axle tractor unit with a two-axle semi-trailer couldn't legally operate beyond 36 tonnes.

M CAB

The 'M' type premium day cab, with provision for folding bunk. For short and medium distances.

Engine: *Mercedes OM 501LA*
Capacity: *12 litre (732 cubic inch)*
Power: *354bhp/394bhp*
Torque: *1276lb.ft/1365lb.ft*
Gearbox: *Mercedes 16 speed*

L CAB

The 'L' type cab is the standard for long-haul transport offering above-standard equipment.

Engine: *Mercedes OM 501/2LA*
Capacity: *12 litre (732 cubic inch)*
Power: *428bhp/476bhp*
Torque: *1475lb.ft/1696lb.ft*
Gearbox: *Mercedes 16 speed*

MEGASPACE CAB

The 'Executive' cab for long-haul transport: with a flat cab floor and unrestricted freedom of movement.

Engine: *Mercedes OM 502LA*
Capacity: *16 litre (976 cubic inch)*
Power: *530bhp/571bhp*
Torque: *1770lb.ft/1992lb.ft*
Gearbox: *Mercedes 16 speed*

Daimler-Benz came to the rescue, being the first German manufacturer to produce a vehicle to match the new regulations. This was the Gaggenau-built, 6x2 LPS 2020 twin-steer tractor unit that first appeared at the 1965 Frankfurt Show. It was coupled to a Schenk air-sprung semi-trailer fitted with a rear steering axle. The LPS 2020 was powered by the 10.8-litre (659-cubic inch) direct-injection six-cylinder OM 346 diesel unit, developing 218bhp at 2200rpm, which was married to a ZF six-speed constant-mesh gearbox, with an optional 11-speed version available. Dual-circuit air-brakes and an air-assisted hand-brake were standard issue, with the added sophistication of a load-sensitive brake valve on the driving axle that rendered the second axle's brakes inoperative when running light. Two models

unveiled at the 1965 Frankfurt Show were the LP and LPS 1418 models, in two-axle, 14.5-tonne truck and truck-tractor format. They were also powered by the OM 346 engine.

Reflecting the trend towards still more powerful engines, the LP 1216 was introduced in December 1966, powered by the 160bhp engine. It was a 12-tonne GVW truck designed for drawbar operation at 26.5 tonnes GTW, and this power-to-weight increase was also applied to smaller vehicles. For example, the LP 911 was fitted with a 110bhp unit that was 10 per cent more powerful than the LP 910 model. But really powerful engines were the province of the heavy brigade, and the switch to 38-tonne semi-trailers coupled with the 6bhp per tonne, power-to-weight ratio ruling prompted the introduction of higher performance

engines. The minimum power requirement at 38 tonnes was 228bhp, and all West German manufacturers contemplated new engine ranges.

HEAVY-DUTY MODELS

New heavy-duty models at the 1967 Frankfurt Show were the LPS 2023 and the LPS 2223 and LP 2223. The engine common to all three models was the 11.6-litre (707-cubic inch) OM 335 long-stroke version of the existing OM 346. The LPS truck-tractor units were intended to operate at 38 tonnes GCW, although one was a 6x2 model and the other a 6x4 layout. At 22 tonnes GVW, the LP 2223 was available in 6x2 and 6x4 format. The new vehicles had a suspension system that was considered to be smoother and more stable than contemporaries, and comprised 1.8-m (6-ft) springs at the front and 1.4-m (4-

ft 7-in) springs at the rear, with telescopic dampers all round and anti-roll bars on the first and third axles.

WÖRTH OPENING UP?

Soon after the new plant at Wörth was opened, Daimler-Benz bought out the commercial vehicle arm of the Rheinstahl group, which included the old Hanomag and Henschel truck firms, which had previously been serious competitors. Hanomag's own vehicles used independent front suspension and front-wheel drive. A new company was formed, called Hanomag-Henschel Fahrzeugbau AG, in 1969. Hanomag was no stranger to corporate acquisition, having itself taken over the light-duty truck and van producer Vidal & Sohn, Tempowerke in 1963, who made the Matador and Wiking models. The take-over was important for Daimler-Benz in that it created an introduction

to the light van sector, and it wasted no time in boosting production levels. This was achieved partly by standardising components and assembly lines. The Kassel plant superseded Gaggenau as the producer of axle gears, providing axles to Mercedes-Benz and Hanomag-Henschel, as well as the Austrian Steyr-Daimler-Puch vehicles, making it the biggest commercial vehicle axle plant in Europe with a daily turnover of 1600 commercial vehicle axles.

Mercedes-Benz P14 light vans were built at the Hanomag-Henschel plant at Sebaldsbruck, Bremen, in what had formerly been the Borgward car plant until 1961, and flatbed and pickup trucks at

The Mercedes-Benz Actros 1835. Service intervals of up to 120,000km (74,500 miles), were a key sales point, since operators only had to have vehicles laid up for the minimum amount of time.

the Hamburg factory. For a time, Hanomag-Henschel medium-duty vehicles were also built at Bremen, but since they duplicated the parent company's vehicles, they were gradually phased out. Similarly, Henschels made at Kassel eventually became Mercedes units. Trucks in the Henschel heavy-duty range were fitted with Mercedes components on the way to complete integration. A couple of 6x6 heavy-construction hybrids, the LAPK 1632 and LAPK 2632, used the Hanomag-Henschel cab but were powered by the 320bhp V10 OM 403 engine and carried the Mercedes three-pointed star logo. They were produced between 1972 and 1973.

A new, light, Bremen-built, commercial range was introduced in 1977, and the Hamburg factory concentrated on component manufacture for trucks and cars. In the 1980s, the 207D and 308 light vans were made at Bremen, as were the T Series estate cars, with volumes in excess of 50,000 units a year.

Meanwhile, following huge investment and a rationalisation of production facilities at Düsseldorf which aimed at grouping components within their own particular department, light vans and pickup trucks like the 319 and 309 began to be manufactured at a rate of around 15,000 a year. That figure had doubled by 1980, and throughout the 1980s, all Mercedes vans and minibuses of 3.5 to 6.5 tonnes GVW and steering units for Mercedes passenger cars and commercial vehicles were made in Düsseldorf. By 1980, output here included no less than 177 variants of the 16 bus and van ranges between 3.5 and 6.4 tonnes.

With the imminent introduction of an 8bhp per-tonne, power-to-weight ratio (which actually came in 1971), and the implication that 304bhp would be required to haul 38 tonnes GVW, the German manufacturers pulled out the stops for the 1969 Frankfurt Show. Detail changes were made to all existing direct-injection, Mercedes engines to gain the extra power at lower engine speeds, consisting of modifications to the injection pump design and the shape of the pistons. But the star of the

show was a completely new engine. It was the water-cooled, 16-litre 320bhp OM 403, a 90-degree V10 unit with direct injection, related to a class of V-cylinder, multi-fuel military units, and despite its capacity it weighed in at only 910kg – 25 per cent lighter than comparable V8s. Unsurprisingly, it was the forerunner of Mercedes-Benz's 1970s 400 Series, modular, truck-engine range, produced in tandem with MAN.

Also on show at Frankfurt in 1969 was a new cab-over range of truck-tractor units for semi-trailers and trailer-hauling, rigid trucks. There were the 6x4 LP 2232 and the LPS 2232, a twin-steer 6x2. Both models were equipped with the new V10 engine and the new hydraulic tilting cab. This could be either a day cab with two bunks or a full sleeper cab. They also had air-assisted clutches and all-synchromesh, four-speed, ZF gearboxes. The Mercedes-Benz stand also featured a complete range of vehicles fitted with an air-suspension system on all axles, which was particularly advantageous for trucks with demountable bodies, where the suspension system was used to raise or lower the body. German operators were among the first to adopt demountable body systems, one of which was called the Rationorm system, equipped with a tail-lift and designed for a producer-to-wholesaler and wholesaler-to-supermarket operation. Models were tailored for industrial requirements, including the construction industry, distribution, utility and municipal work, and refrigerated transport, all of which had a significant influence on vehicle design.

LONG-DISTANCE HAULAGE

For long-distance haulage in 1970, Mercedes offered three drawbar trailer trucks built on the LP and LPS 1519/48 and the 30.8-tonne GTW 192bhp LP and LPS 1519/51 chassis. Two articulated, semi-truck-tractors were offered as an alternative to drawbar trailers with five variations on the theme. The smaller of the two was the 168bhp LPS 1313, designed to operate at 21 tonnes. The larger LPS 1319 units

Heart of the Actros V6 and V8 engine. Four valves per cylinder ensured a more efficient induction and combustion cycle.

were powered by 192bhp engines.

The ruling on the 8bhp per-tonne ratio for truck and trailer combinations of up to 28.5 tonnes GVW, which came into force on 1 January 1971, was highly unpopular with manufacturers like Daimler-Benz, because they weren't on a level playing field with the rest of Europe. These were, after all, the days of the recently expanded Common Market. Nevertheless, the 400 Series of diesel engines was introduced to cover a power band from 130bhp to 430bhp in normally aspirated form, and up to 570bhp with turbocharger. The 400 Series also included a 130bhp in-line four-cylinder, a 160bhp five-cylinder and a 192bhp in-line six-cylinder unit, with long-stroke versions of the two bigger engines. These engines were the subject of a joint production agreement with MAN, which also extended to production of planetary gear hub-reduction axles.

The 400 Series engines, OM 401 V6, OM 402 V8 and OM 403 V10, and axles were fitted in a new range of dual-purpose tipper trucks operating at 16 to 26 tonnes GVW. There were 19 different models, made in cab-over or conventional format, which could be

specified in all-wheel drive and as two- or three-axle versions. All had ZF transmissions, with the S6-80 and the S6-90 six-speed, synchromesh gearboxes with splitter boxes available as options on the six- and eight-cylinder engines, with the nine-speed version for the V10 unit.

A new aerodynamic cab gave Mercedes medium- and heavy-duty trucks a facelift, as well as renewed emphasis on driver comfort. A cab suspension system based on pivoting bearings, with rubber bushes at the front and coil springs and dampers at the rear, isolated the driver from poor road surfaces. The interior was reinforced by pressed-steel parts while a double-shell front panel provided a relative degree of safety.

The 400 Series engines made its debut in the tipper and dumper ranges at Frankfurt in 1973, and the following year a range of heavy-duty trucks known as the New Generation was announced; these were based on rationalised component sources, with operational weights right up to 40 tonnes GCW. The model line included cab-over tipper trucks and general haulage vehicles that shared cabs in common with one another, and was swiftly expanded to include the 1619, the first of the New Generation 16-tonne rigids launched at the 1975 Brussels Show. A medium-duty range encompassing 10, 12- and 14-tonners appeared at Frankfurt later that year. These were fitted with the 130bhp straight-six OM 352, the 168bhp turbocharged OM 352A and the 192bhp V6 OM 401, all using Mercedes-Benz gearboxes. At the top end of the medium-duty range was the 142S, a 14-tonne truck-tractor unit powered by the 240bhp V8 OM 402 engine. Even the redoubtable ten-year-old 2032S was given a facelift, as well as improvements to steering and axle location. Another development on display at the 1975 Frankfurt Show was a four-speed automatic transmission for the Transporter range to ease the work of urban operators.

Hitting the headlines at Frankfurt in 1979 was the new 375bhp twin-turbocharged OM 422LA V8 engine, which was a development of the 400 Series unit. Eaton constant-mesh gearboxes were offered for the first time as alternatives to ZF synchromesh units. New 16-speed ZF gearboxes and lower-ratio rear axles were also aimed at maximising economy.

On the world stage, the Tata joint venture closed in 1968, although Daimler-Benz continued to hold a 12.7

The Atego range was voted International Truck of the Year for 1999. It replaced the LK and MK ranges for medium- and light-duty applications.

per cent stake. Through its connection with Hanomag-Henschel, Daimler-Benz also acquired 25.5 per cent of Bajaj Tempo Ltd of Poona, which built the Hanomag light van range for the Indian market. Meanwhile, Mercedes-Benz Brazil accounted for almost half the Brazilian truck market by the late 1970s, building some 60,000 trucks a year. In Argentina, Daimler-Benz production volumes were much smaller, yet still represented a 35 per cent market share. In Iran, assembly facilities for trucks and buses were established in 1967, leading to the formation two

815 ATEGO LR CAB

Make: *Mercedes-Benz*
Model: *815 rigid*
Type: *4x2, forward cab*
Engine: *Mercedes-Benz OM 904 LA 152bhp at 2100rpm*
Gearbox: *Mercedes-Benz 5 speed*
Suspension:
  front and rear: parabolic leaf springs, shock absorbers, anti-roll bar, optimal Telligent suspension and four pneumatic cushions
Chassis: *parallel side frames with sheet-steel cross-members, assembled with bolts and rivets*
Brakes: *European ventilated disc brakes, dual circuit, pneumatic*
Gross Vehicle Weight: *7490kgs*
Wheel base: *3020mm to 4820mm (118ins to 190ins)*

years later of the Iranian Diesel Engine Manufacturing Company, of which Daimler-Benz owned 30 per cent. Following the revolution in 1979, the market crashed and engine production fell from over 20,000 units a year to below 7000. In Saudi Arabia, the Mercedes-Benz distributor Jaffali & Bros founded the National Automobile Industry Company Ltd of Jeddah in 1975, with Daimler-Benz holding a 26 per cent interest.

In Africa, Daimler-Benz bought a 26.7 per cent stake in United Car and Diesel Distributors (Pty) Ltd, of Pretoria. Daimler-Benz's Australian company was set up in the 1950s but didn't really take off until 1978, when Mercedes-Benz (Australia) Pty Ltd opened a heavy truck plant at Mulgrave, Melbourne. But in a change of policy in the 1970s, Daimler-Benz created its own totally controlled subsidiaries, starting in France in 1969, followed by Britain in 1974, and then Belgium, Holland, Austria and Switzerland in 1979. The Italian subsidiary was Mercedes-Benz Italia SpA, formed in 1973 with Daimler-Benz owning 75 per cent. The Spanish subsidiary was Compania Hispano Alemana de Productos Mercedes-Benz, in which Daimler-Benz held a 50.5 per cent share, and in 1972, it merged with the VW subsidiary IMOSA to form Compania Hispano Alemana de Productos Mercedes-Benz Volkswagen SA (MEVOSA for short). In 1981, a new company was set up called Mercedes-Benz Espana SA following the acquisition of 52.7 per cent of MEVOSA.

Mercedes-Benz's most notable event of the late 1990s was the acquisition of Ford Motor Company's heavy truck division in January 1998. It was the end of an era and, in a sense, the revival of another, because thereafter the marque would be produced and sold under the Sterling trademark in North America. The Sterling range of Classes 6, 7 and 8 heavy-duty trucks would be marketed through an independent network of more than 200 dealers in the USA and Canada, consisting of vehicles for con-

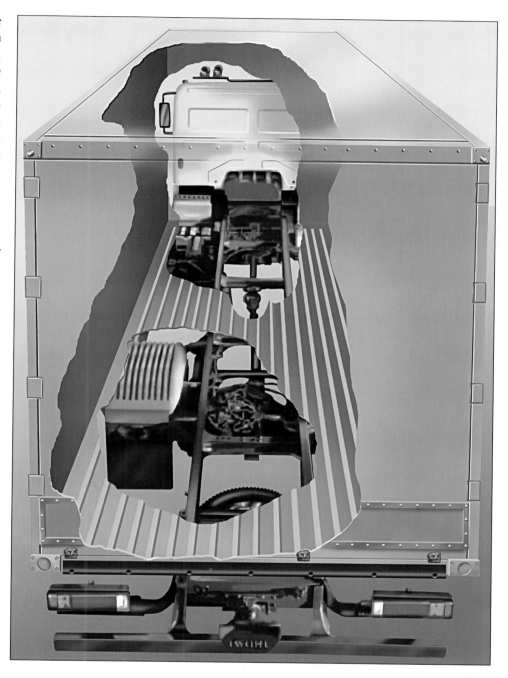

struction-site and long-haul work. It was expected that there would be no conflict with Freightliner, which would expand its market share in the US Class 8 truck segment to nearly 40 per cent. In 1997, Freightliner sold 80,200 commercial vehicles in North America.

Mercedes-Benz's Trucks Europe unit completed its heavy-duty Actros truck range with construction and special application vehicles in 1997, when the Actros was voted Truck of the Year. In revamping the product line, a new six-cylinder version of the 900 Series Powertrain was introduced, coupled

The Atego light truck range has a unique two-piece chassis designed to provide an ultra-low cab floor that gives greater head room for the driver.

with a direct-drive system. The Atego distributor truck was launched early in 1998, and was named Truck of the Year for 1999, while the Citaro was the new-generation, Mercedes-Benz city bus. Trucks Europe production amounted to 78,800 units in 1997, coming largely from Wörth and the plants in Aksaray in Turkey, Arbon in Switzerland, and Molsheim, France.

FREIGHTLINER

Freightliner is a difficult company to pigeonhole, because although it's been part of the Daimler-Benz empire since 1981, for a very short while in 1979 it had a sales agreement with Volvo. The picture is further confused because for 24 years from 1951, Freightliners were marketed and serviced by White trucks, which itself subsequently came under the Volvo umbrella.

Freightliner was founded in 1940 by Leland James, who had been in the truck business himself since the age of 19. He became president of the trucking co-operative Consolidated Freightways, and in the absence of sufficiently durable, lightweight vehicles his workshops in Salt-Lake City, Utah, began building their own aluminium truck and trailer bodies. In 1937, their first cab was fitted to a Fageol chassis run-

ning a six-cylinder Cummins diesel unit, and by 1939 a further 20 were built. These basic angular boxes were dubbed 'Monkey Ward' Freightliners, on the grounds of their amateurish build quality. But in 1940 the firm built a pair of aluminium and magnesium cab-over prototypes that were far lighter than comparable vehicles. Initial production was short-lived because of the advent of the Second World War,

but included the aluminium-panelled 'shovel-nose' model and the 600, which was mostly a steel-panelled cab due to shortages of aluminium. As the Salt Lake City factory went over to make aircraft components and hatch covers for ships, Consolidated Freightways grew so successful that it was sued by the US Justice Department for holding a monopoly in 48 states. All production equipment was relocated from the Salt Lake City plant to Portland, Oregon, to start the new Freightliner Corporation in 1947.

Once again, aluminium and magnesium were used extensively in these post-war Model 800 Freightliners. The cab was redesigned and the resulting bonnet shape earned it the nickname 'bubble-nose' due to the presence of a larger radiator. Fifty of these vehicles were produced in the first two years, and in 1949 came the 5-ton 4x2 cab-over truck-tractor, Model WF800, which was based on a Parrish chassis frame with semi-elliptic leaf springs front and rear. It was powered by a 262bhp Hercules DFXH six-cylinder

1998 FREIGHTLINER CENTURY CLASS 8

Make: *Freightliner*
Model: *Century Class*
Type: *6x2, conventional*
Engine: *732-cubic inch (12-litre) Detroit Diesel or Mercedes-Benz diesel*
Transmission: *Rockwell RM 1-14 5A*
Front axle: *Rockwell FF-961*
Rear axle: *Rockwell RT-40-145*

diesel unit, allied to a Fuller 4B86 four-speed transmission and Fuller 8016 three-speed auxiliary transmission with Timken front and rear axles and Gemmer 500 steering. It was slowed up by Bendix-Westinghouse brakes and the tyres were 10x22 12-ply front and rear. Steering was the Gemmer 500 type. The Model 900 that appeared a year later had much the same specification, except for the addition of an integral sleeper unit.

In 1951, Freightliner made a deal with the White Motor Corporation of 'Cleveland, Ohio, for the sales and servicing of its trucks, electing to concentrate fully on the manufacturing aspect. The new trucks were badged

Cutaway of the 1995 Freightliner FLD120 conventional Class 8 model featuring a 70in (178cm) Mid-Roof sleeper cab, topped by an air deflector. Characteristic fittings are the riveted aluminium cab, flat windscreen panes and three-piece bumper. The front axle is set back under the engine, which could be either Caterpillar, Cummins, Detroit Diesel or Mercedes-Benz.

accordingly, and launched as White-Freightliners in the USA and Canada under the slogan 'Lightweight – More Freight'.

WHITE-FREIGHTLINER
White-Freightliner trucks were available as two basic models. The WF-42 was a four-wheeler truck-tractor capable of hauling two 24-ft (7.3-m) trailers within the 60-ft (18-m) overall length restriction that prevailed in most Western states. The WF-64 was a three-axle, dual-drive truck with 22-ft (6.7-m) body and a single 28-ft (8.5-m) drawbar trailer. The Freightliners' lightweight construction enabled operators to carry nearly a ton more cargo than most commercials. The 4x4 WF-4864 Spacemaker truck-tractor with its 48-in (1.2-m) flat-fronted cab was unveiled in 1948, fitted with the Cummins 'pancake' engine. Because of litigation affecting other companies, Freightliner abandoned the tilt-cab design in favour of three removable engine covers. This was also partly due to the company's roots in the ethics of

the cooperative, which enabled operators, drivers and mechanics to stipulate preferable innovations, such as the roof-mounted sleeper cab, which White-Freightliner incorporated in 1953 in its WF7564 model. This groundbreaking vehicle set new standards for the truck industry. Freightliner reverted to the tilt-cab in 1958 with the 90-degree canting Model 8164T, and its flat glass and sheet-metal monocoque design held sway for nearly four decades.

Meanwhile, a new 47,000-sq.ft (4366-sq.m) plant opened in 1960 in Pomona, California. The first model to roll off the assembly lines was the WFT-7242 cab-over truck-tractor, equipped with a deluxe 72in (1.8m) sleeper unit. The setting up of an assembly plant in Canada in 1961 coincided with production topping 1200 units, while total Freightliner production reached 10,000 units in 1963. The Portland plant had reached full capacity by this time, which amounted to five trucks a day. The first Turboliner appeared in 1965 fitted with a 300bhp Boeing 553 gas-turbine engine. Its chief

1998 'Century Class' Freightliner was a state-of-the-art western conventional model, equally popular in Australia as the USA.

advantage was that it was over a ton lighter than a comparable diesel engined truck, but it also had a prodigious thirst for fuel, and this limited its attractions considerably.

Another new plant was set up at Indianapolis in 1966, which saw the 20,000th Freightliner delivered. Three years later, the Portland plant became a components factory and warehouse, and its vehicle production relocated to Indianapolis for construction of the Powerliner model. In 1973 the Pomona plant shifted to bigger premises in Chino, California. Joining the big Powerliner in the 1974 Freightliner range was a new lightweight conventional truck which shared 80 per cent of its components with the cab-over models. This included the Cummins NTC290 powertrain, which had a Fuller clutch and Roadranger 10-

speed transmission, with 4x2 or 6x4 Rockwell rear axles suspended on Freightliner's own semi-elliptic system.

In 1983, the US Surface Transportation Assistance Act put the truck manufacturing industry back on its feet, and permitted 80,000lb GVW rigs to use interstate highways. Freightliner responded to the new legislation with a raised roof sleeper unit for its conventional trucks and upgrades for the cab-over lines. The 112, its first new model since the German take-over was unveiled in 1985, was also its first medium-duty conventional model.

More specialised vehicles appeared in the 1990s: front-axle conventional trucks for hauling high density commodities; vehicles for the construction and logging industries, which included the FLD120 classic conventional and the FLD1

125D dump truck. By 1995, there were ten basic models in the Freightliner range, with diverse axle and driveline variations and engine options. They supplied 1700 long conventional trucks and truck tractors to the US and Middle Eastern military. Freightliner's Business Class truck range replaced Mercedes-Benz class 6, 7 and 8 offerings in the USA and Canada. In 1996, Freightliner acquired the assets of fire engine manufacturer American LaFrance.

A facelift the same year saw Freightliner's long and medium conventional Century Class models adopt a circular headlight design that differentiated them from the square headlights of early 1990s models, while a new 12-litre (732-cubic inch) engine was developed in conjunction with Detroit Diesel and Mercedes-Benz.

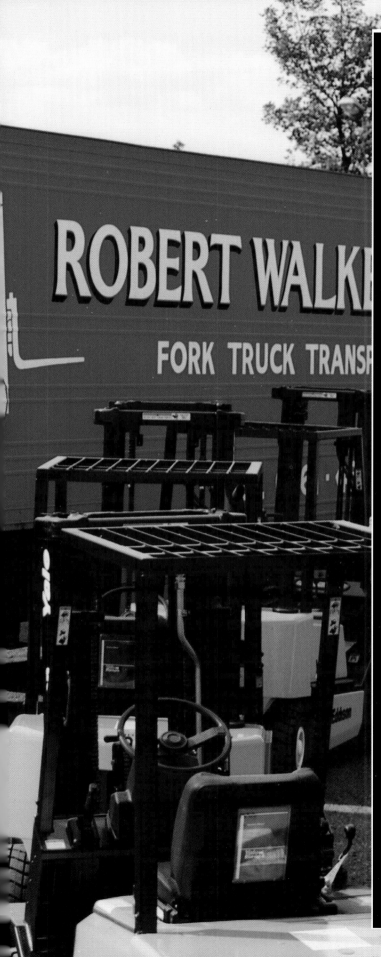

ERF

The letters ERF stand for Edwin Richard Foden, a son of the founder of the Foden dynasty, who was very much involved with the evolution of that company's business in steam traction engines and the transition to diesel power. However, in 1933, after a brief retirement, E.R. Foden was back at work, fronting a new company managed by one of his sons, Dennis, nephew George Faulkner and other key ex-Foden staff. So as not to conflict with the neighbouring Foden concern, they took E.R. Foden's initials as the company name.

By the early 1930s, it was clear that the days of the lumbering steam traction engine were numbered, although they were simple to construct and very powerful, and the diesel engine was the likely new mode of propulsion. ERF's first design was a 12-tonne GVW cab-over, two-axle truck designated chassis 63 (a reference to E.R. Foden's age), and known as the C.I. 4, which stood for compression ignition four-cylinder. It was powered by a Gardner 4L2 diesel engine mounted in a Rubery Owen chassis, with a David Brown gearbox, axles from Kirkstall Forge, and Lockheed hydraulic brakes with a Clayton Dewandre vacuum servo. The Jennings-designed cab was considered quite stylish for its time, and consisted of an ash

The EC Series was launched in 1992 and was the latest incarnation of the SP cab, which was itself four years in the making and the subject of an investment costing several million. The EC10 pictured is powered by a 10-litre (610-cubic inch) Perkins engine.

The first ERF truck came out in 1933 and was given the chassis number 63, which implied that the company had already made a number of vehicles. It was restored in 1971 by ERF apprentices.

frame clad in aluminium panels with steel mudguards, a plywood floor and leather-cloth covered 'stick-and-slat' roof.

SUN WORKS

E.R. Foden was something of a sun worshipper, and the Sandbach, Cheshire plant was called Sun Works, and built adjacent to Jenning's coachworks where the cabs were made. Four chassis were assembled initially, and it didn't matter that the embryo firm had few machine tools at its disposal, as all the major assemblies were sourced from outside suppliers, and ERF-designed components like engine mounting brackets were also made off-site.

ERF's first six-wheeler was built in 1934 and designated C.I.5-6 and powered by a Gardner SLW. The balloon tyres on the double-drive rear bogie could be seen as the forerunner of modern super-single tyres. ERF was also making two-axle cab-over trucks and drawbar trailers and selling them as complete units, although maximum speed was a sluggish 16mph (26km/h),

and a passenger was legally obliged to travel with the rig to operate the trailer brake located in the nearside of the cab. In 1937, the Edinburgh removals firm H&R Duncan ordered a high volume pantechnicon with two steering front axles installed, while retaining the single-rear driving axle. This was the first double-front and single-rear axle configuration in the UK, and became known as a Chinese Six layout.

Towards the end of the decade, Gardner introduced its lightweight 57bhp, 3.8-litre (232-cubic inch), four-cylinder 4LK engine, which was fitted in the new ERF OE4 cab-over 6-tonner, in which the chassis curved over the rear axle. In 1939, ERF developed new tipping gear for the 7.5-tonne tipper trucks for civilian use, but the following year production went over to military vehicles commissioned by the Ministry of Defence. These included two-axle CI.4 models at 12 tonnes GVW for a variety of applications, including wading, and the vehicles were tested on the extensive sands of Southport beach in the north west of England. For the first time there was a serious requirement for truck-tractors to haul semi-trailers, and ERF built complete rigs, designated the type 529, which operated with a fixed fifth wheel, and type 560 with a Scammell coupling.

In order to raise money for the war effort, ERF raffled an OE4 truck, which contributed towards a Spitfire aircraft, which was known as 'Sun Works'.

A facelift in 1948 gave the cab front a V-profile, masked somewhat by the flat radiator that now had a shiny chrome grille. The new range could be specified with Gardner 4LW, SLW and 6LW engines with ratings of 68bhp, 85bhp and 102bhp, allied to a five-speed David Brown gearbox. It was also equipped with Lockheed hydraulic-assisted brakes and 12-volt electrics, and was launched at the first post-war Commercial Motor Show at Earls Court in October 1948.

E.R. Foden, the man who had been at the forefront of two major transport revolutions, from horse to steam-power and from steam to diesel, died aged 80 in 1950. His son Dennis Foden became chairman and managing director in 1951.

In 1952, a modified 44G four-wheeler with GVW of 12 tonnes appeared, powered by a 75bhp Gardner 4LW, with a hydraulic clutch and a removable engine access panel. The radiator grille was now a large oval shape with the logo in the centre, flanked by cromed arrowheads. The cab also included opening quarter-light windows.

EXPORT MARKET SUCCESS

In 1954, a new heavy-duty, 6x4 truck-tractor designated the 66R was introduced for sale to export markets. It was powered by a 184bhp Rolls-Royce C6 NFR engine and rated at 30 tonnes GVW. Among the first customers were South African Railways and Bell Brothers, ERF's Australian distributor and operator. Production volumes had by now risen to over 500 units a year.

A new tipper came out in 1955, equipped with Edbro 6EN multi-telescopic, twin-ram tipping gear, which enabled a dump to be made in just over half a minute. This was followed by a scaled-down KV cab-unit on a model designated the LK44, with 9 tonnes GVW and powered by the 57bhp Gardner 4LK engine. The same year a new version of the twin-steer six-wheeler was introduced, the 46T5R, powered by a four-cylinder Rolls Royce C4 NFL engine. It was the first vehicle to run with this particular engine, and was developed to operate at 17 tonnes GVW or 28 tonnes GCW. Also available was the newly imported, US-made, Fuller R-960 Road Ranger 10-speed gearbox, marketed in the UK by Automotive Products. Power-assisted steering was an option only on trucks with two front axles. By 1956, the KV cab was built with a single section plastic roof and one-piece plastic front panel.

Gardner's *pièce de résistance*, the 150bhp 6LX power-unit, came out in 1958. It was vastly more powerful than previous diesel engines used in the majority of British trucks, yet was no larger and no less economical, and this would remain the standard ERF motor for many years. At the Commercial Motor Show the same year, ERF unveiled its first dump truck – as opposed to tipper truck. The

new model was based on a heavy-duty chassis rated at 15 tonnes GVW, and powered by a Gardner 5LW allied with a five-speed gearbox and a Kirkstall double-reduction rear axle. The 7-cubic yard (5.3-cubic metre) steel dump body had a canopy over the all-steel Jennings cab. Gardner engines were in short supply, so 170 bhp Cummins NH engines made at the US company's new Scottish plant at Shotts became available in ERF chassis.

When Dennis Foden died in 1960, he was succeeded by his 30-year-old half-brother Edwin Peter Foden, who was known as PF.

As well as marketing trucks in Australia, New Zealand and South Africa, ERF also sold in Jamaica, Cyprus, Portugal and Libya through distributor Benkatu & Feitury. This saw its only conventional design, a huge 6x6, all-wheel-drive, oil-field support vehicle specifically for use in the desert.

The Sun Works factory was extended and fitted out with new plant and paint facilities in 1970, with a new service department at Middlewich. ERF made a bid for Atkinson at this point, which was rebuffed, and then Foden made a rival bid, but it was Seddon that came up with an acceptable offer, and Seddon Atkinson was born, which is now part of the Iveco group.

NEW RANGE FOR EARLS COURT

A new cab-over range was unveiled at the 1970 Earls Court Show, known as the A Series. The LV cab was re-engineered for greater comfort and better ergonomics, and in appearance it looked close to a modern truck, while the vehicle used many common parts from across the range to keep production costs down. Power steering and heaters were standard and such was its success that 2000 units were sold in 1973 alone. Another new all-steel cab was sourced from Motor Panels and fitted on certain ERF export models, and in 1973, the Cummins powered 44 tonne GVW Eurotruck was unveiled, with a Motor Panels cab. It was ahead of its time in some ways, as pan-European legislation for heavy-duty trucks would not be standardised until 1983. The SP,

The EC-series truck-tractor unit has sleeping compartment and state-of-the-art aerodynamic roof line and side panels. Interior trim levels include standard, LX or Sovereign options with different designs and different levels of comfort.

or steel and plastic cab, that graced the eight-wheeler B Series trucks of 1975 was styled by Ken Skelton, and was produced by a new technique that bonded sheet-moulded compound panels onto a steel spaceframe. It was strong enough to match newly introduced, EEC 29 roll-over standards.

A recession led ERF to concentrate its efforts on the medium-duty sector in 1978, and at the Birmingham National Exhibition Centre the prototype of the M Series was launched. It was powered by a 180bhp Gardner 6LXB driving through a mid-mounted David Brown gearbox.

But gloom and despondency loomed. Whereas 1979 had been a record year for new truck sales, the market crashed as manufacturers and distributors resorted to discounting in order to shift unsold stocks. ERF's £4.3 million profit in 1980 was wiped out by a £4.25 million loss in 1981, resulting in redundancies for the first time in its history. Production fell from 16 trucks a day to just 16 a week, but despite the downturn, the B Series was superseded by the C Series in 1981, featuring a revised chassis and the 5P3 cab with a new grille. Turbocharged Gardner engines

The EC14 was ERF's most powerful EC model, using 14-litre (854-cubic inch) Cummins or Perkins 500bhp engines allied to ZF and Eaton transmissions. Judging by the weight of the earth-mover on the low-bed trailer, the EC 14 is using all its pulling power.

ERF 54G

Make: ERF – 1974
Model: 54G
Type: 4x2 14 tonne, 16 tonne
Engine: Gardner 5LW 94bhp
  5-cylinder diesel/Perkins 6.354
  105bhp and 112bhp 6-cylinder diesel
Gearbox: Eaton 542 SMA 5-speed
  constant mesh/David Brown 552
  5-speed constant mesh
Suspension:
  multiple leaf springs
Chassis:
  steel ladder frame, bolted cross
  members
Brakes: Lockheed, Clayton Dewandre
  drum brakes
Weight: 4 tonnes
Maximum speed:
  58mph (93km/h) laden

became available for the first time, and in 1983 the M Series went into small-scale production, powered by the Perkins T6.354.4 engine in place of the Dorman unit. Losses continued, although at a reduced rate, but exports were up by 50 per cent, boosted by a Middle Eastern order for 330 heavy-duty, 6x4 truck-tractor units, powered by 290bhp Cummins engines, Eaton RTO.9509 gearboxes and Hendrickson RT380 two-spring bogies.

In the heavy-duty sector, which was ERF's prime territory, the C Series was re-designated the CP Series – CP stood for Common Parts. The basic specification was a Cummins engine, Eaton gearbox and Rockwell rear-axle driveline, and it effectively ended the long-running association with Gardner engines, David Brown gearboxes and Kirkstall axles. The CP Series was superseded in 1986 by the more refined but similarly-specified E Series, designated the SP4 range.

The main visual differences were the squared-off cab lines and rectangular headlights, while in the suspension-mounted cab there was a new facia and a section of the instrument panel was turned towards the driver. By 1988, production was up to 17 trucks a day and increased to 21 units by the end of the year. The ES6 and ES8 light- to medium-duty models came out in 1988, equipped with a new Steyr-built, all-steel cab and powered by Cummins engines.

Around this time, new engines were available in ERFs, including the 325bhp 10-litre (610-cubic inch) Cummins L10 with output lifted by air-to-air intercooling, and the 465bhp 14-litre (854-cubic inch) Cummins L14, as well as the 6-litre (366-cubic inch) Perkins Phaser and the former Rolls-Royce 12-litre (732-cubic inch) Perkins Eagle TX. In 1990, Gardner engines were finally dropped from the UK market as they couldn't comply with emission regulations, although they were still fitted in buses for export.

In 1991, the market for heavy trucks in the UK crashed from 38,000 to a mere 16,000 units, and once again

ERF production was cut back to eight or nine trucks a day. Redundancies inevitably followed, with a £4 million loss on the year.

Keeping up the family connections, Paul Foden, Peter Foden's son, became UK sales director in July 1991. Subsequent investment in new plants at Sandbach and Middlewich, where cab assembly was transferred during 1993, improved production line capacity.

The EC Series was a totally new truck, based on a strong, lightweight, high-tensile-alloy steel chassis with Rockwell axles and redesigned suspension including anti-roll bar and optional air suspension. It was powered by Cummins or Perkins 8-litre (488-cubic inch), 10-litre (610-cubic inch), 12-litre (732-cubic inch) and 14-litre (854-cubic inch) engines with power outputs ranging from 240bhp to 500bhp, with

ZF or Eaton transmissions, including the Eaton SAMT semi-automatic gearbox. The cab styling and structure were derived from the E Series, with taller windscreen, shallower grille, larger doors and three trim levels.

WESTERN STAR TAKES OVER

In June 1996, Western Star Trucks of Kelowna, British Columbia, Canada, acquired control of ERF. It was clear that in order to survive and remain at the forefront of the truck industry, a partner was needed, and the similarly sized Western Star provided such a match. Each had developed export markets in which its particular design of truck was preferred, although both companies used drive trains which were very similar. Western Star's Australian owner Terry Peabody became Chairman in 1996.

Western Star Trucks were relatively new on the scene, having been established in 1967 as the Canadian subsidiary of the White Motor Corporation. Its production and engineering plant was located in Kelowna, British Columbia, and its brief history followed the path of White, until that company was acquired by Volvo AB in 1981, when Western Star was sold to two Canadian resource companies.

Western Star's late-1980s conventionals looked similar to contemporary Peterbilt, Freightliner or Marmon truck-tractors. Although Western Star had made cab-overs, they were few and far between, that was the principal difference – and symbiosis – with ERF.

Western Star is noted for its heavy-duty conventional models like this one. Principal markets are the USA, Canada and Australia.

FORD

Life begins at 40, so they say, and Henry Ford had attained this ripe old age when his newly formed corporation began building delivery wagons in earnest. There had been a couple of previous attempts around 1900, but Ford's trucks really began to roll in 1905, when its first factory-made commercial vehicle chassis formed the basis for the Ford Delivery Car, with a two-cylinder engine mounted under the seat. Models A and B had been converted privately for commercial use, and the Model E was a passenger car that shared their chassis, drivetrain and body parts, but was fitted with a Delivery Top.

In 1907, the Ford Motor Company absorbed its own subsidiary, the Ford Manufacturing Company, and began producing the forerunner of the Fordson tractor, which was known as the Automobile Plough. At the same time, the Model N Runabout light delivery van was in general use.

Ford made a number of passenger cars that year, but in 1908 Henry introduced what was to become perhaps his most famous product, the Model T. The suspension consisted of semi-elliptic, transverse, cantilever springs, and it was powered by a four-cylinder engine with torque tube drive. Although it was made in the factory as a passenger car and taxi, numerous aftermarket conversions existed with chassis

In 1995 Ford introduced the AeroMax 9500 as the first Class 8 truck-tractor designed exclusively for over-the-road use, initially as a 113-in (287-cm) bumper-to-back-of-cab linehaul model.

extensions to build a 1-ton Model T truck.

There was the aura of the maverick about Henry Ford, as he hadn't obtained authority from the Association of Licensed Automobile Manufacturers to build his vehicles, so to run a Ford was to snub the establishment to an extent. However, Ford won the subsequent courtroom battle in 1911, and its victory contributed significantly to the free entrepreneurial spirit of America's automotive industry.

Then in 1917, Ford began to make trucks on a permanent basis. Not surprisingly, the Ford 1-ton Model TT truck resembled many of the aftermarket conversions based on the basic Model T. Its chassis was more robust and its wheelbase was 24in (61cm) longer than the car chassis, with stiffer suspension and artillery-type wheels with solid rubber tyres and a more substantial worm-drive rear axle. Also in 1917, the Model T radiator changed from brass to black painted steel, and the two millionth unit rolled off the production line. It was the year that the

Fordson tractor came out, and during the last two years of the First World War, 7000 Fordsons were exported to the UK. In 1918, Ford built some 39,000 vehicles and various items of military equipment for the war effort, including a submarine chaser boat.

ROUGE RIVER PLANT
The vast Rouge River plant was built at Detroit in 1919, and Model T production attained three million units. By comparison, the much newer Model TT truck output had reached 100,000. Fordson tractors were manufactured in a new plant at Cork in Ireland, and a Danish subsidiary was set up at Copenhagen. On the mechanical front, Model T owners could order the optional starter motor with battery and generator from this point, and in 1920 the Model TT came with demountable wheel rims as a further option. Ford launched its first heavy truck prototype under the Fordson banner. It was a 3-ton cab-over model, and although it never actually went into production, certain Fordson dealers constructed a

Ford's Model TT was its first mass-produced, factory-built truck, based heavily on the Model T but with a longer wheelbase and sturdier chassis. This is a 1923 Ford TT Railway Express Truck.

few similar trucks powered by the farm tractor engine. Other truck makers, including American LaFrance, built fire appliances on the Ford chassis.

The recession of the early 1920s was weathered by slashing prices, reducing output and even closing some plants, while dealers were obliged to maintain excessive stocks. In the middle of this financial crisis, Fordson production was relocated from Dearborn to Rouge River, and the situation was further exacerbated when Ford bought itself the Detroit, Toledo and Ironton Railroad for a cool $5 million. However, control of the railway would enable the company to transport its raw materials more economically.

Ford was on a roll after the recession ended, and its products were now being assembled under license in Japan, and it had acquired the Lincoln Motor

Company. Ford was now making its own batteries, and even bought the town of Pequaming, Michigan in order to obtain its own timber mill, while another parts factory came on stream at Green Island near New York.

In 1924, Ford began building complete truck bodies in-house, based on the Model TT chassis. These consisted simply of a canopy top mounted on the Express body in open, curtained or side-screen versions, and there were eight combinations of complete cabs and bodies available. Buses with 30-passenger capacity were also built on extended Model TT chassis. Also in 1924, the company acquired C.E. Johansson, who made precision machine tool gauges, and two big diesel freighter vessels were launched on the Great Lakes for shipping raw materials to the Rouge River plant. For 1925, an 8-ft (2.4-m) platform stake-bed truck (literally, a flatbed with a fence of stakes around the edge of the platform) was introduced, and Ford's

first closed-cab model came out, along with the first factory-assembled pickup.

Another milestone was passed as the millionth truck chassis was produced, and meanwhile the Model T and Model TT engines were improved, with better lubrication and lighter pistons, soon to be followed by steel valves instead of cast iron and 32x6-in (81x15-cm) rear tyres. The following year, the Model TT light-duty models received new cabs, and the 2-ton cab-over Fordson truck prototype that had been on the stocks for some time was finally given the go-ahead. On the corporate front, Ford was involved in aviation with the Tri-motor Stinson, and new plants were opened in Chester, Pennsylvania, and Plötzensee, Germany, bringing Ford's factories and assembly plants to a total of 88 sites.

MODEL AA
The Model T reached the end of the line in 1927, and factories went over to making the Model A. The Model TT

lingered on for some months until the 1.5-ton Model AA truck was introduced. Initially, both the car and truck models were powered by the same 40bhp engine, which breathed through a Zenith updraft carburettor and had a forged-steel, three-bearing crank and aluminium pistons, and three-speed, sliding transmission. Styling for both cabins included rounded front wings, acorn-shaped headlights and a nickel-plated radiator surround. Along with a stiffer chassis there were heavier springs at the front, and 13- or 15-leaf, longitudinal cantilevered springs at the rear. At first, the Model AA ran on 20-in (51-cm), welded, spoke-steel wheels, but these were soon replaced with five-hole ventilated disc wheels with offset rims,

While car manufacturers updated styling on an annual basis, the truck makers lagged some way behind. This 1953 light-duty Ford pickup truck has rounded cab and wings but a far more utilitarian appearance than contemporary saloons.

with better braking and high-pressure tyres. The powertrain included a two-piece driveshaft and larger, worm-gear rear axle, and in 1930 a four-speed transmission became standard issue. In a bid to create a more robust vehicle, a heavier, spiral-bevel rear axle was fitted and the front axle, radius rods, kingpins and springs were beefed up, while brakes were enlarged to 14in (35cm) in diameter.

The basic Model A car chassis was also available with a variety of light-commercial bodies such as a delivery van, pickup, station wagon and taxi. The Model AA could be specified with hydraulically operated dump truck body, as well as a longer wheelbase chassis that was mostly for the benefit of bus and coach companies. Restyled cabs similar to those of the contemporary passenger car were fitted from 1930, and stainless steel headlights and radiator surround were optional for the trucks – otherwise they were simply painted black. Several commercial prototypes were based on an extended Model A chassis, while the Briggs Company built the Type 78-A utility pickup body. Ford supplied its own versions on the AA model truck.

A Ford provincial truck dealership is almost cut off by snow drifts in the depths of a 1920s winter. Note the old-style fuel pumps under the gallery.

Although by 1930 Ford was finally outstripped for good by GM in terms of car sales, Ford remained comfortably ahead in the truck market. As the Depression loomed, a new manufacturing plant came on stream at Long Beach, California, as did a new assembly plant at Richmond, California. On the global stage, Model AA trucks started to be built under license at the Soviet AMO Plant in Moscow, and the German affiliate Ford-Werke A.G. opened a new assembly plant at Cologne. However, domestic sales crashed in 1931 as the recession hit home.

Meanwhile, the car and truck ranges were revamped as the Model B and Model BB in 1932, along with a sensational new 65bhp 221-cubic inch (3.6-litre) V8 engine. The cylinders were arranged in a 90-degree V, as opposed to the 60-degree Lincoln V8. Further modifications to the spec included a revised chassis, synchromesh gearbox and semi-elliptic springs at the rear instead of longitudinal cantilever springs. A 17-gallon (64-litre) petrol tank was mounted under the seat instead of an 11-gallon (41-litre) tank located beneath the scuttle. This was virtually the last time that car and commercial models bore similar styling cues, as the fashions in the car market moved on rapidly at this time, with

FORD BB

Make: *Ford – 1932*
Model: *BB*
Type: *4x2, conventional*
Engine: *Ford 65hp 221-cubic inch (3.6-litre) V8 petrol unit*
Gearbox: *Ford 3-speed synchromesh*
Suspension:
  front: longitudinal cantilever springs, rear: semi-elliptic springs
Chassis: *parallel ladder-type frame with cross-members*
Brakes: *drums*

designs increasingly more ground-hugging, whereas the truck business focused more on practical aspects. It wasn't until 1935 that commercials inherited the rakish grille styling from the car lines.

CAR-DERIVED COMMERCIALS

Car-derived commercials in 1933 included the Model 40 station wagon and sedan delivery and the longer wheelbase Model 46. The higher compression V8 motor was given aluminium cylinderheads, which in turn improved its performance. There continued to be a call for Ford chassis on which to construct bus and coach bodies of various configurations, and these gradually came to be fitted with the V8 engine instead of the old four-cylinder units. Marmon-Herrington also offered a 4x4 conversion for Ford trucks, known as the All-Wheel-Drive Ford, while the end of the prohibition era found drinks producers swelling the Ford coffers with orders for beer lorries. Companies specialising in third axle conversions included Acme Sixwheeler, Thornton Tandem and Warford Sextette.

The Model BB's 80bhp V8 engine used cast-iron cylinder heads with a lower compression ratio to cope with lower fuel octane ratings, and was improved in 1934 with new manifolds, fuel pump, Stromberg carburettor and fully counterbalanced crankshaft and open-skirt pistons. It was also looking at ways to overcome inherent over-

heating problems with bigger radiators and cooling fans. The new Model 48 came along with a redesigned chassis and powertrain improvements shared with the Models 50 and 51 commercials, which also featured new cab designs. Open cabs now disappeared. Detroit's municipal transit system bought 300 buses based on the Model 51 in 1935, and the following year, Ford introduced the Model 70, its first production line bus. They were built on a forward-control chassis and powered by an 85bhp V8 and fitted with a 25-passenger body made by Union City.

PLASTIC PANELS

In mid-decade, Ford the maverick was experimenting with plastic panels based on soya-bean derivatives, although prototypes thus clad never went into production. It was also investigating the use of alcohol-based fuels that would have been easily distilled in rural areas, but the big oil companies already had a tight grip on patents and distribution systems.

By 1937, Ford had overtaken its rivals Chevrolet, Dodge, GMC and International in truck sales, thanks partly to a workforce that was not obliged by the unions to strike in the spate of industrial unrest that beset the other manufacturers. Henry Ford flatly refused to accept unionisation, but from being the best-paid workers in the industry, Ford's wages fell to below those of competitors in 1938.

Meanwhile, Ford was building a wide range of specialised vehicles, including dump trucks and propane gas tankers, while outside suppliers provided bus and coach bodies. In 1938, Ford trucks appeared with an oval grille and front-hinged bonnets, with wings and headlights restyled accordingly, and the first factory-built, cab-over model came out. The 1.5-ton chassis was reduced to a more popular 1-ton rating and the model became known as the 350, and an Eaton two-speed rear axle was also available.

Hydraulic brakes were long overdue, and in 1939, all Ford vehicles finally got them. This coincided with the

Ford W-series cab-over interstate truck with Cummins NTC-290 engine. This 1975 model came in short cab or sleeper cab variants. An aluminium cab and other lightweight components saved up to 1900lbs (.85 tons) for increased payload capacity.

introduction of the Mercury Model 99 light-duty truck, powered by a bored-out Ford V8 and available as conventional and cab-over layout, also providing the chassis for the Transit Bus.

MILITARY VEHICLES

The first Ford plant to gear up for war production was the Canadian factory, which used components that were interchangeable with GMC and the British Ford operation. Far from being a pacifist, Henry Ford was more of an isolationist, intent on defending the USA rather than Britain. So it was perhaps predictable that Ford-Werke AG was soon building military trucks for the German war effort, just as GM's Opel subsidiary did. In 1940, Ford announced a new range of 3-tonners designated the 018T and 098T, and the very same models were built in large numbers at Cologne and designated V3000 by the *Wehrmacht*. Ford military vehicles were also built in large quantities by GAZ in Russia. In the USA,

Ford won a contract to make 1500 general-purpose reconnaissance vehicles, which gave birth to the name Jeep. The concept was based on a design by American Bantam, and it was originally known as the Blitz Buggy, with an 80-in (203-cm) wheelbase and 45bhp Fordson tractor engine.

For the duration of hostilities, Ford made B-24 Liberator heavy bombers at its new Willow Run factory, taking off at the rate of one an hour by 1945, and they also made CG-4 heavy gliders. Apart from 277,896 jeeps, Ford also built Model GTB cargo trucks, M-8 and T-17 armoured cars, M-4 medium tanks, M-10 anti-tank vehicles, M-20 scout cars and sundry other equipment. It continued to build the Transit Bus Model 29B and Model 49B with blackout trim, and also introduced the 100bhp V8-powered Model 498T and Model 494T trucks in 1944.

Henry Ford II became the corporate figurehead after the founder died in 1947. Ford's peacetime range consisted of 42 different truck chassis, including conventional platform, cab-over and car-based light delivery vehicles, equipped with V8 or six-cylinder engines. A fresh wave of strikes in the US steel industry disrupted production in 1946 and Ford made a loss of $8 million.

FORD DA2114

Make: *Ford*
Model: *DA2114*
Type: *4x2, cab-over*

1 *Suzie connections – lines for air and electricity supply between tractor and trailer: electricity for lights and indicators; air for brakes, signal unit control and main feed (redline) to air tanks on trailer. ABS as appropriate.*
2 *engine air filter*
3 *fuel tank*
4 *chassis*
5 *fifth wheel coupling*
6 *battery*

NEW CAB DESIGN

Ford's heavy-duty trucks were by no means as big as some of the specialists, with just the 1.5- and 2-ton models in 1947. However, a sea change began the following year with the introduction of the 2.5- and 3-ton F-series models. These vehicles sported completely new cab designs incorporating a horizontal-bar radiator grille. They were built on new chassis and, in F-8 'Big Job' format, powered by a new 145bhp 337-cubic inch (5.5-litre) Lincoln V8 Model 8EQ engine linked to a five-speed gearbox, with air brakes, eight-stud wheels and appropriately heavier suspension parts.

By 1949, Ford listed 164 different types of commercial vehicle, and its heavy-duty F-7 and F-8 chassis were now available with a 178-in (452-cm) wheelbase, while two-speed rear axles were replaced by a single-speed version.

As the USA became embroiled in the Korean War, the corporation ratio-nalised component manufacturing into six separate divisions, and a total of 345,801 trucks were built in 1950, the biggest annual output for 21 years. Statistics rose and fell according to extraneous influences, like the steel workers' strikes that reduced production in 1952, or boosts like the military commissions that included a revised Jeep and the M-48 Patton tank. A facelift in 1951 introduced a full-width radiator grille to front the Five Star cab, which had a 50 per cent larger window area, a pair of wipers and a new instrument panel, plus a water-proof ignition system.

GOLDEN ANNIVERSARY

Ford's F Series Economy line trucks came out to mark the company's 50th anniversary with a plethora of new designations. The old F-2 and F-3 Series were combined to create the F-250, and the F-4 was called the F-350. The F-7 was replaced by the F-700, powered by the Big Six engine, and the F-750 was basically the same vehicle running with the V8 motor. The F-900 model was the uprated F-8, rated at 27,000lb GVW and 55,000lb GCW.

By 1954, Ford had beaten its opposition in completing the transition to an overhead-valve engine design, and its medium-duty V8s were similar to the mighty Lincoln V8. Two F-series trucks known as the T-700 and the T-800 appeared with factory-fitted tandem axles using Eaton-Hendrickson dual-axle drive, suspension and power divider.

The latest wrap-around windscreens

The rounded lines of the 1996 AeroMax 9500 were evolved in extensive wind-tunnel testing and when fitted with all aero-dynamic options it resulted in a 9 per cent improvement in drag coefficient over previous L-series models.

Transmatic – as optional equipment.

A new heavy-duty range appeared in 1958, with GVW ratings of 36,000lb and GCW ratings of 65,000lb, 51,000lb and 75,000lb when equipped with tandem rear axles. Three new V8 truck engines powered them, coupled with eight-speed Fuller R-46 and five-speed Spicer 6000 gearboxes and a heavier 13in (33cm) clutch. Externally, their main distinguishing feature was twin pairs of headlights, and they joined the other 370 commercial models listed by Ford for 1959. The first four-wheel drive models produced by Ford, rather than Marmon-Herrington conversions, were the F-100 and F-250 trucks, which came out that year.

In 1961, the range-topping F-1100 and C-1100 were equipped with heavier axles and became strictly off-road trucks, while their truck-tractor siblings were discontinued. The F-, B- and T-series were completely updated with contemporary cab styling, including a reversion to single headlights, and a new diesel-powered cab-over truck-tractor was introduced. This was the first time a diesel engine had been available in a Ford product, and petrol engines remained the norm. Transmissions included eight- and 10-speed Fuller Roadrangers, and 12-speed Spicer with three- and four-speed auxiliary gearboxes were also available, while the Allison-made Transmatic system was discontinued. Most vehicles had longer wheelbases, achieved by moving the front axles further forward, which had the beneficial effect of reducing overhang. Ford set the standards for the industry by offering a 12-month/12,000-mile (20,000-km) warranty for most trucks, and a new company logo reverted to the oval

FORD AEROMAX

Make: *Ford – 1995*
Model: *AeroMax 9500*
Cab: *steel*
Trim: *graphite standard, mocha or cordovan optional*
Equipment: *18in (46cm) leather-bound steering wheel, air conditioning, upper and lower bunks with foam or sprung mattresses, refrigerator/freezer, shore power provision, table, tv, electric fan.*

The 1995 AeroMax driving position was designed for maximum comfort, with instrumentation and switchgear neatly laid out on the dashboard. The AeroMax cab was considered to be more roomy than any previous Class 8 Ford truck.

corporate vice president by 1960.

For 1957, the cab-over models were fitted with new flat-faced tilt cabs built on new chassis with front axles set back, and the design was used by Mack and FWD trucks. Cabs of conventional trucks in the F-, B- and T-series were smoothed off, with wraparound windscreens and wings and doors now flush fitting. All the heavy-duty range trucks were offered with six-speed Allison automatic transmission – marketed as Ford

were applied to the previous year's cab designs in 1956, while more practical evolutions included a 12-volt electrical system, tubeless tyres, four-barrel carburettors and bigger engines, and a new addition was the T-750-series. On the corporate front, Ford sold 10 million shares on the stock market, and at last joined the Automobile Manufacturers Association from which it had always been excluded. The marketing manager of Ford's Truck Division was now the influential Lee Iacocca, who became

F-SERIES ECONOMY LINE

Engine	GVW	Cylinders	bhp
F-900	27,000lb	8	180
B-500/600/700	20,000lb	8	180
B-750	20,000lb	6	150
C-500/600/750	20,000lb	6/8	150/180

design theme of the 1928-48 era.

The N-Series of conventional truck tractors was introduced in 1963 in a bid to capture the Class 8 heavy truck market. Single rear axle versions used petrol engines, while Super-Duty NTD and tandem-axle models used the V6 Cummins 200 diesel engine, which as far as Ford was concerned, was the first instance of a conventional layout with diesel power. N-series trucks were also available as 9ft (2.7m) and 12ft (3.6m) platform and stake bodied vehicles. Ford's Special Military Vehicle Operations unit began producing the M-656, an eight-wheel 5-ton truck.

VEHICLE SAFETY ISSUES

In 1966, the H-series high tilt cab-over model, popularly known as the Two-Storey Falcon, was superseded by the much less glamorous-looking W-series cab-over model that remained in production until 1978. Meanwhile, the F-8000 now had a Cummins 464-cubic inch (7.6-litre) diesel V8 motor at its disposal. But the passing of the Motor Vehicle Safety Act that year was to have a profound effect on US truck manufacturing, as key issues to do with vehicle safety had to be addressed. The following year, Ford's light trucks had completely new cabs, which contrasted with the heavier-duty models that remained unchanged. Some of these models were uprated under the skin, however, with chassis and suspension changes. Low-profile tubeless tyres were fitted on all models up to the 400 series, while medium-duty trucks now received power steering. Heavy-duty trucks were available with the UK-built Dorset diesel engine, which superseded the Dagenham-produced units, and Detroit Diesels were fitted in the 8000 Series. Generally speaking, the 302-cubic inch (4.95 litre) V8 powered light-duty trucks and the Cummins NH 230 was standard fitment in heavy-duty ranges. In

1968, Ford also won a contract from the US military to build M-151 trucks, and it continued to be the largest truck maker in the USA.

LOUISVILLE LINE

A new line of big conventional trucks was launched in 1970. This was the Louisville series, named after the plant that produced them at Louisville, Kentucky. At the time this was the world's largest truck factory with 2.3 million sq.ft (214,000 sq.m), turning out a staggering 336 units a day. The L-series models superseded many of the existing heavy-duty models including the F-800, and the LT-series superseded the T-series, the LN-series superseded the N-series and the LNT-series superseded

In 1995 Ford launched the Louisville range based around a brand new cab design aimed to fit the requirements of Class 7 and 8 operators. This is the 8500-series model.

the NT-Series. The L-9000 and LT-9000 were considered by many to be the company's first genuine long-distance conventional diesel line-haul trucks. They also looked the part, specifications now included stronger electro-plated corrosion resistant chassis, dual circuit brakes, and the largest windscreen of all trucks. They could be powered by 429-cubic inch (7-litre) Cummins or Detroit Diesel engines driving through 6-, 10-, 13- or 16-speed transmissions.

A 450bhp gas turbine engine, designated the Model 707, was tested by Continental Tramways in 1970, but they were never put into production. As Lee Iacocca became corporate president, Ford retained third place in the heavy truck segment behind International and Mack. But the early

A line-up of late 1980s L-series Louisville tankers, an attractive proposition for small fleets and owner-operators.

1970s was a difficult period economically, with the second and third oil shocks leading to fuel shortages, inflation and a cutting recession. Henry Ford II fired Iacocca in 1978.

The LTL-9000, announced in 1976, was a conventional model with tandem axle, powered by a Cummins NTC-350 diesel engine allied to a 10-speed Fuller RT-910 Roadranger transmission,

Rockwell SQHD rear bogie and a front axle rated at 12,000lb. GVW ratings were from 44,800lb to 60,000lb with 82,000lb GCW, and the LTL-9000 was marketed as an attractive proposition for owner-operators and small fleets. Other diesel engine options included the Caterpillar Economy 3406, the Cummins Formula 290 and the Detroit Diesel V8. The LTL-9000 was aimed at competition from the likes of International, Kenworth and Peterbilt.

THIRD-GENERATION CAB-OVER

Ford's third-generation cab-over model in the Class 8 sector was the impressive looking CL model, in production from 1978 to 1991. The heavy-duty CL-9000 was available in five single-rear axle formats, and in nine tandem-axle wheelbases as the CLT-9000. The GVW rating stayed the same as the LTL conventional at 80,000lb and 82,000lb. Cabs including air-suspension for maximum driver comfort and instrumentation were state of the art. Power-plants were normally 600bhp Cummins KT and KTA diesel engines coupled to a range of nine Fuller transmissions with up to 13 speeds, although Caterpillar, Cummins and Detroit Diesel economy engines could also be specified. The heavy-duty AeroMax conventional truck-tractor, designated LA-9000, came out in 1988, and in single-axle form was rated at 80,000lb GCW, while the LTA-9000 tandem-axle model was rated at 82,000lb GCW. By this time the LTL-9000 and CLT-9000 were known as the

AeroForce models, and were as aerodynamic as it's possible for such a large vehicle to be.

During the 1990s, Ford also offered a wide selection of light- and medium-duty commercial vehicles, including pickups and vans, really too numerous and too small to be worth listing here. In 1994, there was a major redesign of F Series medium-duty and B Series bus chassis, and the Ford Commercial Truck Vehicle Centre was set up. At the time, the company was building 22 different Class 7 and Class 8 trucks in 4x2, 6x2 and 6x4 formats, and GVW ratings ranged from 24,500lb to 66,000lb.

The second generation of Louisville Class 7 and 8 trucks rolled off the lines at the Kentucky Truck Plant – or KTP – in 1995, and this model was the first Ford truck prototype to be built using assembly-line tools. The new Louisville was a 113-in (287-cm) BBC medium-duty conventional truck and truck-tractor, available with an aluminium

A/AT 9522 AEROMAX

Make: *Ford – 1996*
Model: *AT 9522*
Type: *4x2 (A), 6x4 (AT) conventional*
Engine: *Caterpillar C-10 of 305bhp or optionally Caterpillar C-12 of max. 410bhp, 3406E-Mt sz of 310 to 380bhp, or Cummins M11-ESP of 280 to 400bhp or Detroit Diesel series of max. 500bhp*
Gearbox: *Eaton with 10 speeds*
Suspension: *multi-leaf springs, optional parabolics*
Chassis: *ladder-type, steel, twin-beam side frames, steel or aluminium cross-members*
Brakes: *drum, Air Cam compressed air, production ABS system*
PTAC: *8 ton to 14.9 ton*
PTRA: *56.6 ton to 70 ton, max. 130 ton*

cab identical to an all-steel cab. Basic engine for the Louisville 8500 was the 210bhp in-line six-cylinder Ford FD-1460 16 diesel, made in association with Cummins since 1992, while other engines were available from Caterpillar and Detroit Diesel. Standard transmission was an Eaton FS-6205A five-speed, direct manual box with optional electronically controlled automatics. Louisville 9500s used the Fuller RT-11709H nine-speed direct transmission.

The KTP factory employed over 3300 people, who produced F and B Series medium-duty trucks and bus chassis, the Ford CARGO tilt-cab medium, and the Ford L Series Class 7-8 trucks. Output was 45 units an hour on the light commercial truck line, and 27 units an hour on the two heavy truck lines.

The AeroMax 9500 of 1996 was introduced as a 113-in (287-cm) BBC conventional line-haul tractor, and could be powered by Caterpillar, Cummins and Detroit Diesel engines. It featured an all-new, welded-steel cab, comparable in weight to some aluminium cabs, with composite doors and multi-piece, glass-reinforced-plastic (GRP), moulded-tilting, front end. An aluminium cab could be specified for lightweight tractor applications, and a full aerodynamics package, including chassis fairings, was also available. Sleeper compartment options included the Able Body Flat-Top Plus and AeroBullet Plus units in 50-in (127-cm) and 68-in (172-cm) lengths with aluminium floors.

In late 1996, 57-in (145-cm) and 77-in (196-cm) integrated sleepers were introduced for the AeroMax, designed as true stand-up and walk-through units, with ample space and storage, optional cable extensions, refrigerator, TV and video. The interior was 4in (10cm) longer and had 2in (5cm) more seat travel than previous Ford Class 8 trucks. The second version of the AeroMax 9500 was a 122-in (310-cm BBC long-conventional model with 'true integrated sleepers' in 57-in (145-cm) and 77-in (196-cm) lengths, a stand-up/walk-through design with no visible exterior seals.

In January 1998, Ford disposed of its heavy truck division to Daimler-Benz, who renamed the range under the old Sterling banner. On the face of it, it was good to see the revival of an old respected make, even though it epitomised the vogue for badge engineering that became commonplace in the closing years of the twentieth century.

Introduced in 1995, the short conventional Louisville 8500 was powered by the Ford FD-1460 diesel, and was intended for rugged construction site duties.

STERLING

ecause the final run of Ford heavy trucks were marketed as Sterlings, this is probably as good a place as any to provide a brief run down of Sterling's history, even though its final incarnation in the 1950s was as Sterling-White. The marque was founded by William Sternberg as the Sternberg Motor Truck Company, building conventional trucks from three-quarter-ton to 7-ton capacity in West Allis, Milwaukee from 1907. But bowing to anti-German attitudes in the First World War, he changed the name to the far more readily acceptable Sterling trademark in 1916.

During the First World War, Sterling built 479 Class B 3- to 5-ton Liberty trucks alongside these other models. A change of ownership in 1919 led to Robert Hayssen taking over, and his first act was to redesign the company logo,

while the special wood inlay that had been developed by Sternberg for the truck frames was patented in 1922.

There were four Sterling engine sizes in the early 1920s, from 286 cubic inches (4.7 litres) up to 464 cubic inches (7.6 litres), and electric headlights and tail-lamps were standard fittings. Tyres were solid rubber, although the three light-duty models could be specified with pneumatic tyres. As the decade wore on, the range grew broader, from the familiar 1.5-ton model up to a 7.5-ton capacity. What transmission was fitted depended on gross vehicle weight: worm-drive trucks were rated up to 27,000lb GVW and chain-drive trucks were rated up to 35,000lb GVW.

The company merged with Corbitt trucks of North Carolina in 1928, and went public in 1929. By this time, 11 different chain-driven models were on

offer, including the DC26, a three-axle Class 8 dump truck with a lightweight aluminium body by Heil. However, a financial debacle in 1931 obliged the Hayssen family to stand down, and in the following year's corporate restructuring, William S. Sternberg, Jr. became vice-president. At any rate, there were sufficient funds available in 1931 for Sterling to acquire the failing LaFrance-Republic Corporation, which was based at Alma, Michigan. In order to satisfy customers, it is likely that when LaFrance-Republic's parts bins were exhausted, a number of Sterling F Series trucks were simply badged as LaFrance-Republics until the name was dropped in 1942. The modern-looking F Series was introduced in 1932, and featured new cabs and a separate radiator housing.

DIESEL ENGINES STANDARD

The first diesel engine used by Sterling was a Cummins H Series unit fitted in the FD195H model in 1932, and it became standard equipment in all models from 4 tons upwards. Sterling was one of the first truck makers to fit diesel engines as standard, and in 1935 it developed its first supercharged diesel engine for use at high altitudes, specifically for a HCS21OH 6x4 dual-chain-drive truck that was transporting lead and zinc ore in Argentina. Sterling also fitted other similar models with Roots superchargers for use as truck-tractors with a GCW rating of 93,600lb.

Sterling's first cab-over model came out in 1934, designated the Model GD97 and popularly known as the Camel Back. It was a 4x2 truck with similar specification to the F Series conventional and rated at 22,000lb GVW. On early models, the cab tilted

When Ford's heavy truck division came under Daimler-Benz ownership in 1998, the revered Sterling badge was adopted to identify the marque, which was expected to increase substantially Freightliner's 28 per cent share in the US Class 8 heavy truck segment.

backwards, splitting at the top of the windscreen, but by 1936 the cab tilted forwards for accessing the 100bhp Waukesha 6D100 diesel engine. To get the weight of the vehicle down to a minimum, much intricate use was made of aluminium in the chassis frame and cross-members as well as the cab and ancillary sheet metal. The actual kerb-side weight of the truck-tractor was just 8070lb, and it could also be specified with a sleeper unit above the cab to maintain the compact BBC dimension.

By 1937, the F Series consisted of 17 basic models of trucks and truck tractors, powered by six-cylinder Waukesha petrol or Cummins H Series diesel units. The largest was the 68,000lb GVW FWS-18OH, which had dual-worm, gear-drive, rear axles. Sterling's H Series sported an F Series cab and served as a dump truck and concrete mixer with other construction site duties. All H Series trucks were chain driven, and the two larger trucks were powered by a 677-cubic inch (11-litre), six-cylinder engine. The following year a smaller, less expensive conventional model known as the M Series was intro-duced, with the similar looking J Series appearing in 1939. In appearance, Sterling conventionals had long bonnets with Rolls-Royce-shaped radiators and flexible, cycle-wing mudguards.

When the once-successful Fageol Truck and Coach Company finally hit the end of the line in 1938, Sterling acquired the business, although production of Fageol trucks ended in January 1939.

Sterling trucks were put to more spe-cialised uses during the Second World War. The US Navy placed orders for Sterling's DDS150, DD5225, DD5235 and 6x4 HC5330 10-ton trucks and low-bed truck-tractors, typically used for aircraft recovery, while the DDS150 worked as a crane carrier for shifting torpedoes. The Ordnance Department also commissioned Sterling to make the 12-ton 85,000lb GVW 8x8 T26 truck and truck-tractor, which had twin steering axles and was powered by a 275bhp American LaFrance V12. Other

Sterlings in use with the US military in small numbers were the mighty 20-ton, 6x6 T29 truck-tractor, powered by a 500bhp Ford V8 tank engine, while the gargantuan T35 used the 750bhp Ford V12 tank unit.

Post-war production continued with the 4x4 D Series, 4x2 and 6x4 H Series and smaller R Series models, using either petrol or diesel engines, and Sterling sales were highest in New England and California. But its days as an independent were numbered, as financial control of the company passed to Donner Estates of Philadelphia during 1947 and 1948, although the Sternberg family still occupied the boardroom with William F. Sternberg and Ernest R. Sternberg as vice-presidents.

The cab-forward TE Series and cab-over TO Series models made their debut in 1948, Both had easily remov-able, insulated engine housings, while the SB Series was introduced in 1949. A range of crane carriers from 10 to 25 tons with tandem rear axles, based on the CC235, was manufactured specially for the Milwaukee-based Bucyrus-Erie Company. Sterling persevered with

STERLING A-LINE

Make: *Sterling*
Model: *A-line tractor*
Type: *medium or long-conventional, unit-construction steel or aluminium cab, 113- (287-) or 122-in (310-cm) BBC, three sleepers available*
Engine: *Cummins M11, N14, Detroit Diesel Series 60, 11.1 (677), 12.7 litre (775 cubic inch), or Caterpillar C10, C12; 280–500bhp.*
Transmission: *Fuller 9–18 speeds*
Suspension: *front: taper leaf or airliner; rear: airliner, Hendrickson or Neway walking beam*

chain drive longer than most of its competitors, building its last chain drive model in 1951.

On 1 June 1951, Sterling was bought out by the White Motor Company, and the vehicles remained the same apart from the new Sterling-White logo. Production relocated to the White fac-tory in Cleveland, Ohio in 1953, and the Sterling make was finally disconti-nued in 1958.

HINO

Hino is the largest Japanese producer of medium and heavy trucks, truck-tractors, special vehicles and buses. There are two separate strands to the company's history, accompanied by innumerable name changes along the way. Basically, its roots go back to 1908, when a car body production plant was set up by Kentaro Wakita in Tokyo, a plant which would be a forerunner of Hino's Auto Body Division. Another founding company, the Tokyo Gas Industry Company, was formed in 1910, and in 1913 its name was changed to the Tokyo Gas and Electric Industry Company. In 1918, it began to produce motor vehicles, and should be seen as the core element of the Hino story.

Wakita Motor Industries was set up in 1930 and re-named in 1938 as Teikoku Auto Industry. In 1939, a new plant was built at Tsurumi, Yokohama, which remains the location of Hino's head office. In 1942, the Kanazawa Aircraft Company was set up at what is now the Hino Kanazawa plant in Ishikawa province, and in 1945 it became Kinsan Industries and began producing car bodies.

Hino's range of Super F Series heavy-duty models were powered by the P11C turbo intercooler engine, and the FS class cab was fitted with a four-point air-suspension system with additional dampers to absorb vibrations.

The next step in the company history was the introduction of the Hino Contessa 900 car in 1961, along with the Hino Briska 900, which was a light-duty truck. The Hamura machinery plant came on stream in 1963, and sales on the Japanese domestic market of the Hino Ranger, a 3.5-ton medium-duty truck, commenced in 1964. It was joined by a 1300 version of the Contessa passenger car. These were still early days in the programme of Japanese redevelopment after the Second World War, and cars and trucks continued to be on the small side. A reflection of this was the Hino Briska 1300, a small truck that came out in 1965.

LINK WITH TOYOTA

A manufacturing and marketing link with Toyota in 1966 bore fruit in the marketing of 11- and 11.5-ton trucks and a luxury high-speed touring coach in 1967, followed by the production of the Toyota Hi-lux and Publica van at the Hamura Works in 1968. This coincided with the marketing of tractors and trucks for road use, and in 1969, they began producing the Hino Ranger KL 4.5-ton medium truck for the home market, as well as a 12-tonner.

Manufacture of trucks and tractors with direct-injection engines began in 1971, including the Ranger KLS 4- and 4.5-tonners, while simultaneously carrying out a research and development programme on electric buses. Hino began selling the Ranger KLSS 4- and 4.5-ton trucks on the Japanese market, and introduced the first Japanese 8x4 truck in 1974. Venturing into Europe, a parts depot was established at Mechelen, Belgium, as Hino Motors Europe NV. This was followed in 1975 by the new 10-ton Spacious Big One series with direct-injection engines. More significantly, two strands of Hino's past came together in 1975 when Teikoku Auto Industries and Kinsan Auto Industries merged to form Hino Auto Body, capitalised at 495 million yen.

The Hino Ranger K LSD medium-duty truck with direct-injection engine was available in Japan in 1977,

Tokyo and Gas Electric Industry Company merged in 1937 with Kyodo Kokutan K.K. to form the Tokyo Automobile Industry Company, renamed in 1941 as the Diesel Motor Industry Company, which went on to become Isuzu Motors Ltd.

The following year, the Hino Heavy Industry Company split to concentrate on the manufacture of trucks, trailer-tractors, buses and diesel engines. The marketing and sales were established in 1948 as Hino Diesel Sales Company, while the firm itself was now known as Hino Diesel Industry Company Ltd. In 1950, came the introduction of heavy-duty diesel trucks, buses and trolley buses, followed by a range of four-

One of Hino's most versatile truck bodies – the large Hi-Wing configuration, known as the gull-wing, was created for dry-goods carriage. It was a more substantial alternative to the curtain-sided body.

wheel drive vehicles. Innovations included buses with underfloor engines in 1953, and a 13.5-ton dump truck was introduced in 1954. Also in 1953, Hino began making the Renault 4CV saloon under licence and the Hino-Renault Sales division was set up, and in 1957 they moved into full-scale production. Hino Diesel Sales merged with Hino-Renault Sales in 1959 and was renamed Hino Motor Sales, quickly rationalised to Hino Motors Ltd.

8X4 FY66-SERIES

Engine	Cylinders	bhp
EF750T diesel direct injection turbocharged	4	250
EF750 diesel direct injection turbocharged	V8	320
EF750T diesel direct injection turbocharged	V8	360

along with the first Japanese body-framed touring coach. Two joint-venture companies were set up in 1977 – Hino Malaysia was established in Selangor, and Jamjoom Hino Motors in Saudi Arabia.

On the home front, the 2-ton Ranger 2 light truck was launched in 1979, and the whole Hino range became subject to sweeping new exhaust and noise-emission control regulations. The Wind Ranger series of medium trucks was introduced the following year, which also saw the start of operations in the casting and production facilities at the Nitta plant. A comprehensive change in the range majored on the Super Dolphin heavy trucks, including an option powered by a turbocharged engine with intercooler.

On the coach side of the business, a complete rationalisation also took place at its bus assembly line at the Yokohama Works in 1982 – the year the Company celebrated its 40th anniversary – and the millionth Hino rolled off the production line on 8 May. A decade on, and it notched up its 500,000th export.

Meanwhile, exports began of the new Econo Line heavy trucks, while on the domestic market the Day-Cab Ranger was available, along with a 3.5- and 4.75-ton medium truck series. A further joint venture in 1984 linked Hino with Kuozui Motors Ltd, Taiwan's leading truck manufacturer. Expanding into North America, Hino Diesel Trucks (USA) was set up at Irvine, California, supported from 1994 by Hino Motors International in Corona, California, acting as a parts depot serving the

USA. Hino Engine Service is at Orangeburg, New York. In Mississauga, Ontario, Hino Diesel Trucks (Canada) was founded in 1985. A second proving ground was completed at Gozenyama in the Japanese Ibaraki province the same year, while another joint venture company, Hinopak Motors Limited, was started up in Karachi, Pakistan.

I CAN SEE A 'RAINBOW'

Production of the world's first full-decked, wide-bodied, mid-under-floor engine mini-bus, the Rainbow 7M began in 1987, and two years later the light and medium Cruising Ranger series trucks became available. At this point, Hino developed the world's first

hybrid, electric-diesel engine system, known as the Hybrid Inverter-controlled Motor and Retarder, or HIMR.

By the early 1990s, the S'elega touring coach and Profia heavy truck series was available in Japan. In 1991, Hino became the first Japanese truck maker to compete in the gruelling Paris–Dakar Rally.

In a round of yet more expansions, the Long Ri Bus Corporation was set up in China in 1993, and Hino Motor Sales Pty in New South Wales, Australia, the following year. While the Rising Ranger medium truck series and the Liesse small touring coach came out in Japan, Hino's third testing facility was completed at Memuro, Hokkaido.

In 1996, the company moved into Vietnam with the establishment of Hino Motors in Hanoi. Its dramatic, new Chaînon 21st Century Centre, incorporating truck museum and training facilities, was opened. The company was on a roll. In 1997, Hino FT trucks took the first three places in the Truck category in the Paris–Dakar Rally.

Trucks are put through rigorous tests like this slalom course to assess handling and stability in extreme driving conditions prior to their launch.

Hino philosophy is that component reliability is achieved by stringent tests carried out by its R&D programme. Here it comes to fruition on the production line, at the heavy-duty integrated plant at the Head Office complex.

TRUCK RANGES

Hino's medium truck range includes 17 different models with increasingly large payloads, including the FB2W, FC2W and GH3M. There is a whole galaxy of configurations, such as flat-beds, crane-mounted, dump trucks, small tankers, fire engines, cement mixers and refuse carts, nearly all of which are 4x2s and cab-over-engine layout. Power units range from 88bhp four-cylinder direct-injection diesel motors to 177bhp six-cylinder units.

Similarly, the heavy-duty truck range includes models designated ZY, a long-bonneted conventional, the cab-over FY27, which are 8x4s, and the biggest Hinos at 30,500kg GVMR are the 8x4 FY66s, which are over 18,000kg payload. These are powered by 265bhp turbocharged V8 diesel engines.

Truck-tractors are a mix of cab-over and conventional models, and include the SG3M 4x2s and the SS635 6x4s, ranging in size from 28,000kg to 50,000kg GVMR, and the biggest of them use the turbodiesel V8 motor. Low-bed trailers, dump trailers, petrol and oil tankers, cement, refrigerated and regular container trailers are available. Special purpose trucks include the cab-over FT3H 4x4, powered by four- or six-cylinder in-line, direct-injection 143bhp diesel engines, and the big, conventional layout 6x6 ZC range with 191bhp engines. Hino produces three coach models, the RR3H, AK17 and HU, all 4x2s with four- or six-cylinder diesel power, and a further ten rolling chassis for bespoke coach and bus bodies.

HINO PLANT

The Hino plant, situated at its Head Office complex, is a totally integrated manufacturing facility for the company's diesel-powered heavy and medium trucks. Here you find the sheet metal presses that form cabs and chassis, the metal-casting operations, heat treatment and machining, the electro-deposition paint process, the chassis-reversal apparatus, and the assembly line where the trucks' varied components, including cabs, interiors, suspension and drivetrain, come together. Finished products are examined on the inspection line prior to dispatch.

Efficiency is achieved by means of a flexible manufacturing system (FMS) — which allows various types of vehicles with differing specifications to be produced on the same assembly line. Productivity is further enhanced by a computerised system that automatically supplies manufacturing instructions to each production area as needed.

An essential part of the Hino factory's production system is its 'Quality Control Circles'. Workers from each area of the plant gather regularly to offer their suggestions on improving operating efficiency or vehicle quality, and these group sessions can often lead to many important innovations in the production process. These operational techniques were instigated by the Japanese in the early 1980s, and it isn't surprising to find they've been copied and are in use at most vehicle

HINO FS2P

Make: *Hino*
Model: *P11C-TE*
Type: *6x4 cab-over rigid, tipper, mixer or cargo bodies*
Engine: *diesel, 4-cylinder, in-line, or 6-cylinder; in-line, direct injection, overhead valve, water-cooled*
Gearbox: *Hino 16-speed all synchromesh*
Suspension: *front: semi-elliptic leaf springs, shock absorbers, anti-roll bar; rear: semi-elliptic leaf springs*
Chassis: *steel ladder frame and torsion bars*
Brakes: *drums all round, pneumatic exhaust brake*
Wheelbase: *3900mm/4900mm (153in/193in)*
GVW: *26,000kg*

manufacturing plants most notably in my recent experience, at Triumph Motorcycles, where it has consolidated that company's remarkable renaissance.

TRANSMISSION PARTS

Hino's Hamura Works, located in the Nishitama-gun area of Tokyo, consists of two basic facilities. The first is an assembly plant where small pickup trucks such as the Toyota HiLux and Tercel and Corsa passenger cars are produced, using a fully integrated robotised manufacturing system. The second is a machining and assembly plant, connected with the Hino Works, which produces transmissions, axles and other parts for diesel vehicles such as the medium trucks made at the Kawashima Works of Mitsui Seiki Kogyo Company. Functions include towering sheet metal presses, machining and multiple robotised spot welding, electro-deposition paint process, transmission and rear axle assembly, engine installation and mounting of the cabs. There is a rear body assembly line for the construction of flatbed and drop-side trucks. And within the Hamura Plant is an integrated corrosion-prevention and painting process for each vehicle.

NITTA WORKS

The Nitta Works is located in the Gunma district, and comprises the two basic facilities of a foundry and a machining plant. The foundry is equipped with state-of-the-art equipment, including a low-frequency, electric melting furnace that creates its own dramatic fireworks display, and a non-vibrating, automatic moulding machine for casting engine casings. High productivity is achieved in the machining shop through a variety of equipment, including the ranks of NC machine tools and roller lines along which the engine blocks and cylinder-head casings travel, plus overhead cranes, gantries and special transfer machines to assist as required. To protect the workforce and the environment, the Nitta plant also features dust collecting and deodorising equipment,

and in addition, cooling water and used sand are recycled in order to conserve vital energy resources.

BODY SHOP

The Kanazawa Plant manufactures truck and van bodies (in aluminium and GRP), trailers, high-wing bodies and medium and small bus bodies. This is an extensive site, and productivity is high. It can also produce bodies for special requirements such as refrigeration and is said to be able to respond rapidly to user needs.

The Mizuho Plant features some of the most outstanding and advanced

technology in Japan. It produces mainly open-truck bodies and medium-sized, aluminium van bodies, which are notably durable. In the world of motor sport, Team Sugawara drove a Hino FT to a class victory in the Under 10-litres Truck Section of the 1998 Paris–Granada–Dakar rally. It was the third consecutive victory in this class for a Hino FT, and brought with it second overall in the Truck Category.

A feature of Hino medium- to heavy-duty trucks like this high-roof Super cab model is the low set window in the door, which provides better visibility when manoeuvring.

INTERNATIONAL HARVESTER

The truck producer with the longest lineage has to be International Harvester. The company's roots are planted in the mechanisation of farming equipment, and it can trace its origins back to 1831, when Cyrus Hall McCormick constructed horse-drawn grain reapers.

The McCormick Harvesting Machine Company built a steam tractor in 1889, and its first motor vehicles were developed by E.A. Johnson in 1898. The International Harvester Company was set up in 1902 when McCormick merged with other competitors, but its first high-wheeler Auto Buggies didn't appear until 1907.

IHC's factory workshops moved from Chicago to Akron, Ohio, and for a brief period it turned out passenger cars, concentrating on Auto Buggies in 1911 and cargo-carrying Auto Wagons from 1909 until 1912.

International began producing trucks in earnest in 1915, turning out five models – H, F, K, C and L – ranging from the three-quarter-ton Model H to the 3.5-ton capacity Model L, which lasted through to 1923. The trucks were based on a steel chassis with semi-elliptic cart springs and pneumatic tyres optional on the tall artillery-style wheels, which only the big 3.5-tonner had as standard fitting. Brakes were self-adjusting. All were conventional layout apart from the 2-ton Model C, which was a forward-control vehicle. Through diligent production, International cornered four per cent of the US truck market by the end of the First World War. International's first brand new post-war truck was

From 1986, Internationals have been made under the Navistar banner, but continued to be badged and marketed as Internationals, like this 1993 ProSleeper 9800 conventional.

the 115-in (292-cm) wheelbase three-quarter-ton Speed Model, introduced in 1921. By now the radiator was housed ahead of a four-cylinder Lycoming engine, while a multiple disc clutch actuated the three-speed transmission. Speed is a relative term, but its 30mph (48km/h) top speed was just fine for a delivery truck of the period.

Principal innovations in 1924 were the centrally hinged butterfly bonnets and the large, front-mounted radiators. Steel spoke wheels were shod with solid rubber tyres, and the final drive was of the double-reduction bevel type, although a small number of chain-drive models were available to special order. All engines and transmissions were of International's own make, with the 40bhp four-cylinder unit being the most powerful.

A bus chassis was introduced in 1925, powered by a six-cylinder engine, spiral-bevel drive, full-floating rear axle and four-wheel brakes. From 1926, the six-cylinder unit was fitted in trucks, and at the same time pneumatic tyres

replaced the solid rubber ones. In the three years between 1924 and 1927, 4700 units of the popular 2-ton Model 43 were produced, with annual output running at around 25,000 vehicles.

THE INNOVATIVE W SERIES

International came out with the A Series line in 1929, powered by either Lycoming or Waukesha engines. Output was now 50,000 units a year, but the Depression had arrived with the Wall Street Crash, and orders dwindled to 29,000 units in 1930. Despite this, another new truck range was launched – the innovative W Series – together with the larger A Series models. The W-series trucks were fitted with overhead-valve engines with removable cylinders, coupled to five-speed transmissions with two reverse gears.

One way to combat falling sales in a recession was to join forces with other manufacturers. In 1932, International made an agreement with Willys, in which International would market the new Willys half-ton C-1 pickup and

When International Harvester bought a 33 per cent share in DAF in 1972, the Paystar 5000 was also badged as a DAF N2500. The shared power unit was the 250bhp DAF diesel with 13-speed Fuller transmission.

panel truck. The arrangement took off in 1934 and the C Series lasted until 1937 when it was superceded by the D Series. More significant was the entry into the diesel engine market in 1933, as International commenced production of its own oil-burners, and the following year began manufacturing its own axles. There were now 18 models in the range, going from a half-ton up to a 7-ton capacity. International was more readily associated with bigger vehicles such as its 10-ton six-wheel design known as the Cornbinder, which used a Hendrickson tandem axle, but for the second half of the decade it also produced a number of station wagons.

Annual production crossed the 100,000 watershed in 1937, when the range encompassed a raft of overlapping models from different series. At either extreme was a new sleeper cab, developed for long-haul applications, while at the bottom end was a new line of Metro delivery vans, with bodies made by the Metropolitan Body Company of Bridgeport, Connecticut. The brief flowering of the characterful D Series trucks was cut short by the arrival in 1940 of the K-series, which proliferated during the Second World War. By 1941, International had built its millionth truck, and ranked third in the US production tables, having sold more trucks over 2-ton capacity than anyone else.

Post-war manufacturing continued with the K Series, which diversified in 1946 into the KB Series with a broader grille and front wings, and some of the bigger models used a butterfly profile bonnet. These vehicles were powered by overhead-valve engines, while the smaller models used side-valve units. Largest was the KB-8, aimed fair and square at the biggest Class 8 heavy-duty segment, and fitted with an International 366-cubic inch (6-litre) 126bhp Red Diamond engine. The larger, three-axle model could also be specified with a Cummins diesel or Continental petrol engine.

WESTCOASTER

International's new plants at Fort Wayne, Indiana and Emeryville, California came on stream in 1947, the latter specialising in heavy-duty Western-style models with a GVW up around 90,000lbs. These new W Series models, known as Westcoasters, were fitted with wider, three-seater cabs, fronted by a flat radiator and flatter V-profile, split windscreen. The conventional model was followed by a cab-over Westcoaster, which was very similar to the bull-nose Kenworth of the same period. Engine options included International and Cummins diesels and Continental petrol units, allied to a wide variety of transmissions and axle configurations.

The L Series made its debut in 1950, and consisted of no less than 87 conventional light- and medium-duty

models. Key stylistic hallmarks of the dumpy, upright cab were wing-mounted headlights and a curved, single-section windscreen. This all-new cab, which contained a concave dashboard, was built by the Chicago Manufacturing Company, and was also used by Diamond T. Buyers could opt for petrol, diesel or LPG fuelled engines. The R Series that quickly superseded it in 1953 used the same cab, but the grille motif was three thick bars. A larger Diamond T cab rejoicing in the name of the Comfo-Vision was fitted on certain cab-over models right up to 1972, and the semi-truck rig included an integral sleeper cabin. The height of the cab prompted the nickname 'Cherrypicker'.

A change of direction in 1961 found International exploring the recreational vehicle market with its Scout model, which was equipped with an integral cab and bed, and could be ordered as a 4x2 or heavier rated 4x4 model. It was powered by a four-cylinder Comanche engine. The same year, the C Series was ushered in alongside the B Series, while the Metro line continued in production as the AB and AM Series.

At the top end of the scale, the conventional M Series was popular with the construction industry, as were the 78,000lb GVW F230 15-ton, 6x6 heavy-duty trucks with their angular tread-plate wings. Both the M Series and the F230 approached the legal length limit of 35ft (10.7m). In the next league up were International's enormous 154,000lb GVW 4x2 and 4x4 quarry dump trucks, which were among the largest four-wheel drive trucks in the world at the time.

STAR TIME

A well-known model in the late 1950s was the cab-over Emeryville – otherwise known as the Highbinder – which had a two-section windscreen and could be ordered with or without a sleeper cabin. In 1962, the Loadstar 1600 truck was available as a

A coast-to-coast journey in the USA can entail several changes of temperature and weather conditions, so sub-zero capability is vital. Navistar's electronically controlled T444E Power Stroke engine guarantees cold starts down to minus 20 degrees Farenheit.

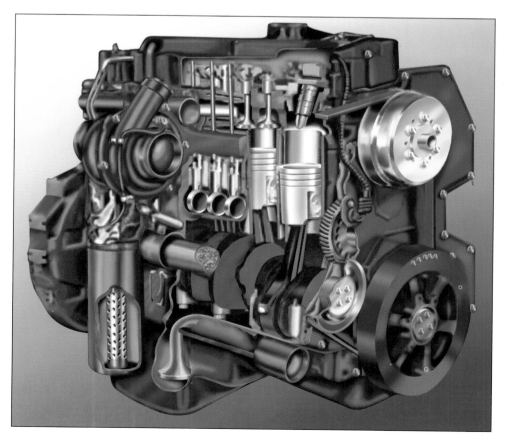

replacement for the B Series, powered by the 193bhp V-304 V8 engine coupled with the T-17 four-speed gearbox. In cab-over format, the Loadstar evolved into the Cargostar. The DC-400 Transtar model of 1963 was a conventional sleeper-cab that achieved a good reputation and which remained in production for a further decade, although not built in any great quantity.

O SERIES

As the Emeryville was phased out in 1965, International brought in a new series designation that included cab-over models like the CO-4000, powered by a 240bhp IH DVT-573 diesel engine. The new range was called the O Series, and it set the trend for the company's future cab-over models. A larger CO-4070A was introduced to facilitate the use of more powerful diesel engines. By the early 1970s, there were seven heavy-duty models ranging from 80,000lb GVW to 168,000lb GVW, powered by 12-cylinder and 16-cylinder diesel engines delivering up to 560bhp. Transmissions could be Allison or Twin Disc nine-speed or 12-speed with International's own axles. The Paystar 5000 appeared in 1973, succeeding the F-230 and M Series heavy

trucks, while the CO-4070B Transtar appeared the following year. By mid-decade, the range encompassed the Scout 4x2 and 4x4, the Travelall, Series 150 and Series 200 pickups and light-duty trucks, conventional Loadstar in 4x2, 4x4 and 6x4 format, conventional Fleetstar as either 4x2 or 4x4, cab-over Cargostar 4x2 and 6x4, conventional and cab-over Transtar 4x2 and 6x4, Paystar construction trucks in 4x4, 6x4 and 6x6 layout, as well as school buses and the CO-8190 fire engine chassis. A grand total of 75 models were available, ranging from 5200lb GVW to 180,000lb GVW, with petrol-fuelled in-line six-cylinder engines up to 215bhp and 200bhp and International V8 diesel units available. Alternatively, diesel engines up to 450bhp from Caterpillar, Cummins and Detroit could be specified, along with transmissions by International, Fuller, New Process and Warner, and axles from International or Spicer.

The 1995 International Eagle 9000 Series of 4x2 and 6x4 trucks could be powered by Cummins M11 or M14 engines or, as in this case, the electronically controlled Detroit Diesel series 60 turbodiesel unit with outputs ranging from 330bhp to 430bhp.

A variety of domestic crises brought about a collapse in the company's fortunes around 1980. A strike lasting from 1979 to 1980 was the first stumbling block, followed by a farm crisis that severely hit International's agricultural trade. Hardest hit was the Fort Wayne plant where the Scout models were produced, and this was shut down in 1980 and the model deleted. From that point, International built only medium- and heavy-duty trucks, and in fact one of the largest made that year was the F-2674 concrete mixer. The financial problems continued into 1981, and in an attempt to offset the difficulties, glider kits were offered, consisting of complete trucks without their powertrains. International wasn't the only company to offer glider kits, but they were never very successful. As a way forward, Iveco began building the new I Series for International in 1982, and although production was interrupted in the USA, the company was reorganised the following year with help from the federal government.

The Paystar, introduced in 1985 and built at Fort Wayne and Wagoner, Oklahoma, was the model for all heavy-duty work, both on and off the road. The Paystar 5000 series, which was available in 4x4, 6x4, 6x6 and 8x4 formats, could be fitted with tag axles that were set back or forward, according to state regulations, or with twin-steering tandems. A whole raft of 20 engines was available, only one of which was an International, while the rest were from Caterpillar, Cummins and Detroit Diesel. The Paystar 5000 was used as a concrete carrier, particularly in the western states where its lighter weight gave it a payload advantage. Use of aluminium in the construction of the chassis and cab saved some 2000lbs. The Weightwatcher was fitted with a 270bhp Detroit Diesel engine driving through a seven- or eight-speed Fuller manual transmission.

The Transtar 4300 cab-over series was the heavy-duty model of the early 1980s with GVW up to 120,000lb. However, state regulations frequently restricted GVW to 80,000lb in defer-

ence to road widths and bridge dimensions. Fourteen diesel engine options were available for the big Transtars, from Caterpillar and Cummins to Detroit Diesel units, and nine- to 15-speed gearboxes were also available.

A CHANGE OF NAME

On 20 February 1986, International's Truck Group changed its name to Navistar International, and sold off its agricultural equipment business to Case-Tenneco, who retained the International Harvester logo. Consequently, trucks have been built under

both names since then. During the following decade, Navistar gradually clawed its way back into contention in the Class 7 and 8 heavy-duty sectors, producing conventional and construction site vehicles at its Chatham, Ontario plant in Canada, and cab-over and medium-duty trucks at Springfield. By 1995, Navistar International had 30 different models.

In 1996, Navistar International's new International Pro Sleeper 9800 highway tractors were fitted with 330bhp 14-litre Cummins N14 CELECT and 430bhp electronically controlled DDC

Following the switch to Navistar in 1986, Class 7 and 8 construction site trucks were built at the Chatham, Ontario, plant. The 8200 models were fitted with Cummins M11-280E diesel engines.

Series 60 diesel engines.

Although Navistar looked decidedly shaky for a while, it appeared to have retained a foothold in the marketplace. One aspect that couldn't be disputed was that the combined tally of International and Navistar products was greater than any other truck maker in the 20th century.

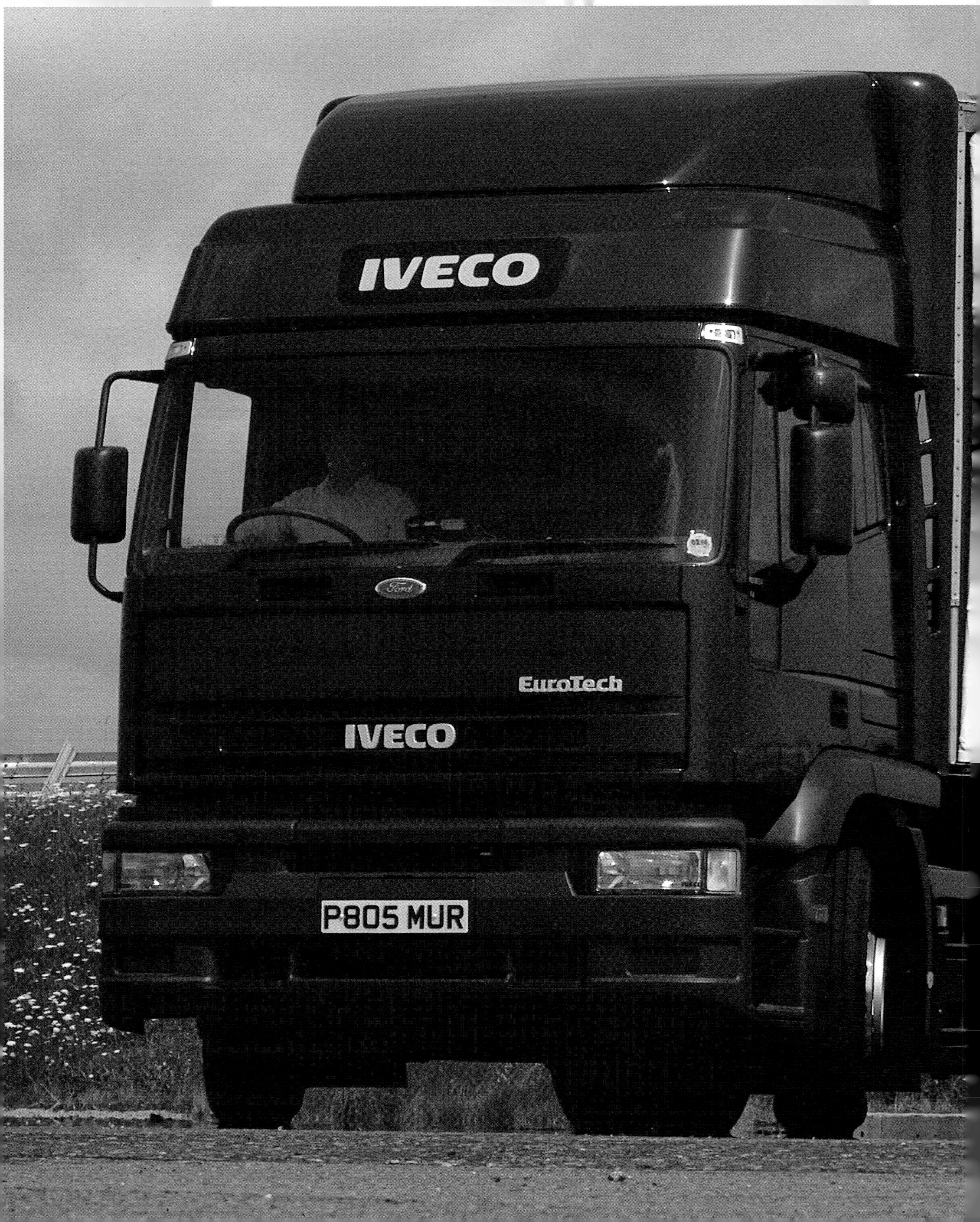
IVECO
EuroTech
IVECO
P805 MUR

IVECO

Iveco was formed in 1975, and is probably the most complex of the major truck building corporations. In the early 1970s, Fiat's Gruppo Veicoli Industriali and Klökner-Humboldt-Deutz's Magirus-Deutz concerns sought partnerships from among the 15 main truck manufacturers then operating. These included five of the world's largest vehicle producers, both European and North American, and 40 or so minor companies of mainly local importance. Fiat's empire included OM, Unic, Lancia and its own truck business. Alfa Romeo also had a small operation for the production of commercial vehicles at Pomigliano d'Arco near Naples, in association with Renault-Saviem. But before going into the Iveco structure and vehicle ranges, it's worth tracing the history of its constituent companies.

The long-running EuroTech series was one of Iveco's medium-heavy ranges in the 1980s and 1990s, and its modular tilt-cab was styled by Giorgetto Giugiaro's Ital design.

FIAT

Fiat goes back to 1899, when Societa Anonima Fabbrica Italiana di Automobili, or FIAT, was founded in Turin. The first real Fiat truck, designed and manufactured in 1903, was a goods vehicle with a cab-forward design that made better use of available space. It was powered by a 24bhp 6.3-litre (384-cubic inch) four-cylinder split-block engine. The truck was followed in 1906 by a 24/40bhp bus, equipped with forward cab and double-decker body.

Typical charabancs of 1908 were made on a conventional chassis, with cab set back and the characteristic Fiat bonnet. There were no passenger doors and the seats were raised towards the back of the bus to give the passengers at the rear a better view.

From 1905, the Italian Army began mobilising, and built up a substantial fleet of military trucks consisting largely of Fiat 'type 15 bis Libia' and '15 Ter' trucks, which were used in the Italian–Turkish war of 1911–12. The 'type 15 bis Libia' was fitted with benches and used as a reconnaissance vehicle. The 17A was derived directly from the 17 model in 1913, yet the military 15 Ter remained in production more or less to the end of the First World War. It was used as an ambulance and mobile searchlight carrier, as well as a troop transport and tanker for the emerging air squadrons. In France during the First World War, more than a quarter of the trucks in active service were made in Italy, and most of these were Fiats. The type 18 BL was the most prolific, and in the seven years prior to 1921 nearly 20,000 were made. The 18 BL had a payload of 3.5 tonnes, with chain drive and a cab fitted with a windscreen, plus a box body with drop sides and hoops for the canvas tilt. It was powered by a 38bhp 5-litre (305-cubic inch) four-cylinder engine, and top speed was 25km/h (15mph) with a GVW of 4.5 tonnes. The post-war truck industry, however, was hit by the saturation of the market with army surplus vehicles. Nevertheless, the splendid new Lingotto plant was opened in 1923, complete with test track on the factory roof.

In 1929, Fiat rationalised its production and came out with the modern-looking 621, which had a stamped steel chassis. This conventional, medium-duty truck endured for the whole decade in various different versions and engines. The basic truck had an enclosed steel cab and hinged sides and tailgate and was powered by a 45bhp 2.5-litre (152-cubic inch) six-cylinder unit, taking it to a maximum of 60km/h (37mph).

In 1932, the 508 Balilla car-derived commercial came out, and was the first real utility vehicle that Fiat had pro-

Commuting anywhere can be hell, but scenes like this one are the norm in northern Africa where Fiat trucks like this 682 provide service long after their normal sell-by date.

duced, spawning a pickup truck with a payload of 0.45 tonne and a van with a payload of 0.4 tonne. It remained in production until 1945. Early in the 1930s, Fiat developed a heavy-duty truck for military use that could operate on any type of terrain. It was known as the Dovunque (meaning 'Anywhere') and was a three-axle, 6x4 cab-forward truck with four rear wheels driven. It was powered by a 40bhp petrol engine, with four-speed transmission and reduction gear, and it could carry a 2.5-tonne payload. A further derivative was the cab-over Spa 10000 of 1945 with identical powertrain and a payload of 10 tonnes. It was available in both military and civilian versions as a 6x4 and a 6x2.

In 1935, the medium-duty 618 and 38 R trucks came out, powered by 1.6-litre (97-cubic inch) four-cylinder petrol engines and having a payload of around 2.5 tonnes. The range included the 4x4 Spa TL 37 military trucks, the Spa CL 39, also called the Autocarretta

Spa 39, and the Spa TM 40 artillery tractor, which was powered by a 9.3-litre (567-cubic inch), six-cylinder diesel engine. These vehicles were also available in civilian versions until 1948.

The tiny Topolino was launched in 1936, and was subsequently used as the basis for a small van with a payload of approximately 3 tonnes. Two years later Fiat introduced the medium-duty cab-over 626 N and the heavy-duty cab-over 666 N. Both new vehicles were powered by straight-six diesel units, of 5.7 litres (348 cubic inches) and 9.3 litres (567 cubic inches) respectively. The chassis were identical, and the cabs were essentially the same. The 626 N could handle just over 3 tonnes and could tow approximately 6.5 tonnes, while the 666 N had double that capacity. Various civilian, military and bus versions were made.

The new Mirafiori plant opened in 1939, but the entire production was turned over to the Axis war effort.

The federation of long-established truck manufacturers that came together under the Iveco banner in 1975 included Magirus-Deutz, left, Unic, Fiat and OM. Lancia and Pegaso completed the picture.

Rebuilding and manufacturing postwar were hampered by an almost complete lack of raw materials and by the need to rebuild or renew most of the plant and equipment, compounded by complex political and social tensions. Once again numerous US army surplus vehicles were available to slow down the truck market.

Fiat resumed production with pre-war models such as the 626 N, the 666 N, the Spa 10000 and, for light transport needs, light-duty trucks and vans such as the 1100 and 500. Between 1948 and 1951, the basic medium- and heavy-duty trucks were the 640 N, 670 N, and 680 N, plus the special 639 N with all-wheel drive, and the light-duty 615.

The truck that made the biggest

impression for Fiat in the mid-1950s was the cab-over 682 N. Powered by a 140bhp 10.6-litre (647-cubic inch) six-cylinder unit with payloads of approximately 8 tonnes, the tractor version could haul semi-trailers with a total weight of up to 30 tonnes. Subsequent updating in 1962 included the fitting of a 180bhp 11.5-litre (702-cubic inch) six-cylinder unit. Bus versions were available with variable payloads and 55 seats or more. Derivatives of this vehicle made it through to the Iveco era and remained in production until the end of the 1980s.

RESTRUCTURING

Following a period of industrial and social unrest in 1969, production costs rose. The repercussions for Fiat were particularly serious, since it had just taken over Lancia, which was faced with serious financial and organisational problems. Fiat Veicoli Industriali section was reorganised accordingly as an independent division concentrating on its Fiat and OM products and also the French company Unic.

First fruits of the revised corporation was the Fiat 619 N, built as a heavy-duty truck and semi-trailer truck-tractor, and the 691 N, a three-axle vehicle with two front axles steering.

The 170 GVW heavy-duty rigid with draw-bar trailer combination was introduced at the time of Iveco's foundation. It also coincided with the expansion of roll-on-roll-off ferries and the onset of containerisation – which changed the face of trucking forever.

Both models used the 260bhp 13.7-litre (836-cubic inch) six-cylinder diesel engine. The 697 N was another truck and semi-trailer truck-tractor with three axles, including a pair of rear-drive axles, and it used the same engine but with slightly lower carrying capacity.

From 1973, Fiat and OM models took on a decidedly modern aspect. New models of medium-duty trucks were launched, including the 50 NC range and its derivatives the 1155 N and 65 N, equipped with 81bhp 3.4-litre (207-cubic inch) four-cylinder

diesel engines. These were followed by the 80 NC, 90 NC, 100 NC, 110 PC and 110 NT, all running with the same 122bhp 5.1-litre (311-cubic inch) six-cylinder diesel engine and a power output of 122 HP at 3200rpm. They were all available in truck or van format. The bigger 130 NC was equipped with a 145bhp 7-litre (427-cubic inch) six-cylinder diesel with five- or ten-speed transmission, and was available as a truck, semi-trailer truck-tractor and cab chassis, with different wheelbases. Although these were all really medium-duty vehicles, they were equipped for the first time with many devices only previously seen in heavy-duty transport applications. In this way they had the advantages of manoeuvrability with lower operating costs and good payload capacities.

At the 1973 Turin Show, Fiat Veicoli Industriali launched its new 4x4 amphibious truck, the 6640 A. It had a sealed integral body, and was designed for transporting army and civil defence personnel and goods on land and on water. It was powered by a 177bhp 5.1-litre (311-cubic inch) straight-six direct injection diesel unit and had a payload of 2 tonnes and 6.26-cubic metre (221-cubic feet) loading platform. On the road it could do 90km/h (56mph), while on the water it used a screw propeller to reach 11km/h (6.8mph).

In July 1974, an agreement between Fiat and Klökner-Humboldt-Deutz of Cologne was reached for setting up the Iveco multinational holding company. The majority share of the equity belonged to the Fiat Group, its registered offices were in Holland and the company was operational from the 1 January 1975.

FIAT TRUCKS 1958-1962

Year	Model	Engine	Power output
1958	C40N/C50N	4.6-litre six-cylinder diesel	90bhp
	682N	10.6-litre six-cylinder diesel	150bhp
1960	690N	19.8-litre six-cylinder diesel	200bhp
1963	662N	4.6-litre six-cylinder diesel	110bhp
	643N	9.1-litre six-cylinder diesel	156bhp

OM

Production of OM trucks started immediately after the First World War and centred on the acquisition of Züst cars of Brescia in 1917 by Societa Anonima Officine Meccaniche of Milan. The latter's roots went way back to 1849 when it produced railway rolling stock. Züst's antecedents were equally as old, and the firm began making cars and commercials in 1905.

The first OM trucks were the S 305 models, derived from car chassis, and the 469F light-duty truck was the first purpose-built commercial vehicle. The 665 model used the 1.9-litre (116-cubic inch) six-cylinder engine. Derivatives of this carried the company through the 1920s until it introduced the distinctive OM-Saurer 5 BLD conventionals in 1929 with their long bonnet and flat-cab profile. The first OM vehicles equipped with diesel engines produced under the Saurer licence were launched at the Motor Show in Milan in 1931. These were the 5 and 6 BLD 6-tonne trucks and the 3 BLD 30-seater buses, equipped with the 80bhp 8.5-litre (519-cubic inch) six-cylinder diesel engine.

In 1933, OM sold its Brescia plant to Fiat, which provided useful capital, but it also ceased producing passenger cars. In 1934, it came out with a medium-duty truck designated the 1CRD, which was equipped with a 4.5-litre (275-cubic inch) diesel engine still made under Saurer licence, with five-speed transmission and hydraulic brakes. The truck version had a 3-tonne payload and the bus had 25 seats. The C30 coach was a charming rotund vehicle with curved four-section windscreen and horizontal louvres along the bonnet. The BUD heavy-duty model was shown in 1936, and powered by the 130bhp 11.5-litre (702-cubic inch) diesel unit, joined by the Titano 137

truck the following year, which remained in production until 1939. It was superseded by the Taurus in medium- to heavy-duty truck and bus versions, equipped with the 5.3-litre (323-cubic inch) four-cylinder diesel engine, and the more powerful Ursus truck with a 100bhp 7.9-litre (323-cubic inch) six-cylinder diesel unit.

With the outbreak of the Second World War, OM produced military versions of the Taurus, using a petrol engine instead of a diesel. All factories suffered extensive bomb damage, but a new Taurus 340 went into production in 1945 using the new cab-over design. The Supertaurus of 1951 was equipped with an 80bhp 5.8-litre (354-cubic inch), four-cylinder diesel engine allied to four-speed transmission with reduction-gear and pneumatic pre-selection control. The hydro-pneumatic brakes were integrated with the engine exhaust brake. Two bus versions were also made,

Wonderful 1950 illustration of Leoncinos on the dockside, advertising both OM and Pirelli tyres. The 52bhp Leoncino cab-over was head of OM's 'Zoo' family of trucks, all named after wild animals.

with structural modifications to dimensions and wheelbase and also changes to gearbox and suspension.

One of the stars of the 1950 Turin Show was the new light- to medium-duty cab-over Leoncino. The engine used was a 52bhp 3.7-litre (226-cubic inch) direct injection four-cylinder diesel unit. Suspension was by leaf spring with four double-acting shock absorbers, and a whole raft of variants was available, from dumper trucks, vans, municipal vehicles, and no fewer than 10 buses all based on the Leoncino chassis. The range was extended to include four-wheel drive and front-wheel drive versions and also local and long-distance buses with varying capacities.

The Leoncino was the head of a family of models of similar style and structure, all named after animals and known as The Zoo, including the Tigrotto, which also had an elongated cab with bunk. The more powerful Tigre was available as a 135bhp super-charged version. In 1961, the Titano

was introduced, powered by a 260bhp 10.3-litre (628-cubic inch) six-cylinder direct injection diesel unit, which was probably the most powerful truck on the European market at the time. The range included trucks and truck-tractors with two and three axles, buses and 4x4 dumper trucks. The Cerbiatto medium-duty cab-over model of 1964 was designed for truck, van and bus applications, along with the similar Daino with the same drive train. A host of versions were made by specialist aftermarket coachbuilders from mobile shops to drinks vehicles, refrigerated trucks and gown vans. But there were no buses. The Orsetto of 1967 was the lightest vehicle of the Zoo collection. It had a 2.6-litre (159-cubic inch) four-cylinder diesel engine, and was also available as a chassis for specialist conversions. Another truck ripe for conversion was the larger 8-litre (488-cubic inch) OM 150, launched at the 1967 Turin Show.

In 1968, OM finally became part of the Fiat Group, for a short time as Fiat Azienda OM and then as Gruppo

The Taurus models first appeared in 1939 in medium- to heavy-duty format, and this conventional was powered by a CR1D four-cylinder 5320cc diesel unit. The similar-capacity petrol engine was available only from 1941 to 1944.

Veicoli Industriali Fiat, which combined Fiat and OM production and also that of the French company Unic. However, OM 100 and OM 120 trucks were still being marketed in 1970, and the heavy-duty 292bhp 14.8-litre (903-cubic inch) V8 OM 190 and OM 260 were still going in 1971. Many were built as tankers and crane carriers. Both models were available in cab-over truck and semi-trailer truck-tractor versions. The tilt-cabs were three-seaters, the first time that OM cabs had this facility. The OM 190 was a two-axle 4x2 with a 28-tonne payload while the OM 260 was a three-axle 6x4 with a 44-tonne payload. They were widely used in quarries and construction sites, and were the last models designed and built by OM.

LANCIA

Lancia is more commonly regarded as a sporting make, with numerous World Rally Championship titles to its credit, as well as being Italy's prestige carmaker. But it was also a significant producer of commercial vehicles.

The company was founded in 1906 by ex-Fiat employees Vincenzo Lancia and Claudio Fogolin to make cars. Along with Wagner, Lancia was one of Fiat's most successful racing drivers and continued to race Fiat until 1909, when Snr. Agnelli vetoed their activities. The first Lancia car was built in 1907, and its successors were full of innovative technical and design solutions. The first Lancia commercial was a small van using the strong chassis of the Eta passenger model with suitable modifications, such as strengthening the suspension brackets. Known as the Z, this vehicle was equipped with a 70bhp 4.9-litre (299-cubic inch) Type 61 straight-four engine with a payload of 2.1 tonnes, which was increased to 2.2 tonnes for the 1 Z military version used in the Italian–Turkish war in Libya from 1912.

At the outbreak of the First World War in 1914, the Lancia factory began to make new military vehicles such as the Jota and Diota in addition to the 1 Z, though they were powered by the same engine. Differing only in chassis lengths, these models served as artillery tractors, ambulances and mobile searchlights, and they were fitted with armour plating by the Turin coach-building Carrozzeria Stabilimenti Farina and Ansaldo of Genoa. The Jota was equipped with a range of electrical equipment and pioneered a series of vehicles, and it was in production up to 1935. Some 2131 of these robust trucks were produced during the First World War. The Diota model was also equipped as a bus and 170 were made between 1915 and 1919.

In 1921, two new models known as the Triota and Tetraiota were launched, both using the Tipo 64 engine. They were simply available as basic 2.4-tonne chassis, and bodywork was produced by outside coachbuilders. They were sometimes fitted out as buses and

coaches. Lancia unveiled its first conventional heavy-duty vehicle in 1924, known as the Pentaiota, which used the gearbox and central rear axle unit of the Tetraiota, but with a longer wheelbase. Payload was 5.3 tonnes, and it remained in production for ten years, during which time 2191 units were produced, including bus versions for local, long-distance and tourist services. The Esaiota derivative of 1924 was the first Lancia commercial to be equipped with brakes on the front wheels as well as the rear.

The Eptaiota was intended for use at low speeds to transport goods that were light but bulky, and 1827 units were made up to 1935, including bus versions. In 1927, Lancia launched a new, more powerful truck engine. It was the 91bhp 7-litre (427-cubic inch) six-cylinder petrol engine and was immediately set to work in the new conventional bus chassis known as the Omicron. Lancia's first commercial six-cylinder unit had double overhead camshafts and a centrifugal rev limiter so the engine couldn't over-rev. The

Lancia's medium- to heavy-duty Esadelta cab-over model came out in 1959 and remained popular throughout the 1960s. It was upgraded in 1962 and power from its 8.2-litre (500-cubic inch) six-cylinder engine increased to 132bhp the following year.

brakes were mechanically assisted on all four wheels, and up to 1935, 552 chassis were produced and mainly used for buses. The public transport department in Rome was a keen customer. It was a thirsty engine, however, and from 1930, Lancia acquired a licence to make the Junkers diesel unit. The stocky conventional RO-series was launched at the 1932 Turin Show, powered by the efficient 3.1-litre (189-cubic inch) two-stroke flat-twin unit. The 65bhp Junkers engine had no glow-plugs or air heaters, and had automatic direct injection without a pre-combustion chamber. The lightweight chassis could carry a 6-tonne payload or 12 tonnes with a trailer, and the compact engine allowed for a particularly short bonnet. Between 1932 and 1938, approximately 1418 units were produced, supplied in numerous wheelbase and payload versions and also as a bus.

Before he could produce his own diesel unit, Vincenzo Lancia died suddenly in 1937, aged 56. His widow, and brother Arturo took over the company reins. Technical director was the brilliant Ing. Vittorio Jano, who had previously been at Alfa Romeo and remained at Lancia until 1956.

In 1938, Lancia launched the 3 RO truck, equipped with its own Tipo 102 diesel engine, which was a 93bhp 6.8-litre (500-cubic inch) five-cylinder

The Esatau B of 1960, powered by a 122bhp 8.2-litre six-cylinder diesel engine, was available as a tractor and semi-trailer unit for hauling items like these chemical drums.

unit. The 3 RO was available in both civilian and military versions, with different wheelbases and payloads, and with or without a trailer facility. It could also be specified with petrol, producer gas and even methane engines, and the company also experimented with electric power. In 1941, some models were equipped with 90-mm (3.5-in) long-range guns. The post-war 3 RO was equipped with a more comfortable cab and a bunk for the second driver for long-haul applications.

Meanwhile, bombing raids on Turin in 1942 forced Lancia to transfer its operations to its Bolzano plant, which remained the commercial vehicle factory. The Esaro medium- to heavy-duty truck was a survivor from the war, and was available in two versions and structurally identical to the 3 RO model. It was produced with the original diesel engine, and some 2000 units were made between 1942 and 1947. That year, the Esatau conventional heavy-duty truck went into production, with rounded cab and mudguards fronted by the imposing Lancia grille. It was also used as the basis for forward-control buses, and was the first of a long

series, some of which were cab-over designs. The engine grew from five- to six-cylinders and to 8.2-litres (500-cubic inch), and up to 1963, 15,525 units were made. These included a modern, cab-over design that appeared in 1957 with a completely flat front and with the windscreen projecting beyond the radiator plane.

Commercial derivatives of the Appia passenger car began to appear in 1955, available as a van and light-duty pick-up truck, powered by the 37bhp 1-litre (61-cubic inch) V4 unit. The same year the Lancia family sold up to a finance group controlled by cement industrialist Ing. Carlo Pesenti, and their Formula 1 racing cars were acquired by Ferrari. The new regime launched its first commercials in 1959, including the cab-over 4x4 medium- to heavy-duty 506-series truck. It was used by the military for rugged duties and as a fire engine, snowplough and street sweeper, and was powered by a 170bhp 6.7-litre (409-cubic inch) six-cylinder petrol engine. One version used 115–145 octane aircraft fuel, which increased power to 195bhp. The cab-over Esadelta version replaced the obsolete 3 RO and was powered by a 115bhp 8.2-litre (500-cubic inch) six-cylinder diesel engine, and it was available as a truck or truck-tractor for semi-trailer work.

The cab-over Esagamma was introduced in 1962 with a powerful 187bhp 10.5-litre (641-cubic inch) six-cylinder diesel engine, with four-valves per cylinder, and a GVW of 14 tonnes.

Lancia's final fling as an independent producer was in 1969, with the Esagamma 718.441 local bus and Esagamma 718.641 long-distance bus. They used the 10.5-litre (641-cubic inch) engine in a central location with automatic or semi-automatic transmission. The Fiat take-over was announced on 29 October 1969 and after joining the Fiat Group, Lancia's production of buses continued at the Bolzano factory. From July 1972, this plant was known as Lancia Veicoli Speciali and was responsible for research and development on civil defence and military vehicles.

UNIC

The French truck maker Unic goes back to 1904, when Georges Richard et Cie was set up to produce Voitures Legères et Cycles Unic (or light vehicles and Unic cycles). Between 1905 and the outbreak of the First World War, the majority of Unic commercial vehicles were powered by 2.6-litre (159-cubic inch) or 3.4-litre (207-cubic inch) four-cylinder petrol engines. They frequently took the form of buses, with bodies made by outside suppliers, or elegant taxicabs. The C9 camionette served as an ambulance from 1914 and throughout the First World War.

In 1936, Unic launched a 4.9-litre (299-cubic inch) four-cylinder to power the medium-duty Z-series of conventional trucks and buses, and the same year introduced engines that could run on charcoal, anthracite or coal gas. The following year, Unic brought out its own diesel engine, a 10.2-litre (622-cubic inch) six-cylinder pre-combustion chamber unit, coupled with an eight-speed transmission.

Volumes were decreasing however,

and on the eve of the Second World War, the Unic catalogue listed only three types of chassis for cars, and 32 types of chassis for commercial vehicles. Production of ambulances and military vehicles began in anticipation of hostilities, and one of the most notable was the P 107 Kegresse half-track. This came out in 1937 and was bought in quantity by the French Army. During the following two years, 3276 were built. However, in June 1940, the Puteaux factory was badly damaged, but production resumed under the supervision of the occupying forces. Peacetime production at Unic was problematic.

Unic clearly needed help to carry out a modernisation programme and in 1949 the Simca Corporation stepped in, providing capital and new plant. Unic thus became Simca's commercial

After Unic came under Iveco control in 1974, cabs were standardised, and this 340bhp 14.8-litre (903-cubic inch) V8-powered Izoard cab-over model has a similar appearance to comtemporary Fiat products.

vehicle division. Simca was a company on the move, and having been a Fiat distributor before the war it acquired the Ford France operation in 1955. Production of trucks continued at Poissey and then at Suresnes with components sourced from both Unic and Ford Cargo models. In 1956, Unic merged with Saurer France, effectively tying together the neighbouring Puteaux and Suresnes factories. Unic's heavy-duty models continued to be made as conventionals, such as the ZU 121 and 101 models which bore no resemblance to any other truck design. Viewed from the front, the grille and wing configuration was more or less triangular, with the front axle set back under the front of the cab.

In 1960, Simca was divided into Simca Automobiles, which became a part of Chrysler France, and Simca Industries, which included Unic Industrial Vehicle Division, and from this point Unic no longer produced light vehicles for Simca.

In 1960, Simca Industries was taken over by Fiat France, which included Unic trucks, and the exchange of products with Italy increased accordingly. A few months after the takeover, at the Paris Show, Unic introduced the Izoard 6x4 three-axle chassis fitted with a new cab-over unit, a 35-tonne GVW heavy-duty model powered by the 225bhp 10.7-litre (653-cubic inch) V8 M62 diesel engine, which was equipped with the Saurer injection system.

Following a restructuring at Turin, production was partially transferred from the Unic factories at Puteaux-Suresnes to Trappes, 30km (18.6 miles) south of Paris, between 1971 and 1973. Puteaux-Suresnes became the engine plant, and the last Unic product was the 8220 engine, a 9.5-litre (580-cubic inch) straight-six producing 201bhp at 2600rpm, launched in September 1975 at the Frankfurt Show under the auspices of Iveco. Just before changing to Iveco, the Unic division was set up under the name Unic FIAT S.A.

MAGIRUS DEUTZ

This truck company is a key piece in the Iveco jigsaw, and has its origins in Ulm, Germany, the birthplace in 1824 of Conrad Dietrich Magirus. From 1864, Magirus made agricultural machinery and began producing equipment specifically designed for fire brigades. The first Magirus truck was a 3C, launched in September 1917, with a 3-tonne carrying capacity. It was powered by a 40bhp 6-litre (366-cubic inch) four-cylinder petrol engine, designated the V 110. In the post-war period, Magirus enlarged its range to include 18-seater buses with a superstructure mounted on a 2C chassis equipped with the V 110 engine.

A Magirus-Deutz M310 D22 FLL 6x2 prepares to receive a 6m (20ft) container, having just parted company with a 7m (23ft) Kögel interchangeable body unit. This truck is powered by the 305bhp air-cooled V10 engine.

The first Magirus six was the 55bhp 4.2-litre (256-cubic inch) S 85 petrol engine that appeared in 1929, and the first Magirus diesel was a six-cylinder engine based on the 4.5-litre (275-cubic inch) S 88 petrol engine, introduced in 1932 and known as the S 88 R.

In order to offset debts incurred during the depression, Magirus started to produce a light-duty cab-over truck in 1933, known as the M 10, with a pay-

load of approximately 1 tonne. It looked uncannily like a modern milk-float, and was powered by an 18bhp 670cc (41-cubic inch) two-cylinder air-cooled two-stroke engine, supplied by Ilo-Werke GmbH of Pinneberg, Schleswig-Holstein, and designated the P 2334. In five years, 1022 units were built.

The finance houses that effectively controlled the company sacked Adolf von Magirus as Chairman in 1934, and from then on the Magirus family no longer had any dealings with the company. The following year, Magirus AG was taken over by Humboldt-Deutz-Motoren AG of Cologne. The take-over increasingly favoured the excellent Deutz diesel engine, in preference to those made by Magirus.

With an eye to future military requirements, the German government introduced a rationalisation plan for the production of trucks and buses, involving standardisation of components for joint production between different companies. It also laid down a basic standard for various types of vehicle in terms of payload and application. A typical example of a vehicle built jointly by several companies, including Magirus, was the 33 GI model, a three-axle 6x4 vehicle made under licence from Henschel, and powered by the 100bhp 9.1-litre (555-cubic inch) Deutz F6M516H six-cylinder diesel engine.

Between 1937 and 1941, Magirus produced 3860 of these 33 GI trucks with various equipment and bodies. In the same period, the three-axle 6x6 was also made, which was equipped with the 80bhp 6.2-litre (378-cubic inch) direct injection six-cylinder Deutz HWA526D diesel engine. Magirus produced 18,568 units of the 3-tonne 3000 model between September 1940 and September 1944. Its versions included a regular truck, semi-trailer truck-tractor, dump truck and bus, as well as all-wheel drive military vehicles, Maultier half-tracks, fully tracked personnel carriers, and fire engines. All these vehicles

MAGIRUS DEUTZ 1950S CELESTIAL RANGE

Year	Model	Engine	Power output
1951	Mercury	5.3 litre four-cylinder	85bhp
	Jupiter	10.6 litre V8	175bhp
1955	Uranus	10.6 litre V8	175bhp
	6x4, 6x6		
	Sirius	5.3 litre four-cylinder	85bhp
	Saturn	7.9 litre V6	130bhp
	643N	9.1 litre six-cylinder diesel	156bhp

were equipped with the 70bhp version of the Deutz F4M513 diesel unit.

Production ended in 1945, and in the reconstruction that followed, Magirus made tractors for the agricultural division of the parent company, KHD, and bus bodies on General Motors chassis and a forward-control half-track designated the RS 1500 and known as the Phöenix aus der Asche. Under the guidance of chief engineer Adolf Wunsche, Magirus began to make trucks and buses again, based on the pre-war 3-tonne vehicles and equipped with the new F4L514 air-cooled engine. Its first authentic post-war models were unveiled at the 1951 Frankfurt Show,

and featured an imposing curvaceous bonnet and distinctive ovoid grille with the Magirus space-rocket logo, and known as the Mercury and Jupiter models. All were equipped with Deutz air-cooled diesel engines.

In 1953, KHD bought a factory from Westwaggon AG at Mainz, and in 1955 it transferred the entire production of Magirus buses to Mainz, following which Magirus bus body construction was thoroughly revised.

At the beginning of the 1960s, Magirus underwent a vast renewal programme and the range of vehicles was also rationalised to encourage standardisation of components.

A new series of direct injection air-cooled Deutz diesel engines went into production in 1969, and a modern factory came on stream at Ulm-Donau to build these engines and later on to manufacture trucks.

In 1974, an agreement was signed between Magirus, Saviem, DAF, and Volvo to produce fully interchangeable components. The project was officially known as the Euro Truck Development Group, but was also referred to as the Club of Four. In practice, the benefits were limited, and Magirus just used axles, springs and cabs that were also supplied to DAF.

On 18 November 1974, KHD transformed its Magirus division into a totally independent company which became known as Magirus-Deutz-Motoren AG, which then transferred its Ulm and Mainz factories to the new multinational, Iveco.

A typical heavy-duty all-wheel drive off-road construction site vehicle is this Magirus 232 D26AK, featuring a high-articulation rear bogie and powered by a 228bhp air-cooled V8 engine with 12 forward speeds.

PEGASO

The Pegaso marque was founded in 1947, as the Spanish industrial restructuring body INI set about getting the country back on its feet after the Civil War and Second World War. Responsibility for the car development was entrusted to the brilliant engineer Wifredo P. Ricart, who had recently resigned as manager of Alfa Romeo's technical department. This restructuring led to the creation of SEAT, Sociedad Espanola de Automoviles de Turismo, and the production of cars under licence from Fiat.

Commercial vehicles and buses were considered to be of national strategic importance and the Centre De Estudios Tecnicos de Automocion (CETA) was set up in Madrid in January 1946, also under Ricart's control, for vehicle production and testing. This led to the founding the same year of ENASA, the acronym of Empresa Nacional de Autocamiones S.A., with a management and design centre in Madrid and a production plant in Barcelona in the old Hispano-Suiza works. The agreements between ENASA and Hispano-Suiza didn't include a marque name, so in 1947 the name Pegaso was registered.

The last lorry developed by Hispano-Suiza, the 660 was introduced as the Pegaso I, followed by the cab-over Pegaso II in 1948, designated the Z-203 and powered by a 110bhp 5.6-litre (342-cubic inch) six-cylinder petrol engine. In 1949, the first Pegaso Diesel engine came out. It was a 125bhp 9.3-litre (567-cubic inch) six-cylinder unit based on the similar Hispano-Suiza 66 engine, and was nearly twice as economical as the petrol equivalent.

In 1949, a 70-seater bus body was fitted to the Pegaso II truck chassis and designated the Z-410. It was powered by a 110bhp petrol engine or 140bhp diesel unit. The Z-403 bus appeared in 1950, fitted with an innovative monocoque body, and it marked a significant development of the long-distance coach, both in terms of safety and comfort.

Pegaso introduced its first cars in 1952, including a prototype Z-101 six-seater limousine fitted with a 4-litre (244-cubic inch) 12-cylinder engine. Two sports cars, the Z-102 and the Z-103, both used highly sophisticated 160bhp 2.5-litre (152-cubic

In 1966 Pegaso introduced a new generation of trucks with panoramic cabs and one-piece windscreens, while retaining the classic corrugated steel panelling and cruciform radiator motif. Pictured is a 1065 model with dumper body.

inch) V8 aluminium engines.

In 1953, a facelift for Pegaso trucks saw the frontal styling altered, as the horizontal grille was replaced with the cross motif that would identify the marque for the next 30 years. The Madrid-Barajas plant finally came on stream in 1954, when it began to produce the Z-207 trucks and buses. The bodywork was made from corrugated steel sheet, which became a characteristic of Pegaso vehicles, and power was supplied by a new fuel-injected 110bhp 7.5-litre (458-cubic inch) V6 aluminium engine. This was an advanced specification indeed, further refined by a contra-rotating balancing shaft positioned below the crankshaft to reduce vibrations. It was also fitted with independent front-suspension, which gave an excellent ride. The Z-702 truck-tractor with semi-trailer had a payload of up to 10 tonnes, remaining in production until 1962, by which time 4412 units had been produced. In 1955 the prototype of the first rear-engined Pegaso bus, the Z-407, was built, based on the Z-207 Barajas chassis.

THE WINGED HORSE IN ORBIT
In 1957, ENASA entered into a joint venture with Leyland for importation and distribution on the Spanish market by Pegaso of a number of Leyland models. Hybrid models included the 5022 bus, equipped with a Leyland engine and Pegaso mechanicals. The Pegaso Comet 1090 was launched, powered by a 125bhp 6.5-litre (397-cubic inch) six-cylinder Leyland engine and fitted with a new panoramic cab with single-section windscreen. The bodywork was in corrugated steel and the two Pegaso hallmarks − the stripes and the broad cross on the grille − were prominent. Also based on the Comet 1090 design was a truck designated the 2030 truck-tractor with a payload of 10 tonnes, and an off-road vehicle with integral transfer box, designated the 3040, designed for construction sites and off-road transport.

Pegaso introduced a new heavy-duty range in 1964, designated the 1061 4x2, and the 1063 6x2, with GVW ratings of 20 to 35 tonnes, and the 2011 4x2 truck-tractor, seen by many as the ancestor of modern truck-tractors, with a GVW of 38 tonnes. Common power-unit was the 9105, a 200bhp 10.5-litre (641-cubic inch) six-cylinder unit with four valves per cylinder. The naturally aspirated version was soon followed by Pegaso's first turbocharged engine, a cast-iron block unit producing 260bhp.

In 1966, ENASA acquired just over half of Sociedad Anonima de Vehicluos Automoviles or SAVA, which provided Pegaso with access to the light-duty truck and van market.

The new cab-over 1080 range was unveiled at the 1972 Barcelona Show, all fitted with a new six-cylinder 12-litre (732-cubic inch) engine and a new all-steel rubber-mounted cab. The engine was accessed via a frontal flap,

and was available in naturally aspirated 250bhp and 352bhp turbocharged format, with four valves per cylinder.

Economic difficulties led ENASA to link up with International Harvester in 1980, with the US firm taking 35 per cent of ENASA shares. The following year, ENASA signed an agreement with the German ZF company to produce its gearboxes in Barcelona.

At the 1983 Barcelona Motor Show, the extensive Ti range of heavy-duty vehicles from 14 to 40 tonnes GVW was introduced. Engines ranged from 6.5-, 10.5- to 12-litre (397-, 641- to 732-cubic inch) units in naturally-aspirated or turbocharged format, with outputs from 135bhp to 310bhp. Transmissions were ENASA-produced 16-speed ZF S-130 gearboxes, and disc brakes were fitted.

In 1984, Pegaso introduced the prototype low-floor 6420 bus, which was developed in co-operation with MAN, and ENASA and DAF formed the joint

Formula 1 teams transport their cars from base to Grand Prix circuits in articulated rigs like this 1990 Giugiaro-designed Troner-cab Pegaso powered by a 12-litre (732-cubic inch) engine.

venture company CABTEC to manufacture a new Giugiaro-styled cab in a new factory at Madrid-Barajas, and production started in 1986. It was intended for the top-of-the-range Pegaso Troner, and would later be used on the DAF 95 range. Launched in 1987, the Troner was a heavy-duty truck with GVW of 44 tonnes, powered by a 360bhp 12-litre (732-cubic inch), 24-valve engine. Air conditioning was standard on all models. ENASA had acquired Seddon Atkinson from International Harvester in 1983, as a result of which the Strato model appeared in 1988, powered by Cummins, Gardner or Perkins engines and fitted with a revised Troner cab.

SEDDON ATKINSON

A word or two on Seddon Atkinson is more than appropriate. The company goes back to 1907, when Edward Atkinson began servicing steam engines in Preston, England. His firm subsequently progressed to the manufacture of diesel trucks in the late 1930s, about the time that Edward Seddon began a truck importing business in Salford, which became a

manufacturing plant by the end of the decade. During the Second World War, both companies won contracts from the British government to produce commercial vehicles for civilian use. Following the war, Seddon moved to Oldham, occupying the Woodstock mill, which was previously used to produce engine parts for the Spitfire aircraft. Atkinson produced heavy-duty

tractors while Seddon concentrated on producing lighter vehicles. In 1971, Seddon bought out Atkinson and began to build a wider range of vehicles at its Oldham plant, and later in the decade the company was sold to International Harvester. It enjoyed a healthy market share during the 1970s, which all went sour at the end of the decade when the recession ravaged the

SEDDON ATKINSON T7

Make: *Seddon Atkinson*

Model: *23.380M*

Type: *6x2, cab-over road relay, twin-width bunks*

Engine: *Cummins M11 10.8-litre (659-cubic-inch) straight-six charge-cooled 279bhp*

Gearbox: *Eaton RTSD 14316, 16 speeds*

Suspension:

axle 1: parabolic leaf springs

axle 2: parabolic leaf springs, double-convoluted air bellows

axle 3: drive-axle two-bag air suspension with raise/lower facility. Shock absorbers on all axles

Chassis: *forged steel beam ladder type*

Brakes: *dual-circuit air brakes, Jacobs engine brake*

GVW: *23,000kg*

GCW: *44,000kg*

heavy industries that Seddon Atkinson vehicles traditionally supplied. In 1991, Seddon Atkinson was acquired by Iveco, and became more entrenched as a bespoke manufacturer, producing niche vehicles tailored to customer requirements, mostly in the 17- to 44-tonne GVW range. In 1999, capacity was running at 1300 units per year.

Meanwhile, Pegaso's range of light-duty Ekus vehicles was produced in association with MAN and Volkswagen in 1988, replacing the old J4 series and trucks of SAVA origin.

The medium-duty Mider appeared at the 1989 Barcelona Show, with variants in the range from 20 to 26 tonnes, powered by the 257bhp version of the 10.5-litre (641-cubic inch) Pegaso engine. The following year, INI and Fiat signed an agreement that brought Pegaso into the Iveco Group. Not only was this worth 30 per cent of the

Spanish market in the over 16-tonne segment, but they also got six production facilities in Madrid, Barcelona, Valladolid, Mataro, Oldham England and Cumana Venezuela. Subsequently, the Ekus was replaced by the Daily range, partly produced in Spain, partly imported from Italy. The Tecno was replaced by the EuroCargo, while the Troner continued to fulfil the heavy-duty role, powered by an inter-cooled turbo version of the 400bhp 12-litre (732-cubic inch) Pegaso engine. The Trakker range of construction site trucks was available with two, three and four axles. Iveco-Pegaso offered two bus chassis: the 5226, with a 257bhp 10.5-litre (640-cubic inch) engine and a 320bhp 12-litre (732-cubic inch) engine, and the 5237 with 370bhp engine. In 1992, the Barajas works began work on the heavy-duty EuroTech assembly lines.

IVECO INTEGRATES OPERATIONS

At first it was unclear for Iveco whether to create a completely new identity or continue with the existing makes, with OM making specialist light-duty vehicles, Magirus Deutz in the construction sector, and Fiat building heavy-duty road trucks. Between 1975 and 1979, Iveco concentrated on converting factories and their respective specialisations into groups of components and finished product lines. Difficulties were compounded by cultural differences between the constituent companies, but integration was achieved between 1979 and 1984 by a committee made up of representatives of the national companies, together with managers of the central divisions.

There continued to be problems in transferring the image of the old marques to the Iveco brand, which lacked an image in the heavy truck industry, but by the end of the decade all the old makes had been replaced by the Iveco marque. Meanwhile, Iveco continued to set up operations worldwide, in China, Turkey, India, Africa, Asia and the USA.

The TurboStar was Iveco's most prominent heavy-duty model of the late 1980s. Launched in 1984, it went on to become a best seller on the Italian market, and over 50,000 were sold in Europe by 1992. It was powered by the 330bhp turbo after-cooler version of the 13.8-litre (842-cubic inch) six-cylinder 8210 unit, and the 420bhp turbocharged 17.2-litre (1050-cubic inch) 8280 V8 engine.

The acquisition in 1986 by Ford of Britain's truck division resulted in the formation of Iveco Ford Truck, which opened up the European market for the company once again. The ubiquitous Cargo series was manufactured at

IVECO EUROTECH

Make: *Iveco*
Model: *EuroTech*
Type: *4x2, cab-over*
Engine: *Iveco TCA 8250 V8 17.2-litre (1050-cubic inch) 520bhp*
Gearbox: *Eaton Twin Splitter 12 + 3 speeds, or ZF-Ecomid 16 + 2 speeds, or ZF-Ecosplit 16 + 1 speed, Rockwell or Iveco rear axles*
Suspension:
front axle: parabolic leaf springs, shock absorbers and anti-roll bar
rear axle: pneumatic shock absorbers and anti-roll bar, or pneumatic front and rear
Chassis: *modular, bottleneck side frames with cross-members,*
Brakes: *discs front, drums rear*
Weight range: *16–26 tonnes*

Ford's sophisticated Langley plant to the west of London, which first built commercial vehicles in 1960. The Cargo quickly became Britain's top selling truck and altogether some 100,000 units were built in its 12-year production run.

Iveco's other large family of vehicles for the 1980s and 1990s was the exten-

sive Euro range. These covered the weight ranges from 6 tonnes up to the medium-duty vehicles of 12 tonnes to 17.5 tonnes, followed by the medium-to heavy-duty vehicles at around 17.5 tonnes for a twin-axle vehicle and 35 tonnes to 40 tonnes for vehicle combinations. Heavy-duty vehicles ranged from 18 tonnes up to the limit of 44

unit. Transmissions included the Eaton Twin Splitter gearboxes and ZF Ecomid, both with nine- and 16-speeds, or the Ecosplit 16-speed box. By 1999, the 12-speed EuroTronic automated transmission was available for the EuroTech and EuroStar truck ranges, and the 16-speed version was available on EuroStars running with the 470bhp engine.

CONSTRUCTION SITE APPLICATIONS

Construction site applications were the province of the EuroTrakker models. The range incorporated weights from 19 to 40 tonnes, and included truck-tractors and heavy-duty all-wheel drive vehicles designated HT and HW in 4x2, 4x4, 6x4, 6x6 and 8x4 configurations. Articulated vehicles and semi-trailer combinations ranged from 40-tonne 4x2 tractors to 88-tonne combinations derived from the 380 model. Heavy-duty combinations were designated 440, 560 and 720, referring to the maximum gross weight. For example, the 560E37HT was a 56-tonne tractor with a 370bhp engine.

The EuroTrakker shared the cab of heavy-duty on-road models but was fitted with a stronger, shallower front bumper. EuroTrakker also shared the same engines and gearboxes with the heavy-duty on-road EuroTech range, while the chassis, front and rear axles and the braking system were specifically developed for construction site work, including concrete mixers, tippers and snowploughs.

The chassis were of the traditional ladder frame construction and made from high-tensile steel and flitched for extra strength. The Iveco rear axles used double reduction for better ground clearance and uniform torque distribution. The front suspensions were parabolic springs with conventional semi-elliptical springs available, while the rear suspension was a two-spring design which, depending on the model, could have parabolic or semi-elliptical leaves. Either type could have anti-roll bars fitted. The braking system used drums on all axles in conjunction with Simplex type units.

tonnes for vehicle combinations and construction site vehicles.

Iveco developed a range of modular tilt-cabs styled by Giugiaro's Italdesign. Each model had a short and long version, a top sleeper, medium or low roof for the EuroTech and the EuroStar and a high roof for the EuroStar. The EuroCargo cab equipped the 16- to 17.5-tonne vehicles in the light- and medium-duty ranges. The EuroStar cab was used for heavy-duty vehicles.

The medium-heavy and heavy-duty models were powered by three engines. These were the 300bhp, 345bhp and 375bhp versions of the 8460, and the 306bhp, 420bhp and 470bhp versions of the 8210, and the 514bhp 8280

MAN

MAN is an acronym of Maschinenfabrik, combined with the two cities of Augsberg and Nürnberg. The company began by building steam engines, and its commercial vehicle operation started in 1915. Some 20 years earlier, Rudolf Diesel invented the oil-burning engine that was named after him, and **MAN** was one of its chief exponents. It's probably no idle boast that **MAN** has been at the forefront of truck evolution for some eighty-five years. In 1995, its 600bhp 19.603 model was the most powerful series production truck in Europe.

The milestones of MAN's innovations follow on from its first truck offering in 1915, and in 1923 it became the first manufacturer in the world to offer a diesel engine with direct injection. The following year a M.A.N. truck was unveiled with a direct injection diesel engine, and again, this was a world first. After a gap of nearly thirty years, it came out with the first German turbocharged truck diesel engine in 1951.

Four years later the MAN plant was set up in Munich, and from this point the company name lost the punctuation that had previously meant it was called M.A.N. In 1971, it acquired the Büssing Motor Company, and in 1979 it introduced air charge intercooling on its turbodiesels.

MAN F2000 semi-trailer truck-tractor with sleeper cab and Fruehauf curtain-side trailer unit.

Typically, MAN was up with the latest technology.

A corporate coup took place in 1990, when MAN bought out the famous Austrian specialist truck and engine maker Steyr Nutzfahrzeuge AG. The following year the MAN Commercial Vehicles Group was set up as a subsidiary company, incorporating the long-established Austrian companies Steyr Nutzfahrzeuge and ÖAF-Gräf & Stift. The company's Lion's Star model won the Coach of the Year accolade in 1993 and, in 1995, MAN lifted the Truck of the Year award for the fourth time.

MAN's seven production plants were interdependent. Each plant had its own specialised work-areas, and the workforces contributed ideas and solutions to production issues. The company's head office was in Munich, southern Germany, and it included the assembly line for the F 2000 heavy-duty range, as well as the research and development and the marketing and sales depart-

ments. Within the MAN Commercial Vehicles subsidiary, ÖAF made heavy trucks, buses, special-purpose vehicles, and manufactured transfer boxes. Steyr produced its own trucks from 6 to 40 tonnes, and it also assembled the M 2000 medium truck and constructed cabs for the L 2000 light-duty range. The actual assembly line for the L 2000 was at the Salzgitter plant.

Buses and coaches came under a separate corporate division, with production concentrated at Salzgitter. Diesel engines were developed and built at the long-standing Nuremberg plant. Pressings such as the chassis frame and cross-members were made at Gustavsburg, where there was also a tool-making facility, and wiring harness and various components for cabs and other areas of the vehicle were manufactured at the plant in Penzberg.

By 1998, MAN had three model ranges, which were, logically, light, medium and heavy truck lines, and all

of which were among the European leaders in terms of cab design, driveline technology and chassis construction. There were many different versions of each individual model, and they were available with a wide variety of superstructures for optimum payload and tasks.

The L 200 light truck range encompassed the 6- to 10-tonne category, and was developed for urban and localised transport requirements. It was a typical all-rounder, emphasised by the presence of a 4x4 model in the range. Engine power outputs ranged from 102bhp to 115bhp and 220bhp.

The MAN M 2000 medium truck range encompassed the 12- to 25-tonne band, and cab alternatives available included that of the L 2000 model, designed for town use, and the more specialised M 2000 cab. A variety of engines provided the M 2000 with power outputs ranging from 155bhp to 260bhp.

In the 1990s, MAN experimented with lean-burn technology to ensure that its engines operated within Euro 2 standards. This is the Eco 370 truck tractor and semi-trailer rig undergoing trials.

MAN TRUCK RANGE 1998

L 200 light truck range: *6–10 tonnes, 102, 115, 220bhp*
M 2000 medium truck range: *12–25 tonnes, 155–260bhp*
L 2000 light-duty truck range: *7.5–10 tonnes including 4x4 model*
F 2000 heavy-duty truck range: *18–48 tonnes, 270–600bhp – at time of launch, the most powerful series production truck in Europe*

The F 2000 heavy-duty range went from 18- to 48-tonne vehicles, and these really were high-performance trucks. At the time of its launch, the 600bhp F 2000 was the most powerful series production truck in Europe. As you might expect, the German makers paid close attention to safety, environmental compatibility, driver comfort, convenience and economy, as well as the detailing and ergonomics within the cab. The Euro 2 engines were rated from 270bhp up to 600bhp, with EDC management fitted as standard equipment.

Thus, MAN had pretty much a vehicle to suit most applications. Its special-purpose vehicles included ten-wheeler chassis or eight-wheeler, semi-trailer truck-tractors, which found a ready market in the construction industry, and for hauling heavy and unusual loads. The key features of MAN off-road vehicles included torsionally rigid chassis frames, generous suspension travel, permanent all-wheel drive, and knobbly tyres. The company's Lion's Star highliner coach contained state-of-the-art equipment for comfort, safety and economy, and featured a completely level floor. The single-decker coach carried the same styling characteristics as the Lion's Star, while the Lion's Coach model was more of an all-rounder. This coach was manufactured by MAN Kamyon ve Otobus Sanayi AS in Ankara, Turkey, in accordance with the parent company's strict quality standards. All MAN coaches and its inter-city scheduled-service bus bore the family hallmarks of similar aerodynamic styling, frontal design and exterior mirrors.

The MAN city-bus concept was aimed at making this form of public transport more attractive to passengers,

as a way of increasing urban mobility. The important aspects here were good ergonomics, spatial integrity and passenger comfort. For its current generation of low-floor busses, MAN was able to draw on more than 20 years of experience in this type of construction. A variety of bus concepts were being tested and developed during the late 1990s, using contemporary low-floor engineering in combination with innovative, extremely low-emission drive systems. These were developed in order to make travelling by bus a more attractive experience for the passenger and less damaging to the environment – we've all seen plenty of city buses churning out clouds of black diesel fumes. Among MAN's successful projects in this area were natural gas powered low-floor buses that found operation with a number of public transport authorities. Buses with diesel electric power and a completely level floor from front to rear were also in the frame. This system reduced fuel consumption and emission levels considerably.

MAN ON THE MOVE
The company's special-purpose coaches included modern airport apron buses built by ÖAF, the specialist-vehicle arm. Articulated buses were able to have a particularly low floor at the revolving section because of the company's patented rotating joint. A damping and anti jackknifing system ensured that both sections of the vehicle

Safe braking. Dual-circuit brake system with discs at the front (top) and efficient drums at the rear (bottom). Linings are asbestos free. ABS is standard on the M 2000 tractors.

remained under control in emergency situations or simply in tight curves and on icy roads. An Adaptive Cruise Control (ACC) system was developed to keep the truck at an electronically controlled distance to the vehicle ahead. It was based on a radar distance sensor with an integrated signal-processing unit.

MAN's research and development division's concerns ranged from the ecological situation, economic considerations and mobility, to the technical features of commercial vehicles and the traffic situation. It was also active in materials research, electronics and information and communication technology, development work on vehicle drivelines, design and ergonomics, traffic guidance and navigation systems, fleet management and satellite-link communication.

MAN bus chassis ranged from 8-tonners to the large three-axle 24-tonners, in versions with front or rear engine. The chassis were sold to vehicle manu-

facturers all over the world to be fitted with locally produced bodywork, including luxury coaches, inter-city and city buses or even double-deckers. They were sufficiently adaptable to be used for other special-purpose bodies; too, like horseboxes, conference rooms, mobile homes and touring exhibitions.

MAN drivetrains included high-speed, water-cooled diesel engines for road vehicles, ships, construction equipment and agricultural machinery, as well as many different industrial applications. There were also natural-gas-and liquid-gas powered engines. The water-cooled diesels were made as in-line or V-cylinder layouts and power ratings ranged from 47kW (64hp) to 882kW (1200hp). The gas-powered units were in-line six-cylinder and V12 units.

MAN offered two series of driven axles, depending on load capacity,

torque and operating principle. They consisted of planetary-hub front or rear axles and single-reduction, hypoid rear axles, and both types of axle were available with through-drive for use in tandem or multiple assemblies. There were non-driven front axles of either straight or dropped, solid-end pattern, and also a double-wishbone, independent, front-suspension system. Other manufacturers used MAN axles as well, and they were available with ABS and ASH (wheels-up control). Developed jointly with the ZF Company of Friedrichshafen, MAN transfer boxes were of short, compact three-shaft construction.

The pressings for MAN truck cabs and other body sections came from its Gustavsburg plant, which also supplied chassis elements and frame girders produced from heavy- and medium-gauge steel plate. The company designed and

MAN F 2000 RANGE

Make: *MAN*
Model: *F 2000*
Type: *4x2, forward cab*
Engine:
   MAN 10-, 12- or 18-litre (610-, 732- or 1098-cubic inch) in-line six or V12
Gearbox: *MAN, ZF or Eaton*
Suspension: *progressive parabolic springs with stabilizers and dampers at front and rear. Air suspension available on all 4x2 and 6x2 models in all weight classes, with ECAS automatic adjustable ride height*
Chassis: *flat-topped ladder-type with tubular-steel cross-members*
Brakes: *discs and drums, ABS*

MAN provided complete back-up facilities, like full service leasing, long-term vehicle hire maintenance and repair agreements for the benefit of operators running rigs like this F 2000.

monoxide (CO), but a precondition for its installation was the use of the low-sulphur diesel fuel.

MAN engines which ran on natural gas (CNG) or liquid petroleum gas (LPG) produced low emissions, and an optional rape-seed oil, methyl-ester (RME) equipment package was available, which diesel engines could run on without a problem. Providing a zero option for exhaust and noise emissions was the low-floor, battery-powered midibus, which was squeaky clean, pollutant free and gave more or less silent running. In the late 1990s, a MAN scheduled-service bus with a hydrogen-gas engine was undergoing field tests at Erlangen, on the basis that hydrogen was the most environmentally friendly fuel on which to run an internal combustion engine. In the manufacturing environment, MAN used modern, spray-coating booths, and CFCs, asbestos and solvents were abolished wherever possible. Marking of recyclable components enabled subsequent sorting into separate groups of materials.

Its systems consultancy advised on technical matters and vehicle options for specific trades and work areas, providing mobile data-communication systems. If a convincing demonstration

were required of a MAN product, the Eco-Challenge Tour of 1995 would do nicely. The 2800-km (17,400-m) route took competitors from Edinburgh in Scotland down to Bari on Italy's Adriatic coast, and the specially equipped MAN F 2000 established a world-record fuel consumption of 25.2litres per 100km or 9.3miles per gallon. This was quite a remarkable feat for a fully laden, 40-tonne, semi-trailer train with a body height of 4m (157in).

MAN vehicles competed regularly in Super Truck races, and to increase the efficiency and power output of the 12-litre (732-cubic inch) in-line six-cylinder engine, four-valves per cylinder were used, together with twin turbochargers. The truck's radiator, intercooler and electronically controlled injection system were sourced from the company's marine engine sector. In the speed range from 1800rpm to 2600rpm in which it is operated, this engine develops over 1000bhp.

Eddie Stobart, a large UK operator, favour MAN F886 truck-tractors, hauling strapless curtainside trailers. An air-powered tensioning system is quicker to open and close as well as being streamlined.

manufactured its own forming and press tools, and the finished chassis were treated with modern spray-coating systems.

EMISSION CONTROL

The company has experimented with lean-burn technology, EDC engine management, high-pressure direct injection through multi-hole nozzles, optimised turbochargers or wastegate charge-air regulation, enabling its engines to operate well within the Euro 2 standards. Mercifully, those clouds of exhaust fumes that used to be generated on moving off and accelerating were virtually eliminated. MAN evolved an oxidising catalytic converter for vehicles for the F 2000 heavy-duty line in 1996 that was present throughout the entire range by 1997. This achieved a reduction of 70 to 90 per cent for hydrocarbons (HC) and carbon

OSHKOSH

For many people outside the USA, the news that Oshkosh is a maker of trucks rather than merely a brand of kid's dungarees comes as a surprise. However, it is in fact one of a number of small specialist North American manufacturers whose products have weathered the test of time, and its products are among the most fascinating trucks you can get.

Oshkosh was co-founded by William R. Besserdich in 1917, having abandoned the FWD Company he'd previously started in 1908 with Otto Zachow in Clintonville, Wisconsin, due to disputes over patent rights. His new partner was Bernard A. Mosling, and their speciality was four-wheel drive vehicles produced under the name of Wisconsin Duplex Auto Company. Their first truck was built in a Milwaukee workshop, and Old Betsy, as she's known, is still in working order. This 1-tonner was powered by a four-cylinder LeRoi engine mated to a three-speed transmission, and shod with Firestone gum-dipped pneumatic tyres, which were always standard equipment on Oshkosh trucks.

In 1917, a factory was leased in Oshkosh, about 50 miles south of Clintonville, and the name was changed to the Oshkosh Motor Truck Manufacturing Company. It was derived from the Red Indian Chief Oshkosh of the Menomonee tribe, who lived from 1795 to 1858. The company built the Model A, its first four-wheel drive truck with an automatic centre-lock differential in 1918. It was based on an A.O. Smith chassis, and was powered by an unusual 72hp Herschel–Spillman four-cylinder engine.

This dramatic-looking vehicle is a four-wheel steer Oshkosh HB snowblower, an essential tool for airfields, capable of dispersing 3000 tons of snow per hour.

The mighty HEMTT (Heavy Expanded Mobility Tactical Truck) proved its worth in action in the Gulf War of 1991. She was the first Oshkosh truck and is seen here giving Old Betsy a lift.

Oshkosh relocated to its present factory in 1921, and the University of Wisconsin-Oshkosh was subsequently built on its old site. The new Model B light-duty truck went straight into production, but despite a strong publicity campaign that promoted the truck's versatile off-roading abilities, sales suffered due to the generosity of the US Government, which was busy donating army surplus, four-wheel drive vehicles to construction companies.

New vehicles were the 5-ton Model F and the Model H, which appeared in 1924. The Model H was eventually powered by a six-cylinder engine with double reduction axles, and it sustained the company for the rest of the decade. As a utility vehicle, the Model H was often used as a snowplough and in road-construction programmes. The Great Depression of 1930 led to the restructuring of the company, and the rationalisation of its name to The Oshkosh Motor Truck Company Incorporated. Meanwhile, trucks were getting bigger, and in 1932, Oshkosh came out with its FC and FB models, rated at 44,000lb GVW. Powered by six-cylinder Hercules engines ranging in output from 102bhp to 200bhp, coupled to a wide selection of transmissions from four- to 12-speed. Snow-clearing accessories included gigantic V-shape,

wing and rotary ploughs and bulldozer blades. Oshkosh trucks excelled at snow clearance, and were utilised in many states to keep roads clear for dairy farmers' milk collection.

In 1933, Oshkosh launched the Model TR truck, specifically for earth-moving and construction-site work, and for use in conjunction with bottom-dump semi-trailers. Its Goodyear tyres were the largest pneumatics ever seen, and through its four-wheel steering, the TR could perform a 180-degree turn in just over 31ft (9.5m). The tyres were wrapped with chains where necessary to provide extra grip in mud and snow. As well as construction companies – including 100 units sold in the UK – the TR was also tested by the US military as a 105mm (4in) gun tractor.

FIRST DIESEL TRUCK

The first Oshkosh truck to run with a diesel engine was the G-series fitted with a Cummins unit in 1935, and the 2- to 3.5-ton J Series model with its new one-piece windscreen cab, large swept-back, cycle-wing mudguards and rounded-top grille came out the same year. The FB Series was brought up to date when it came to be fitted with the J Series' cab.

One of its most enduring models was the W-Series, which went into

This T-1500 ARFF vehicle is in service with Los Angeles City Fire Department and has a 3000 gallon (11,300 litre) capacity. It is equipped with both roof and bumper mounted water cannon turrets.

production in 1940, and lasted for 20 years. It featured a new cab with V-shaped windscreen (instead of a flat single pane) and an Indian-head grille. The W-700 derivative was used by the US Army Corps of Engineers who fitted them with snow blowers for clearing airfield runways. Typically, a Klauer TU-3 snow blower was mounted on the front of the truck, and powered by a petrol-fuelled 175bhp six-cylinder Climax R61 engine balancing it at the rear, which was actually more powerful than the W-700's own 112bhp six-cylinder Hercules RXC unit.

The company built military vehicles during the war, culminating in the W-1600 of 1944, which was a large 6x6 off-roader that was often to be seen hauling trailers laden with heavy machinery, public utility gear like power lines or oil field derricks. The Model W-2200 of 1947 was a seriously big truck-tractor. It was powered by petrol or oil-burning Buda or Hall-Scott engine that was mounted well

OSHKOSH SPECIAL VEHICLES

Model A: *powered by the 115bhp S9w 702 engine*
5-ton Model F and the Model H: *six-cylinder engine with double reduction axles*
FC and FB Models: *44,000lbs GVW – 102bhp to 200bhp*
Model TR truck: *4x4, four-wheel steering, 31-ft (9.5-m) turning circle*
G Series: *6x6 cab-over for oil-well servicing*
J Series: *4x4 conventional, 2-3.5 ton*
W Series: *112bhp Hercules RXC engine plus 175bhp Climax powered snow blower*
C, F and D Series Models: *8x6, 8x8 and 10x6 drives*
D Series model, 16-cubic yard (12-cubic cm) capacity: *12x10 drive*

forward in the chassis, and it was altogether superior to its rivals. As well as being an excellent highways department snow-clearance vehicle, the W-2200 was also used by sugar-cane producers and mining operations for heavy-duty off-road work, and it was sometimes converted as a concrete mixer, airfield fire truck or garbage carrier. As a truck-tractor the W-2205 would haul enormous excavators on its low-loader trailer.

The ever-larger capacity mixers that followed were the C, F and D Series models, which were offered with 8x6, 8x8 and 10x6 drives. The largest of all was the 16-cubic yard (12-cubic m) capacity D Series model, which had two tandem steering front axles and four rear axles, which created a formidable 12x10 drive. The last axle in the rear set could be hydraulically retracted after the barrel was emptied.

Oshkosh vehicles underwent a complete exterior facelift in 1960. At this time, the Cold War with the Soviet Union was at its height, and the US defence system required early warning radar stations in far-flung outposts in Canada and Alaska. Oshkosh trucks were just the vehicles to provide access

R Series of the 1980s, was also recognisable as a regular truck rather than some giant extra-terrestrial Tonka Toy, and was also assembled in South Africa and Australia.

STANDARDISATION

In 1973, Oshkosh standardised its engine range, fitting diesel units from Caterpillar, Cummins and Detroit Diesel. Then in 1974, they came out with the new 6x6 J Series conventional layout models, the Desert Prince and Desert Knight truck-tractors, aimed at the oil field market. These were very big trucks indeed, and were actually based on the F Series but powered by 325bhp or 485bhp diesels.

to such remote sites, and the company won a contract to supply the US Airforce with its new model, the WT-2206. These tall, short-wheelbase trucks were fitted with big, roll-over snow ploughs (they could be rotated after one sweep so as to push away the snow all in one direction) or rotary snow blowers, and operated in echelon at up to 55mph (88km/h) to clear away snow from runways. They used 325bhp Hall-Scott engines coupled to Allison TG 602-RM automatic transmissions. Around 1000 were built, and many ended up at commercial airports.

A new all-wheel-drive utility truck-tractor with the set-back, front-axle long-nose design, designated the U-44-L and otherwise known as the 'Pogo Stick', appeared in 1962, designed for use in conjunction with earth-boring machines. It had solid suspension to give stability while drilling, and was fitted with giant hammer drills – hence the nickname – and was used by the US Navy and telephone companies.

As early as 1953, Oshkosh had supplied purpose-built Aircraft Rescue and Fire-fighting (ARFF) trucks to the US Coast Guard, but in 1968 it was contracted to supply 300 units of the utilitarian MB-5 to the US Navy. It could carry 400 gallons (1500 litres) of water, which when mixed with a foam concentrate increased fire-damping capacity to 5000 gallons (19,000 litres).

This S Series concrete carrier of 1982 superseded the B Series model, with its rear-mounted engine, central mixing barrel and chute above the single-seat cab for accurate deposition in out-of-the-way building sites.

Another larger crash truck, the 1500-gallon (5700-litre) 6x6 P-4, was sold to the US Navy and the Australian Air Force in the early 1970s. It was superseded by the massive forward control 66-ton P-15 in 1977, which was powered by a pair of 492bhp Detroit Diesel V8s, and had a 60,000-gallon (227,400-litre) foam capacity. The extinguishing foam was directed at the target by a 'gun' mounted in an exposed turret mounted above and to the rear of the cab.

Meanwhile, back in 1968, Oshkosh was building trucks of a very different kind. The U-30 was a large tow-tractor made specifically for pulling aircraft such as the giant C5A cargo plane. It had four enormous wheels shod with huge, all-terrain pattern tyres, a winch at the front and a power unit amidships. Only 45 were made.

In 1971, contrary to the trend towards enormous, heavy-duty, specialised trucks, Oshkosh made the E Series, a relatively small, tilting, cab-over highway tractor powered by a Cater-pillar diesel, which came to be made in South Africa. Its successor, the

Possibly the most significant contract was awarded in 1981, Oshkosh's largest government deal of the decade, which was to produce a range of Heavy Expanded Mobility Tactical Trucks (HEMTT). These gigantic, futuristic-looking vehicles featured significantly in Operation Desert Storm in 1991, acting as refuelling tankers and long-distance-front-line supply trucks.

Production of HEMTTs had risen to 13,000 units by 1992, and included five variants of the 8x8 truck, from cargo carriers and a tanker to a truck-tractor and recovery vehicle. The tractor version was used for hauling the Patriot missile launcher, and was powered by the 445bhp Detroit Diesel V8 engine linked to a four-speed Allison HT-740 automatic transmission. In 1985, the US Marines corps took delivery of 1400 Logistics Vehicle Systems (LVS) trucks. These were articulated at the centre in order to provide better mobility on difficult terrain.

In 1990, Oshkosh won a contract to produce a new 8x8 Heavy Equipment Transporter (HET), the M-1070 model, for the US Army, superseding the M-911 HET that saw service in the Gulf War. Its 500bhp power-unit endowed it with greater hauling capacity, and it was built with a five-person cab.

Oshkosh was awarded another US Army contract in 1990, to build 2626 Palletised Load System (PLS) vehicles. The 10x10, 500bhp PLS was equipped with an hydraulic load-handling system, including a crane for hoisting a flat-rack cargo palette onto its back. In 1996, Oshkosh expanded its operations into trailer manufacturing and developed a new combined recycling, and, refuse truck with its forward-control cab mounted far ahead of the front axle. Strange-looking beasts, these Oshkosh trucks, yet they were hugely competent.

The impressive snow-clearing fleet at Chicago's O'Hare International Airport is comprised of Oshkosh PA Series conventionals and HB Series forward-control vehicles, featuring snowblowers, plough blades and rotating brooms.

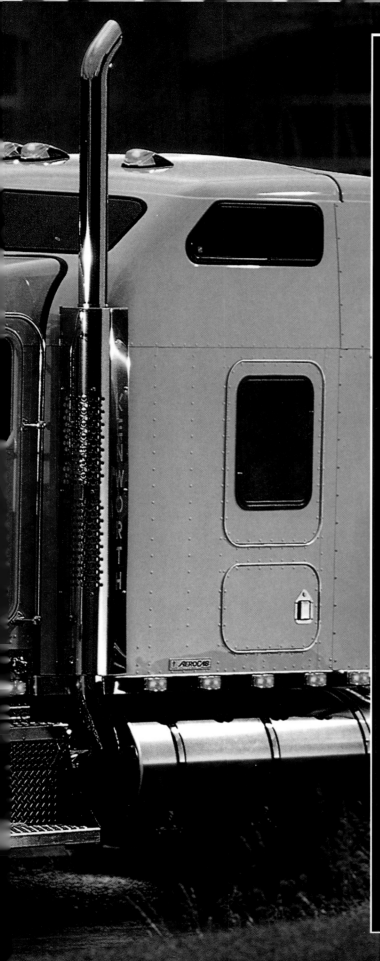

PACCAR

In the late 1990s, PACCAR – the Pacific Car and Foundry Company – had become the second largest manufacturer of heavy trucks in the world, an $8 billion global corporation that turned a profit every year since 1938, and in 1997, its share value increased by 71 per cent. PACCAR'ss prominence rested on its ownership of four of the best-known names in the trucking world. These were Kenworth, Peterbilt, DAF and Foden, all of whom had at some point been at the pinnacle of the trucking business in the USA, Europe and Australia.

PACCAR's status rests on the reputations of its constituent makes. Their individual fame was established by celebrated models in the 1950s like Kenworth's Bull–Nose cab-forward and Narrow–Nose conventional, and Peterbilt's custom-built Model 334 conventional and model 352 cab-over. DAF's more recent rise to international prominence was marked by its 1986 Paris–Dakar rally winning 3600 Turbo Twin II, and Foden, with its origins in steam engines, specialised in classic eight-wheeler rigids in the 1950s and 1960s. What follows is a potted history of each of these makes, indicating the point at which PACCAR gained control, as they continue to prosper under the corporate umbrella.

No mistaking this heavy-duty Kenworth T800 72-in (183-cm) AeroCab conventional, which has been a major presence on West Coast highways since its introduction in 1986.

KENWORTH

Kenworth was derived from the surnames of Harry Kent and Edgar K. Worthington, who were stockholders of the Gerlinger Manufacturing Company of Portland, Oregon. This firm moved to Seattle in 1917 and called itself the Gersix Manufacturing Company – its truck had a six-cylinder engine – and in 1923 the name was changed to Kenworth.

Output for 1926 was 99 custom-made units, and production rose by nearly 50 per cent with three vehicles a week leaving the factory. As maximum capacity was reached, a new plant was opened in 1927 in Vancouver, which potentially doubled the West Coast market potential. However, the Wall Street Crash was just around the corner, and economic circumstances were dire in the truck market. But in spite of the Depression, Kenworth introduced new torsion-bar suspension and vacuum-assisted hydraulic brakes. Six-wheel trucks now became available, with either a tandem drive axle or third trailing axle, and Kenworth's repertoire expended in 1932 to encompass fire engines and a small number of

inter-city buses. Among these were forward-control models and conventionals with engines mounted under the floor, as well as exotic one-and-a-half-deckers. In the early 1930s, diesel fuel was about a third of the price of petrol, and diesels had superior torque, which enabled heavily laden trucks to negotiate steep gradients more easily. A milestone was reached in 1933, when Kenworth became the first US manufacturer to offer a diesel engine as standard, and the specific unit was the 100bhp Cummins HA4. Here was a company on the move, and it also produced its first sleeper cab that year.

The Federal Motor Carrier Act of 1935 empowered the Interstate Commerce Commission to introduce legislation that prompted Kenworth to start using aluminium components in a bid to reduce weight, and accordingly its cabs were panelled in sheet aluminium.

Kenworth's K Series cab-over model of 1974 was very similar to Peterbilt's 352 model, and it was the forerunner of Kenworth's Aerodyne cab-over of the 1990s.

The so-called shovelnose radiator grille was introduced on conventionals, and the first Kenworth bubblenose cab-over model appeared in 1936, designated the Model 516. The justification for this was to circumvent the length restriction in Arizona.

Kenworth built 10 different truck models in 1937, ranging from the 2-ton Model 88, powered by an 83bhp Hercules JXC engine, to the 7-ton Model 241C, powered by a 125bhp six-cylinder Cummins diesel. Petrol-fuelled six-cylinder Buda and Herschell-Spillman engines were also available for the 4-ton Model 146B and 7-ton Model 241A. From 1940, a new flat radiator grille replaced the previously curved format and would see the company through to the 1980s. The following year, Cummins was prompted by Kenworth to make the world's first aluminium diesel engine.

As the USA entered the Second World War, Kenworth was commissioned to produce 1930 units of the M-1 and M-1A1 heavy-duty, 4-ton wrecking trucks, and 6x6 crane-carriers equipped with spotlights and winches front and back as well as cutting and welding equipment. From 1943, it manufactured components, including nose assemblies, for the Boeing B-17 Flying Fortress and B-29 Super Fortress aircraft and, being fairly exposed on the Pacific coast, it was persuaded by the US government to relocate some of its plant further inland. As hostilities came to an end, the company built a further 484 military vehicles and 427 commercials.

But a corporate matter was to impact more on Kenworth than the Japanese did. Following the death of its President, Phil Johnson, in 1944, Kenworth was acquired by PACCAR, and became a wholly owned subsidiary. Coincidentally, the chassis frame made from aluminium extrusions was introduced that year, and aluminium was also used for transmission cases. Kenworth returned to Seattle in 1946, and occupied the

redundant Fisher Body plant, where 705 trucks were made, a number of which found buyers in the Hawaiian sugar-cane plantations. The US military continued to request prototype heavy-duty trucks from Kenworth, and one example was the T30 truck-tractor with a 30,000-lb GCW rating, powered by a 290bhp water-cooled OHV six-cylinder Continental X6748 petrol engine. As its more familiar conventionals and cab-overs became more refined in the post-war years, in 1949 Kenworth launched a vehicle known as the Bruck, which was a hybrid bus and truck. For the next decade or so, it also experimented with gas turbine engines in association with Boeing, on behalf of the US Navy and West Coast Fast Freight. The 175bhp Boeing 502-8A turbine was significantly lighter than a comparable diesel engine, but high fuel consumption and high development and maintenance costs ended the project. In 1953, a prototype was in service with West Coast Fast Freight, running between Seattle and Los Angeles.

By this time annual output was up to 1000 units, many of which were cab-over, semi-truck tractors, as the marque gained popularity with owner-operators and larger fleets. The double-ended T-10 heavy equipment transporter which had a truck-tractor at either end, was manufactured for the US Army. Another oddball was the single seater cab-beside-engine CBE model, introduced in 1954, and almost all were produced as truck-tractors, with a few 6x4 versions, and others had sleeper units behind the engine.

In 1955, Canadian Kenworth Limited was formed as a wholly owned subsidiary of PACCAR, centred on a new plant at Burnaby, British Columbia. Kenworth built the four-axle Dromedary with twin-steering axles in 1956, at the request of Pacific Intermountain Express. Like the Peterbilt version, it included a short cargo van between the cab and the fifth wheel coupling for the semi-trailer. At the same time, PACCAR annulled Kenworth's independent charter, so it became a division of Pacific Car and

Foundry. Next new model was the 521, a flat-fronted cab-over launched in 1955, intended to replace the Bullnose model as that was phased out towards the end of the decade. The CSE or cab-surrounding-engine was yet another configuration – an advanced concept at the time. The heavy-duty Model 923 was powered by the Cummins NH 200 diesel engine and fitted with compression brakes, and was ideal for the robust conditions of oilfield exploration in the frozen wastes of the Yukon. While cab-over models got full tilt facility in 1957, Kenworth conventionals were available from 1959 with all-fibreglass Uniglas front ends, which could be hinged forwards to expose the engine, and this meant the old butterfly bonnet could be phased out. Also introduced at this time was the Model 900, a conventional model based on a new chassis with a sloping bonnet section. Powered by a Cummins NTC 350 diesel engine, the Model 953 represented the peak of truck development for the oil exploration industry.

In 1959, favourable regulations prompted Kenworth to open a plant in Mexicali, Baja California. Two years on, the W900 conventional truck-tractor and the K100 cab-over were launched, and the latter proved popular in the eastern seaboard states. The W Series conventionals and the K Series cab-over models continued in production into the late 1970s, with

Kenworth aerodynamics were greatly improved in models like this range-topping T2000 75in (190cm) Aerodyne, which had the lowest drag coefficient of the model line, plus a radiator grille reminiscent of a passenger cars.

GVW ratings from 50,000lb up to 89,000lb for the construction site vehicles, and GTW rating with semi-trailers from 76,800lb up to 130,000lb. By 1979, the W-900 was most often fitted with the 300bhp turbocharged six-cylinder Cummins NTC-300 engine, combined with a Fuller RT-910 10F 1 R transmission and Rockwell single-reduction, hypoid, tandem rear axle.

THE 'HUSTLER'

The L700 model was also known as the Hustler. It was introduced in 1961, and built at the Quebec plant together with the almost identical Peterbilt 310 model, with Caterpillar, Cummins and two-cycle Detroit Diesel power-units. In 1962, the first wide bonnet was introduced for conventionals, and it was first featured on the Model 925, which blended the traditional appearance of the smaller cab with the Uniglas front and larger radiator. A favourite with classic truck fans, this model was only available for a few years. A restyled conventional cab ushered in a couple of years later with a larger windscreen spelled the end for the traditional look. It could be recaptured, however, by the

This C500 is typical of a heavy-duty tractor used in the North American and Australian logging industries, normally powered by 450bhp Cummins, Caterpillar or Detroit Diesel engines and fitted with a sleeper cab. The piggyback derivative is found in Australia, where regulations prohibit a second trailer on the road; it comes into action in forest tracks.

Aero-dyne cab-over model, a fabulous retrospective design of the 1990s.

Another new plant came on stream at Kansas City, Missouri in 1964, and 2037 units were built in its first year of production. A couple of years later, Kenworth invoiced 3900 trucks in one year. These really were boom times and, in 1968, again attracted by favourable regulations, a factory was opened in Melbourne, Australia, to build right-hand drive conventionals and cab-overs.

The PD Series was introduced in 1971, and its no-frills, cab-forward design, which it shared with the Peterbilt 200 line, made it ideal for the medium-duty urban delivery market.

1973 marked Kenworth's 50th anniversary and the occasion was commemorated with gold emblems known as Kenworth Bugs replacing the polished aluminium ornamentation on the bonnet. The conventional 6x4 Brute series appeared in 1973, destined for on-site use in the heavy construction industry. Further expansion saw Kenworth open another factory, this time at Chillicothe, Ohio, which raised annual capacity to 16,000 units. The following year, Kenworth trucks set new

speed records of 154mph (248km/h) for a truck-tractor and 92mph (148km/h) for a truck-tractor and semi-trailer.

The so-called Very Important Trucker or VIT series came out in 1978, offering cabs with standing room, double beds, refrigerators and cooker hot plates. Each truck bore the name of a different state, effectively making them a limited edition series for that year. The range was extended with the introduction of the Arctic Transporter, designated the ATX, which was equipped with six-axle steering and torsion-bar suspension. Its contemporary, the C500, was designed for construction site duties and was available in 6x4 and 6x6 versions, and powered by Caterpillar, Cummins or Detroit Diesel engines in straight-six, V6 and V8 formats. Typically, a C500 would have run

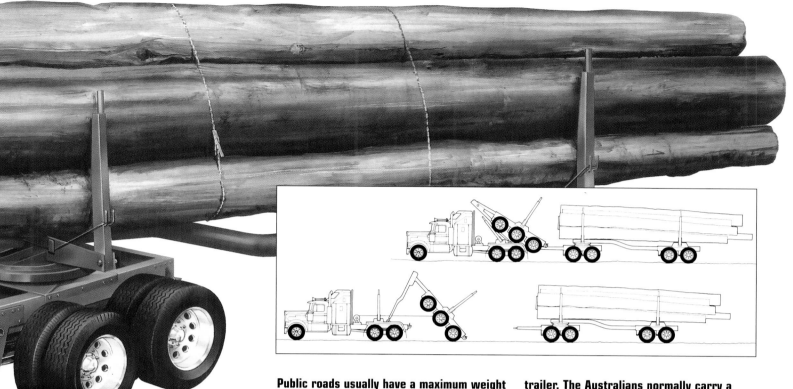

Public roads usually have a maximum weight limit and a maximum length for trucks, so a logging truck can usually tow only a single trailer. The Australians normally carry a second trailer piggyback on the tractor unit for use on forestry tracks.

with a 270bhp turbocharged six-cylinder Cummins NTC27O diesel, coupled with a Fuller RTO1 157DL 8F 1R constant mesh transmission and Eaton single-reduction, spiral-bevel, tandem rear axle.

GVW was rated at 40,000lb, and the three-axle version's front axle was set back and it was fitted with a steel and glass-fibre cab rather than the aluminium cab of the standard C500. This model was also known as the Brute, and frequently served as a concrete mixer.

The K-184 was fitted with twin steering axles and a relatively short sleeper cab. Power-units were 350bhp to 450bhp Cummins diesels or 270bhp to 435bhp Detroit Diesels, with five- to 15-speed Fuller and Spicer transmissions and Eaton or Rockwell single- or double-reduction, tandem rear axles. A facelifted W900B was unveiled in 1982 and the K100E cab-over was introduced in 1984, featuring aerodynamic developments that were further refined a year later, including fairings between cab roof and semi-trailer unit. Nowhere were these improvements more evident than in the T600A, which

was a slope-nosed conventional with set-back front axle that rejoiced in the name of the Ant-Eater. In wind tunnel tests, the T600A's styling was shown to be an amazing 40 per cent better aerodynamically than the conventional W-900, yielding a 22 per cent saving in fuel consumption.

The T800 that was launched in 1986 was fitted with a set back front axle, geared for heavy-duty operations and for on- and off-road applications. Another monster was the C500B conventional construction site truck of 1988, most often seen with a dumper body, which sought to combine the rugged elements of the previous C510 model with the comforts of the T800 cab. In the same year, the T400A was introduced for the benefit of the short-haul operator. This was followed in 1989 by the second-generation T600A and the T450 construction site truck. For 1990, Kenworth brought out W900L long-nose conventional model with a 130-in (330-cm) BBC dimension, and the all-wheel drive T884 construction site truck followed in 1991. This model incorporated two steering axles, front

and rear, facilitating a tighter turning circle – a bonus in off-road applications such as mining and heavy industry.

In 1992, 500 truck drivers took part in Kenworth's advanced driving programme, known as Board Members. The same year the K300 Class 7 cab-over model was launched, and the Class 7 plant was moved from Brazil to Ste Therese, Quebec. Later on, the B Series trucks and their Quiet Cab were introduced. The following year, a new production line came on stream at Renton, Washington, and production of the T600 AeroCab began. This configuration reduced drag by a further 3 per cent over the T600B, and the AeroCab format was augmented by the ergonomically improved Studio Sleeper.

The mid-1990s range was headed by the T2000 Aerodyne and brought up by the relatively small T300 conventional, which had a GVW rating of 30,000lb and was fitted with the T600 cab. Taking the company up to the turn of the century, the AeroCab range was expanded to include the FlatTop sleeper, in which a six-foot person could stand upright.

PETERBILT

Time had run out for the old Fageol Truck and Coach Company of Oakland, California and, in 1939, logging merchant Theodore Alfred (Al) Peterman bought the company from Sterling. The first Peterbilt trucks came out the same year, and included the chain-drive Model 260 logger, and were virtually identical to conventional Fageol models, but lacking the Fageol's distinctive, round-topped grille. The first Peterbilt chassis was designated S-100, and sold to the O.M. Hirst Company in Sacramento, who bodied it as a fire engine. The following year, production was around 100 units, including ten cab-over Freightliners powered by supercharged HBS-600 Cummins diesels on behalf of Freightways. It was

early days for Peterbilt, and volumes were insufficient to service military requirements, but a rugged tandem-axle dump truck was built for the US Army in 1942, coinciding with the introduction of the Model 270. Specifications included Cummins, Waukesha and Hall-Scott engine options, in petrol or butane gas format, allied to Brown-Lipe, Spicer and Fuller transmissions, with dual-reduction worm-drive Timken-Detroit axles, Ross cam-and-lever steering, and Westing-house air brakes. A further 225 trucks were supplied to the US Government in 1944 from the factory in Oakland.

The majority of early Peterbilt trucks were conventional 6x4 load carriers

and truck tractors used in the logging industry, where Peterman's expertise rested, as well as sugar-cane transport, quarrying, mining and oil-drilling applications. Much use was made of aluminium in Peterbilt chassis and cabs, and also peripheral components such as wheels and bumpers in order to save weight. They could be as much as 1500lb (680kg) lighter compared with a steel-built truck. The founder died in 1944 with 225 truck units to his credit,

In the mid-1990s, Peterbilt's one model that made a concession to aerodynamics was the Model 377A/E, which featured rounded bonnet edges and streamlined wings. It's standard engine was the Caterpillar C-10 3176B-350 unit.

and his widow Ida took over the company. Two years later she sold up to a consortium of five Peterbilt employees, and by 1947, the company's turnover exceeded $4.5 million. The switch of ownership brought a corporate name change, from Peterman Manufacturing Company to Peterbilt Motors. The following year the Model 350 was launched, joining the existing range which included Models 270DD, 344DT, 345DT, 354DT and 355DT. All were available as two- and three-axle versions with GVW ratings from 27,000lb to 77,000lb.

CAB SIZES ENLARGED

In 1949, the cabs were substantially enlarged, and what were already big vehicles gained even more presence by the lowering of the bumpers, which revealed more of the squared-off radiator. Accordingly, headlights were relocated from above the bumper to either side of the radiator. Preferred power-plants were the Cummins diesels or Waukesha petrol engines, with Hall-Scott 400 petrol or butane engines also available. Peterbilt bought out the

PETERBILT MODEL 362E

Make: *Peterbilt*
Model: *362E*
Type: *6x2, cab-over*
Engine: *Caterpillar C-10 350bhp at 1800rpm*
Gearbox: *Fuller RT13710B 10-speed*
Suspension:
Eaton front axle, tapered leaf springs, shock absorbers and anti-roll bar
Eaton rear axle, Peterbilt Quadraflex tapered leaf springs
Chassis: *steel rails, steel cross members with gussets, tapered end of frame*
Brakes: *drums all round, Rockwell/WABCO ABS*
Cab options: *90in (229cm) and 110in (279cm) BBC, cab/sleeper configurations*

MacDonald Truck Company of San Francisco in 1949, and for three years it continued to build a small quantity of low-bed semi-trucks.

The first Peterbilt cab-over was launched in 1950, based on the Model 280/350 chassis, and although the cab tilted forward, it was easier to access the engine by swinging the front mudguards outwards. Around this time, Peterbilt began developing the Dromedary design, which consisted of a long-wheelbase truck-tractor with a sleeper cab and a substantial amount of cargo space, and which could also pull a semi-trailer. The Drom tractor unit might be fitted with a box unit or tanker body, and one example of this configuration was the Model 451 Dromedary, which carried a fuel-oil tanker and had two axles at the rear and twin-steer tandem axles at the front. It also had a penthouse sleeper above the cab. Other cab-over models included the off-road Model 381 with front axle set back for better angle of approach. The tilt-cab Model 352 was available from 1952 to 1956, when the second-generation cab-over range appeared with improved ergonomics.

The Model 379 conventional was designed very much along traditional Peterbilt lines, with riveted aluminium cab and seamless roof panel. Customary chromed exhaust stacks and external engine air filters are prominent.

Two conventional models, the 281 and 351, were introduced in 1954 and remained in production for eleven years, and cab-over versions with curved two-section windscreens came out the following year.

A big move was imminent, when Peterbilt Motors was acquired by the Pacific Car and Foundry Company (PACCAR) of Renton, Washington in 1958. Two years later, Peterbilt relocated to a new $2 million factory at Newark, just south of its Oakland plant, which came on stream in 1960. One of the first vehicles to be built under the new regime was the Model 341 in 1962, a lightweight chassis regularly seen as a dump truck and cement mixer. The following year the cab-over models 282 and 352 received a facelift, which majored on twin headlights and a wraparound windscreen in four sections. Ergonomics hardly featured in this revision, as the

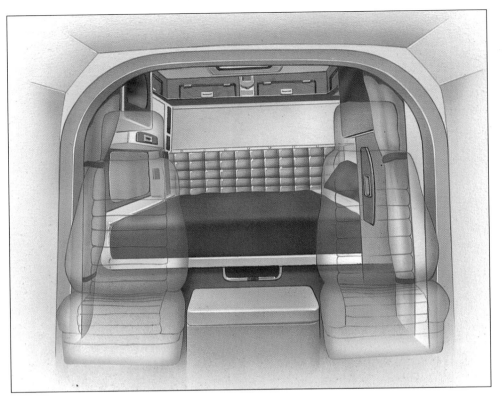

bumper-to-back-of-cab dimension was somewhat cramped. On certain 4x2 truck and drawbar trailer rigs, the sleeper was integral with the cargo body directly behind the cab. The H-versions had higher cabs and larger radiators, and prefigured the tilt-cab models 288 and 358 that were introduced in 1965, followed two years on by the 289 and 359. During the 1960s, the most commonly used engine was the Cummins NH 220 diesel unit, mated to a Spicer 12-speed transmission and Timken full-floating hypoid or double-reduction axles.

The conventional Class 8 truck-tractors made a comeback in 1967 in the shape of the Model 359, and were fitted with aluminium or glass-fibre bonnets, large rectangular radiator grilles, angular bonnets, two-piece wind-screens and a sleeper compartment. Like all self-respecting highway trucks, the massive exhaust pipes pointed sky-wards and were invariably chromed. At this point, another assembly plant opened at Nashville, Tennessee in 1969, and during the decade that followed, Peterbilt produced around 21,000 units.

In 1973, the heavy-duty 6x6 and 8x6 Model 346 construction site truck

Over the years, Peterbilt cab interiors evolved from the cramped confines resulting from short BBC dimensions into luxurious cabins and sleepers. They could be equipped with all the creature comforts and accoutrements required by long-haul truckers, making them as palatial as any contemporary motor home.

appeared, which was often used as a concrete mixer and dump truck. It was powered by the standard 255bhp Cummins V-555 unit, driving through a Rockwell Standard FDS1800 front axle and Rockwell Standard SQHD rear axle. Other engine options included the Caterpillar 1673 and 1674, Cummins VT-555 and Detroit Diesel 6V53 and 6171.

During the early 1970s, certain Peterbilt trucks were manufactured for particular uses. For example, models designated the 200 and 300 LCF were built as refuse trucks, while the Model 353 was introduced specifically for logging and construction site duties, and Model 387 was intended for off-road mining and oilfield applications. By this time Peterbilt's highway conventionals were fitted with Kenworth cabs, apart from the off-road models that retained a

more upright stance. As specifications improved with the implementation of modern components such as radial tyres, the Fuller 15-speed transmission became standard equipment, complementing regular Caterpillar, Cummins or Detroit Diesel engines varying in power-output from 210bhp to 450bhp. By 1978, the GVW rating for highway work was between 34,000lb and 62,000lb, and the GCW rating was between 55,000lb and 125,000lb. In 1980, Peterbilt's output was around 9000 units, while total production for the previous decade numbered 72,000 units.

A new facility at Denton, Texas came on stream in 1980, coinciding with the phasing out of the Model 352 and the introduction of the cab-over Model 362. What passed for a facelift included twin rectangular headlights and a broad three-section wraparound windscreen with triple wipers. In 1986, production ceased at the Newark plant, but it carried on as an engineering, development and administration centre for a few more years. As Caterpillar and Cummins engines took precedence over Detroit Diesel, the conventional series, including the Models 375, 377 and 379, was revamped. The traditional prominent radiator grilles were retained, but a grudging deference was paid to aerodynamics with the deepening of the bumper to act as an air-dam. The aerodynamic direction was more readily apparent in the cab-over Model 372 introduced in 1988, featuring a curved front, sloping windscreen and integral fairing above the cab, although the earlier Model 362 remained popular.

By the mid-1990s, seven basic models were available, including the Models 362E cab-over, 357 conventional construction industry truck-tractor, 375 conventional, 379 conventional, 377 A/E aerodynamic conventional, and 378 conventional, all of which were powered by the Caterpillar C-10 3176B-350 engine. All models were available in 4x2 or 6x4 format, apart from the 6x6 Model 357. The aluminium ladder chassis also featured Fontaine and Holland fixed and air-slide fifth wheels.

DAF

While its two most prominent charges were the heavy-duty producers Kenworth and Peterbilt and, until 1984, Dart trucks, PACCAR had a broader canvas to paint with its ownership of DAF trucks, which came about in 1991. The Dutch concern recorded excellent results in 1997, with sales of its 65 Series to 95XF models reaching an all-time record of 23,700 units, up 41 per cent on 1996.

DAF's origins were in trailer manufacture and it only began producing trucks after the Second World War. These facets made it a unique phenomenon in European truck manufacturing.

The founders were the brothers Hub J. van Doorne and his brother Wim. Hub was the driving force, he was born in America, which just happened to be the name of a small village in the southern Dutch province of Limburg.

In 1928, the brothers founded a motor workshop at Eindhoven and were soon designing and building drawbar trailers, known as the Featherlite design. An interesting feature of its twin oscillating axles was that each pair of axles could be rotated on its own axis for easier maintenance. The company name was registered in 1930 as Van Doorne's Aanhangwagenfabriek, meaning the Van Doorne trailer factory – or DAF.

The trailer designs were very innovative, and in 1934 DAF assembled its first powered vehicle incorporating such original thinking. It was known as the Daflosser, and consisted of a tractor unit and short swan-neck semi-trailer low-loader. It was fitted with a tilting platform superstructure that enabled containers to be loaded and unloaded

from railway trucks. Soon afterwards DAF produced another prototype known as the Trado, a 6x4 designed for military uses. The Trado system could be applied to virtually any civilian vehicle in a matter of four hours by substituting the Trado's two tandem wheels for the existing axle and locking in a set of separate drive shafts. Derivatives of the Trado design included an ice-breaker truck, fitted with a disc saw in place of one of the wheels, to work on the Dutch canals. DAF's first military vehicle was a prototype armoured-car, of interest to the British Army, but stymied by the outbreak of the Second World War.

DAF 1983 SPACE CAB

Make: *DAF*
Model: *3600 Space Cab*
Type: *4x2, forward cab*
Engine: *DAF six-cylinder DKS 11.6-litre (708-cubic inch) turbocharged, intercooler 360bhp*
Gearbox: *Fuller RTO 9513 13 speeds*
Suspension:
  front axle: parabolic leaf springs, shock absorbers and anti-roll bar
  rear axle: electronically controlled pneumatic

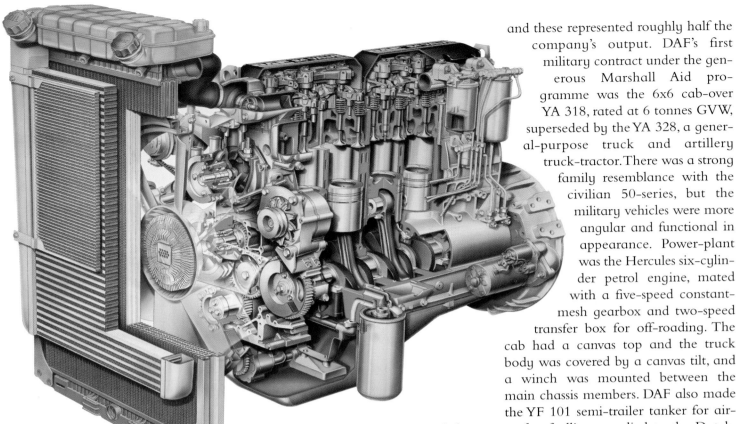

The power-house of the 95XF is the 12.6-litre (769-cubic inch) straight six, with four valves per cylinder, plus turbo and inter-cooler. Outputs are rated at 380, 430 and 480bhp. Injectors are centrally located, while off-set valve configuration provides better air intake.

DAF was ideally placed geographically for making a success of the truck business, located so close to the major international ports of Antwerp, Rotterdam, the nascent Hook of Holland, and the major European waterways, including the Rhine and Maas. At the time, there was a strong demand for long-haul, heavy-duty trucks to deliver cargoes to central Europe and the Middle East. Accordingly, the company set about producing them. In 1950, DAF opened a brand new state-of-the-art factory in Eindhoven, and by the end of the year, 746 units had been built. The 10,000th DAF truck left the factory in 1953, a figure which was a measure of the plant's efficiency. The first trucks off the line were 5-tonners, designated the 50 Series, a 4x2 configuration with GVW

rating of 7 tonnes, powered by a 102bhp 4.6-litre (280-cubic inch) four-cylinder Hercules petrol engine or an 83bhp 4.7-litre (287-cubic inch) Perkins P6-80 diesel unit. Both were allied to a four-speed, heavy-duty gearbox, and one model was distinguished from the other by the prefix A for the petrol-engine and D for diesel. The chassis was an electrically welded pressed-steel frame similar to that used on the Featherlight trailers, and it had vacuum-assisted hydraulic brakes, a fully floating, hypoid-bevel-gear rear axle, and cam-and-lever-type steering gear. The eight-bolt steel disc wheels, twinned on the rear, were shod with 8.25-20, 12-ply tyres, and suspension was by semi-elliptic springs, plus telescopic dampers at the front. In addition to the regular trucks, the 50 Series was also available as a truck-tractor for semi-trailer use at 13 tonnes GCW. The distinctive DAF cab of the next decade was enshrined at this point. It was an upright cab-over design with a panoramic window configuration made up of flat panes, and a seven-slat, horizontal grille arrangement.

During the 1950s, DAF expanded its business by making military vehicles,

and these represented roughly half the company's output. DAF's first military contract under the generous Marshall Aid programme was the 6x6 cab-over YA 318, rated at 6 tonnes GVW, superseded by the YA 328, a general-purpose truck and artillery truck-tractor. There was a strong family resemblance with the civilian 50-series, but the military vehicles were more angular and functional in appearance. Power-plant was the Hercules six-cylinder petrol engine, mated with a five-speed constant-mesh gearbox and two-speed transfer box for off-roading. The cab had a canvas top and the truck body was covered by a canvas tilt, and a winch was mounted between the main chassis members. DAF also made the YF 101 semi-trailer tanker for aircraft refuelling, supplied to the Dutch, Norwegian and Danish airforces. In 1956, it came out with the 6x6 YA 616, 6-tonner, which was available as a general-purpose truck, tipper, radio truck, truck-tractor and crane-carrier. Somewhat later it developed the twin-steer 8x8 YP 408 as an armoured car and troop-carrying gun tractor, radio truck and ambulance. The DAF Pony, or YP 500, was a basic flatbed with balloon tyres, seat and controls that could be parachuted from an aircraft, and it was powered by the flat-twin DAF engine and Variomatic transmission. The general-purpose military vehicles of the 1950s lasted through the 1960s, and were only replaced in the 1970s.

Other commercial vehicles included buses, and in 1953 the municipal bus range was introduced.

TIME FOR A FACE-LIFT

The range was given a facelift in 1955, and the 1100, 1300 and 1500 models were introduced, with GVW ratings of 8.4, 10.1, and 11 tonnes respectively. They were powered by the Leyland 0.350 engine, which was part of a joint agreement between DAF and Leyland, which prefaced DAF's taking out a licence to build Leyland engines. By the 1970s, DAF would be self-sufficient in everything other than clutches and gearboxes. It began to make its own axles in 1958, coinciding with the launch of the little DAF 600 car, and the following year the engine range was extended with the introduction of the DA 475 and the DS 575 units. With these engines DAF moved up the chassis weight scale to the 1600- and 1800-series. The 1600 was rated at 12 tonnes GVW and replaced the 1500 Series. The 1800 Series powered by the DS575 motor had a GVW rating of 14 tonnes.

Although the majority of DAF trucks were cab-over designs, two medium-duty conventionals appeared in 1959, designated the 13- and 15-series, powered by 83bhp and 115bhp petrol engines. They had round-topped panoramic cabs with single-piece screens, rounded bonnets, and mudguards verging on the cycle-wing type, fronted by a peculiar shrouded grille with five horizontal slats. It was not only distinctive but also redolent of US designs. All conventionals were powered by Leyland and Perkins diesels, and a typical example was the 125bhp 15DD, powered by the DAF DD575 unit.

DAF products were influenced largely by vehicle weights and dimensions legislation, and this was evident in the specifications of the 1500-, 1600- and 1800-series that took the company into the 1960s. As well as the cars, DAF continued to build trailers, and in 1962 it doubled its trailer production through the construction of a new factory at Geldrop. However, by the mid-1960s a variety of capacity, labour and manufacturing issues to do with car

DAF 95XF

Make: *DAF*
Model: *95XF Super Space Cab*
Type: *6x2, cab-over*
Engine: *DAF 12.6-litre (769-cubic inch)*
Gearbox: *16 speeds, single reduction 13-tonne rear axle*
Suspension:
front axle: parabolic leaf springs, shock absorbers and anti-roll bar
rear axle: four bellows pneumatic

manufacturing prompted DAF to open a cab and axle plant at Oeval in 1966, just inside Belgium. A new car plant was built at Born, near Sittard in Limburg, Hub's home territory, to make the DAF 44 and 66 models. The diminutive DAF 33 had also been produced as a light-duty van and pickup truck. DAF launched its air-and-leaf-spring suspension system at the Amsterdam Show in 1966 on a bus chassis, later adopted in modified form on goods vehicles.

In 1960, DAF introduced the 2000 series, fitted with its first sleeper cab, and

PACCAR promo shot of three of its finest; a Kenworth T2000 Aerodyne on the left, a DAF 95XF cab-over at centre, and Peterbilt 379 conventional on the right. Even at the turn of the millennium the stylistic differences between typical US and European trucks remain quite distinct.

available in two cab-over and a single conventional design. Two years later, weight limits were raised in the Netherlands to permit articulated semi-trailers to run at weights of up to 34 tonnes and more, subject to axle-spread and bogie-weight requirements. DAF began to build trucks to match that could handle freight containers, 20-ft, 30-ft and 40-ft long weighing up to 30 tonnes. The first of these was the 2600 Series. This model was fitted with a new cab-over design and powered by the 220bhp Leyland 0.680 engine and fitted with power-assisted steering and air brakes. The contemporary 1800 and 1900 Series trucks could be fitted with a 10- or 13-tonne axle to give a maximum GVW rating of 19 tonnes. Of the 69 vehicles in the DAF range in 1970, many were construction site rigids, including the AZ 1900 DS, the first 6x6 tipper chassis, followed a year later by

the extra heavy-duty 6x4 version for the French market.

DAF's test track at St Oedenrode, near Eindhoven, included sections for functional tests, hill sections, skidpans, a water trough for wading tests, high-pressure douches to test for dust and water-tightness, and an off-road section.

The early 1970s proved difficult for DAF – 33 per cent equity was sold to International Harvester. This provided capital for further growth, and it gave both partners a foothold to market their vehicles in another continent, and the symbiotic arrangement would allow both companies to share engineering and development facilities. However, exchange rate fluctuations meant that DAF products became too expensive for the North American market, and differing views on technical matters meant that the arrangement was financial. In 1971, the

company was split into DAF Personen-wagen BV, or DAF Cars, and DAF Bedryfswagen BV, which was DAF Trucks. The car company was sold to Volvo in 1976.

The most significant model of the latter half of the decade was the F 2800 Series, unveiled in 1973 with long-haul applications in mind, and powered by 11.6-litre (708-cubic inch) DAF diesel engines ranging from 230bhp to 320bhp outputs. It was available in two-axle and three-axle formats, with single-drive or double-drive tandem axles, and fitted with a 70-degree tilt cab. This could be either a long cab with sleeper compartment or short cab, general-purpose version.

CLUB OF FOUR

DAF participated in the European Truck Design programme, known as the Club of Four venture, with Magirus

Deutz, Saviem and Volvo in 1972. A common cab design was envisaged, but engines and transmissions were down to the individual companies. In the mid-1970s, a new headquarters, including offices and factory extension, was built at Eindhoven. The founders died soon after it opened: Wim aged 72 in 1978 and Hub a year later aged 79. At this stage, the van Doorne's Holding Company Vado Beheer held 42 per cent of DAF shares, International Harvester had a 33 per cent interest, and the Dutch, state-owned mining company DSM held the remaining 25 per cent. In 1980, the IH share rose to 37.5 per cent. When the loss-making trailer plant was closed in 1979, the whole complex was reorganised. Also in 1979, DAF Trucks and Dodge's European trucks operations, manifest as the PSA Peugeot-Citroen Group, announced a joint technical and manufacturing co-operation.

The mainstay of DAF's military truck range of the 1980s was the 4x4 diesel-powered 4-tonne YA 4440, which was to be the main DAF military vehicle for the 1980s, replacing the YA 314 and YA 328 trucks of the 1950s. The YA 4440 was powered by the 153bhp six-cylin-

Truck racing is hugely entertaining, producing close racing and many thrills and spills per lap. The DAF Fina Racing Team's 1200bhp 12-litre (732-cubic inch) twin-turbo (straight-six engined) 95 racers compete in the eleven-round European Championship.

der DAF DT615 turbocharged diesel engine, allied with a ZF S535/2 five-speed synchromesh gearbox and ZFVG 250/2 transfer case that allowed front-wheel drive to be engaged or disengaged as required. Liaison with ENASA led to Pegaso producing DAF military vehicles under licence in Spain, and in Portugal, DAF trucks were assembled from CKD kits by Proval in Lisbon.

One vehicle popular in developing countries and for rugged, construction site duties was the conventional N 2800 series, which could be specified as a 6x4 rigid and a 6x4 truck-tractor. It was powered by the 230bhp 11.6-litre (708-cubic inch) DAF DKA naturally aspirated unit, and from 1981 with the DRS 320bhp turbocharged and intercooled unit. Transmission was the ZF S-160 eight-speed unit with splitter. The rear bogie was a Steyr double-drive

mergers and takeovers, Leyland was itself made up of a host of famous names, including Albion, AEC, Thornycroft, Austin Morris, Daimler and Guy. As British Leyland, it was effectively sucked into the morass of the British Motor Corporation (BMC) and a host of bankrupt car producers, despite which it still managed to come up with the 1981 Leyland Roadtrain that won the Truck of the Year award. Fortunately, DAF was on hand to pick up the pieces.

unit. The robust steel cab was purpose-built by Magirus Deutz for off-road operation in hot climates. The bonnet section was made of plastic by Norcem in Norway, and assembled at Eindhoven.

In 1991, DAF came under the PAC-CAR umbrella, by which time the ever more sophisticated DAF trucks were equipped with ECAS electronically controlled air suspension and E-Gas cruise-control system. Coming to the end of the decade, the DAF heavy-duty range was represented by its 95 Series trucks, which comprised the 95.360, 95.400, 95.430, and 95.500. A variety of wheelbases and axle configurations was available, including 4x2 and 6x2 twin-steer truck-tractors and drawbar models, lifting rear axle and low-deck truck-tractors. Engines based on DAF's Advanced Turbo intercooling – or ATi – technology, compatible with the environmentally focused Euro 2 specification, powered the whole 95 Series. The 11.6-litre (708-cubic inch) ATi engine came in three versions, 364bhp, 401bhp, or 428bhp, and a 507bhp 14-litre (854-cubic inch) Cummins VF373 unit could be specified. The DAF 95.500 could be specified with a C brake, which operated via the exhaust valves and produced a braking effect. The 95XF long-distance haulage model was powered by DAF's 12.6-litre

(767-cubic inch) 24-valve XF engine, available in 380bhp, 430bhp and 480bhp format, as well as the 530bhp Cummins VF engine, and it was mated to a driveline with 13-tonne single-reduction rear axle. Drum brakes were fitted all round. The 95 Series Super Space cab featured four-point cab suspension with rear horizontal dampers for better ride comfort, with a smaller 45-cm (17.7-in) diameter steering wheel. Volumes were considerable at the DAF Assembly Plant at Eindhoven, where over 100 units left the factory every working day in 1999, amounting to 25,000 vehicles each year from The Netherlands alone. All DAF cabs and axles were manufactured at its state-of-the-art facilities in Westerlo, Belgium.

LEYLAND DAF

Leyland DAF is all that's left of a once great British truck manufacturer, laid low by the Labour government in 1968 when it was obliged to attempt to salvage the failing UK car industry single-handedly. Through a series of

In spite of all its corporate problems, Leyland still managed to win the International Truck of the Year award in 1981 with its Roadtrain model, seen here at high speed on the banking at the MIRA test facility.

Leyland DAF Trucks was a wholly owned subsidiary of DAF Trucks N.V. of Eindhoven in the Netherlands, which by the 1980s had become firmly established as one of the most prestigious truck makers in Europe. Leyland DAF was based at Thame, Oxford, with a national network of 122 dealers.

In the late 1990s, DAF Trucks was the largest producer and exporter of trucks in the UK, and claimed that it outsold any other marque in the UK for vehicles over 6 tonnes GVW, and that it had around 20 per cent of the market. In 1997, no less than 8938 Leyland DAF trucks were registered in the UK.

State-of-the-art factories had the capacity to produce 35,000 trucks every year. Leyland DAF and DAF light- and medium-weight models were built at the Leyland Assembly Plant near Lancashire, with output reaching 10,000 trucks a year. Leyland DAF Trucks offered a complete range of commercial vehicles from 7.5 to 44 tonnes. Among these was the British designed and built, light-duty 45 Series 7.5-tonner, launched in 1996 and powered by the six-cylinder engine. The 12- to 15-tonne 55 Series model was available in rigid, drawbar or truck-tractor format, and could also be specified in 18-tonne format as a high-capacity, two-axle truck. The 65CF model was designed for medium-duty urban goods distribution, while the 75CF was powered by the 9.2-litre (560-cubic inch) 24-valve XF engine. This model was available in rigid and truck-tractor format with various axle configurations, and was used for national fleet distribution, construction industry, town cleansing and removals applications. The 85CF heavy-duty model was available in the same range of power units and axle configurations for medium- and long-distance operators, and was also powered by the 12.6-litre (769-cubic inch) 24-valve XF engine for even greater fuel efficiency. Leyland DAF's flagship in 1998 was the 95XF, launched in mid-1997 and providing the same specification as the regular DAF model.

1981 LEYLAND ROADTRAIN

Make: Leyland
Model: Roadtrain T100
Type: 6x2, cab-over
Engine: Leyland TL11 280bhp turbodiesel
Gearbox: Spicer 10 speed
Cab: Ogle-designed motor panels

FODEN

The man whose name originally fronted the trucks with the kite-shaped logo was Edwin Foden, a Cheshire engineer who patented a compound steam traction engine in 1880 and demonstrated a running prototype in 1887. His son Edwin set up the steam traction engine and threshing machine company under the name of Edwin Foden & Sons Co. Ltd, and began building steam-powered wagons in the late 1890s that culminated in the 5-tonne Overtype model of 1901, which could cruise at 6mph. In 1902, a factory site was acquired at Sandbach, Cheshire, and all amenities were available for the workforce, including a much-vaunted work's brass band.

Edwin Foden died in 1911, and during the First World War, the British Army requisitioned virtually every Foden steam traction engine. Fodens also manufactured vast quantities of munitions. After the war, Foden was penalised to some extent by the glut of ex-army vehicles and a new scale of taxes, imposed in 1920, assessed vehicles according to unladen weight; steam traction engines were heavy beasts. On the domestic front, the Foden family had been in turmoil in the wake of the founder's death and the growing tendency of his widow – known as Black Annie – to assert control of the business. Willy Foden resigned in 1923 and emigrated to Australia to take up farming.

Foden persevered with steam power because the concept, where placing less stress on internal components, was simple, powerful and easy to build. With

MAN, Deutz, Daimler-Benz and, later, the British Gardner marine engine producer building practical diesel engines by the early 1930s, the writing was on the wall for steam power and Foden's great workhorses. The government-sponsored Salter Report of the early 1930s recommended that any road-going vehicle weighing over 4 tonnes should face swingeing taxation. Foden managed to strike up an association with Gardner for a supply of diesel engines in 1930.

The first Gardner-powered Foden lorry (truck) was delivered in 1931. Three years later, Willy Foden returned from Australia and became managing director. During the Second World War, Foden built 1750 vehicles for the army, including 770 Crusader and Centaur tanks and millions of shells.

In the post-war period, Foden built a number of prototypes, while Gardner perfected its four-cylinder diesel. There was a ruling in 1947 that no vehicle could be sold on the home market

Above: The Foden FG seen here in fuel tanker format was a classic, British eight-wheeler, cab-over model from the 1950s and 1960s, powered by Gardner 8LW diesel engines.

Right: By 1973 Foden offered a choice of cabs that included all-steel S90 and Motor Panels versions. This 32-ton 4x2 artic is powered by a Rolls-Royce 220 MkIII diesel and Foden 8-speed gearbox.

unless a similar one was exported, so J. E. Foden successfully marketed the company's products in Rhodesia, South Africa and Australia.

At the 1948 Commercial Motor Show, Foden unveiled its two-stroke diesel, and following tests, a large number was ordered by the British Admiralty. Foden engines had become established in the nautical world, with 32 shipyards installing marinised Foden engines for the Admiralty and other clients.

The 1950s was dominated by big eight wheelers, including the Foden FG and DG models, with chief rivals the AEC Mammoth Major and Leyland Octopus, and in a sense these were the heydays of old-fashioned British models. The advent of larger turbocharged trucks from Sweden and Germany in the 1960s drove many of them to the wall. At the 1956 Commercial Motor Show, a Foden with air brakes and power steering was introduced. In 1958 a new department at the Elsworth plant was turning out reinforced plastic cabs, a trend that Fodens helped to initiate.

New plant and workshops came on stream in 1963, the fruits of three years of planning. The Foden Dynamic engine was introduced at the 1964 Commercial Motor Show, along with a tilt cab, the first on the British market, and a 17-tonne semi-trailer truck-tractor known as the Superpayload. During the mid-1960s, Foden production was running at between 25 to 30 units a week, made up of various types ranging from two axle truck-tractors to low-line crane carriers. A new assembly plant opened in 1972 and lifted capacity to 120 units a week. The following year, Foden was commissioned by the Ministry of Defence to make £10 million worth of heavy-duty trucks for the British Army. These low-mobility trucks were fitted with the new S90 steel cab and powered by Rolls-Royce diesel engines.

In 1975, the oil crisis and consequent recession caused Foden to seek a £2 million loan from the Department of Industry, eventually underwritten by City Institutions, enabling the company to continue trading independently.

This 4380 4x2 tractor is one of the Alpha 4000 range. It's powered by an 11-litre (671-cubic inch) Cummins M340E six-cylinder intercooled turbo engine, allied to Eaton 12-speed transmission with Spicer driveshafts and Rockwell rear axle.

Foden's range of products included road-haulage trucks and construction industry vehicles with GVW ratings ranging from 20 to 100 tonnes, as well as truck-tractors and four and six axle tippers and concrete mixers.

Another financial crisis loomed in 1979, and Foden was given a helping hand by PACCAR in 1981. The culmination of synergies with its other European subsidiary DAF led to the launch in 1998 of the much-acclaimed Foden Alpha. It was fitted with the DAF 75/85 all-steel cab, also used by the Iveco EuroTech and Seddon Atkinson Strato. More significantly, it signalled the end of Foden's days as a niche market manufacturer. The Alpha 2000 and 3000 ranges included 17-tonne rigids and 38-tonne semi-trailers, equipped with synchromesh gearboxes as standard. The Alpha cab was differentiated externally from other users by distinctive stamping in the door panel to provide extra rigidity, and a new front panel featuring the famous Foden kite symbol. The finished cab units were shipped from DAF's main cab plant at Westerlo to Sandbach to be mated to the Foden chassis on the Moss Lane assembly line. Somewhat ironically, Foden was already fitting the same cab on the 17-tonne Leyland DAF 65 Series. The Alpha was initially powered by the 215bhp 5.9-litre (360-cubic inch) Cummins B-Series engine, but Foden became the first UK manufacturer to fit the 300bhp 7.2-litre (439-cubic inch) Caterpillar 3126 straight-six. It was coupled with Eaton or ZF 95109 six- and nine-speed all-synchromesh boxes and Rockwell Mentor or Si80E back axles with an 11.5-tonne rating. Suspension was by steel parabolic springs with the optional Hendrickson air system on the rear, and drum brakes all round. The Alpha six- and eight-wheelers maintained Foden's presence in the tipper and mixer markets, with vehicles like the lightweight 6x4 model powered by the Caterpillar 3126 with a ZF nine-speed transmission. At the turn of the century, Foden's fortunes are as high as the proverbial kite.

RENAULT VÉHICULES INDUSTRIELS

The corporate name and identity of Renault V.I. was established in 1992. The Renault V.I. Group is comprised of several enterprises that started up in the nineteenth century. Through reasons of industrial or financial expediency, these companies linked to form one of the largest makers of road haulage vehicles operating in Europe and the United States.

The oldest of the constituent companies was founded by Marius Berliet in Lyon in 1895. Berliet would pave the way for France's commercial vehicle technology in many countries, particularly in Africa, bringing about progress in heavy trucks through diesel engines and innovations such as Stradair – the first air-suspended vehicle – a technology now widely used on most vehicles.

The Renault branch was formed from three companies set up early in the twentieth century. They were Renault itself, Latil and Somua. In 1906, Renault began building heavy trucks and buses, and produced thousands of vehicles of all weights for civilian and military uses. Latil's reputation stemmed from 1898, when it launched its famous front drive axle assembly, and from the First World War, when it specialised in all-wheel-drive tractor vehicles (it remained a specialist in this field after the war). Somua was an important maker of long-distance trucks and brought about

Routier ruler. Renault V.I.'s slogan at the 1998 Mondial du Transport Routier in Paris was 'One Hundred Years of Innovation', and that is evident here in one of its heavy-duty Premium cab Magnum Integral models, designed for long-distance haulage duties.

significant breakthroughs in the forward-control cab concept by increasing comfort and visibility. The three companies grouped together in 1955 under the name of Saviem, which remained the group's heavy truck subsidiary for twenty years. It was noted for efficient medium-duty vehicles, coaches and buses.

Another player in the Renault V.I. camp is the legendary Mack, which started out in New York in 1900 and quickly built up a solid reputation as the maker of near indestructible trucks, a reputation which it has never lost. 'Built like a Mack truck' is an expression that has remained in popular language to describe sturdiness. Mack AC models played a significant part behind the lines on the battlefields of the First World War, which is where the trucks with the original bonnet earned their nickname 'Bulldog' and inspired the brand's famous emblem.

There's no question that Mack's contribution to technological advances in road haulage is considerable. The launch of the Maxidyne engine in the 1960s was a decisive step in fuel economy. In the early 1980s, Mack designed the V-MAC electronic system which controlled engine operation in order to further reduce fuel consumption and cut down pollutant emissions. Today, Mack

Trucks Inc. has successfully diversified its operations within the market for heavy-duty trucks.

Several other companies including Chausson, Floirat, Laffly and Citroën Poids Lourds, joined the different branches of Renault in the course of various consolidations, bringing with them new ideas and products. Karosa, which first specialised in body making, and has been manufacturing coaches and buses for more than 70 years, joined the Group in 1993 as yet another centenarian. Karosa was the first company to build buses using the complete panel assembly process, which is used today to make Renault's Agora buses. Heuliez Bus, a bus body building company from western France, was the most recent addition to the Group when Renault V.I. acquired a majority share in the company in early 1998.

Many of Renault V.I.'s innovations have made a significant mark on truck technology, including air suspension, the introduction of disc brakes on heavy-duty trucks, and the revolution that was the Magnum cab. In 1998, it launched the 'Single' cab concept on road tractors, which combined a rational and ergonomic driver station with far superior quality of life on board.

CHRONOLOGY

The company chronology goes something like this. In 1894, Marius Berliet built his first automobile, and in 1895 came the foundation of the Latil Company in Suresnes, followed by the launch of the famous Latil front drive axle assembly in 1898. The same year saw the foundation of the Czech company Karosa in Visoke Myto, a company which specialised in body making. The founder, Louis Renault, presented his 'Voiturette' on Christmas Eve, 1898. This small car, initially built for Renault's own pleasure, soon started to acquire orders and in March 1899 Renault set up the company Renault Frère. Meanwhile, in New York the Mack brothers were readying their first vehicle, which was a bus powered by a four-cylinder engine and launched in 1900, when Louis Renault unveiled his first utility vehicle.

In 1905, the US company Alco built the Berliet 22hp car under licence, while the following year the first Berliet trucks and coaches rolled off the assembly lines of the Montplaisir plant in Lyon. At the same time, the first Renault truck and bus chassis appeared. In 1910, Berliet launched its

An example of a chain-drive Berliet CBA, many of which were used in the First World War. Design was conventional with robust 4-tonne chassis, four-cylinder 25hp engine mounted over the front wheels and driver protected by a canopy.

M model, often cited as the true fore-runner of commercial vehicles.

The Berliet CBA appeared in 1913, and quite naturally a large number were drafted into service in the First World War. Berliet's production centre was set up in 1915 at Vénissieux near Lyon, bringing together all the trades involved in truck manufacturing. The same year, Renault built its first EP truck for war requirements, and Georges Latil unveiled his multi-role TAR four-wheel drive tractor. Around this time hundreds of Mack AC trucks were active behind the battlefields of north eastern France and Belgium, confirming the 'Bulldog' nickname and inspiring their memorable emblem. In 1917, Renault manufactured the FT 17 for military service, and the Somua company was formed at St Ouen near Paris.

After hostilities ceased, the first production event of any note was in 1923, when the original Renault type LH road tractor came out. In 1925, Renault fitted its MZ tractor with all-wheel brakes, while Mack became the first company to do the same in the USA. By 1928, Karosa had started making

coaches, and in 1931, Berliet produced its first truck with a diesel engine, the GPCD. The following year saw the launch of the highly successful Renault TN6 bus. Also prior to the outbreak of the Second World War, the Latil H2 heavy truck powered by a six-cylinder Gardner engine was introduced.

TRUCK OF THE CENTURY

In 1946, Somua launched its JL 15 and JL 17 forward-control trucks, and in 1949 the famous Berliet GLR truck made its debut and went on to achieve considerable international success. It was even named Truck of the Century in 1994 by a group of European journalists. Berliet acquired Laffly in 1952, and fitted its first turbocharger on a diesel engine in 1956. This was just after the merger of Latil, Somua and Renault had taken place to form Saviem LRS. The first vehicle to appear under the new regime was Somua's JL 19.

Berliet's huge 100-tonner, the T100, was unveiled in 1957, as was Saviem's Galion. In 1959, Berliet embarked on its expedition to the Sahara desert using 6x6 Gazelle trucks, while in the world of

The sloping bonnet was characteristic of all early Renaults, and this 1909 model with solid rubber tyres and five-spoke artillery wheels is no exception. The radiator is to the rear of the engine by the bulkhead, where it was better protected from stone or impact damage.

boardroom diplomacy, its directors were busy acquiring Rochet-Schneider.

That same year, Saviem launched its Tancarville models which were derived from the Renault diesel R41.90 of 1949. Two years on, Saviem bought out Floirat, the coach maker that was itself the product of Isobloc and Besset, and the Annonay plant in the Ardèche. Another bus-maker, Karosa, became the first company to assemble buses by complete panels. Meanwhile, Berliet set up its Research & Development Centre in St Priest, near Lyon, while Saviem and the German truck maker MAN signed manufacturing agreements regarding components and vehicles. Saviem also bought the Limoges plant from the Ministry of Defence in 1964, and launched its S 45 coach. This was the year that Berliet opened its new factory at Bourg-en-Bresse, Ain, and 1965 witnessed the debut of the Berliet Stradair, the first air-suspension truck. The same year also saw the release of Saviem's SG2 and SG4 low ranges, and the company's restructured Normandy plant at Blainville was opened in 1966.

Also in 1966, Mack launched its constant-torque Maxidyne diesel engine, and Saviem and Alfa Romeo reached agreements on the distribution of low-range vehicles and the production of engines in Italy. It was a time of joint ventures, and under the sponsorship of Michelin Tyre Company, Citroën and Berliet made an agreement of association. In 1968, the joint Saviem/MAN high range with the 860 cab first appeared.

A couple of years later, Berliet set up an axle plant in St Priest and a gearbox plant in Bouthéon in the Loire, while Camiva set up a factory in Chambéry, Savoy, for assembling road maintenance and fire-fighting vehicles. In addition, Berliet's TR 300 road tractor with the new KB2400 cab was shown for the first time.

A 1960 Saviem Mondragon with tipper body is loaded up in a quarry. The same year Saviem entered into a joint venture with busmakers Chausson.

RENAULT COMMERCIAL VEHICLES 1998

Master B115.33 van and chassis cab: *powered by the 115bhp S9w 702 engine*

Messenger B110.35 construction and public works vehicle: *with the 106bhp 8140-23 motor*

Messenger B120.35

Midliner S150.08/A4: *powered by the 150bhp Renault MIDR 04.02.26*

Midliner M250.16/C: *with 250bhp motor*

Premium 250.19 Distribution vehicle: *with the same engine*

Premium Distribution 340.19 TD Tanker: *with the MIDR 06.20.45 at 338bhp*

Premium Distribution 300.26 6x2 Refuse Collection vehicle: *with a steered rear axle, and 298bhp version of the same engine*

Premium Long Distance 400.19 T Privilège Single Cab: *with more powerful 392bhp MIDR 06.23.56 engine*

Premium Long Distance 400.19 T High Volume H=1 100

1972 marked the foundation of the ETD company – European Truck Design BV – that served as the framework for the DAF, KHD, Saviem and Volvo conglomerate, also known as the Club of Fours, with a view to jointly developing an intermediate truck range.

Things were gathering pace on the corporate merger front, as Citroën Poids Lourds was bought by Berliet in 1974, and the following year Berliet became a subsidiary of Régie Renault. In 1976, Saviem set up the Batilly plant in Lorraine, where Masters and Messenger

vans were made in the late 1990s. A major piece of the jigsaw fell into place in 1978 with the merger of Saviem and Berliet to found Renault Véhicules Industriels. This coincided with the launch of the Renault VAB (Wheeled Armoured Vehicle) programme. The following year came the initial agreements between Renault V.I. and Mack on the marketing of Midliners in the USA, and the purchase by Renault of a 20 per cent stake in Mack.

In 1980, Renault introduced its F van, the forerunner of the Master and Messenger ranges, while the long-established Berliet name disappeared, along with Saviem, as their products came to be badged as Renaults. Another major acquisition took place in 1981 as Renault V.I. bought US giant Dodge's heavy truck operations in Europe. Simultaneously, the first Midliners were marketed by Mack in the States, while Karosa's new 731 bus range appeared.

The Renault G 260 was named Truck of the Year in 1983, and the FR1 coach was launched, notable for being fitted with disc brakes along with other medium-range trucks. The R 312 city bus appeared in 1985. Two years on, in an internal financial arrangement, Renault V.I. bought 44 per cent of Mack's stock from Renault, and in 1988 Mack launched its 12-litre (732-cubic inch), 24-valve E7 engine

along with its CH over-the-road range. Its Winnsboro plant in South Carolina came on stream at the same time.

Renault V.I. became the first manufacturer to fit disc brakes on a top-of-the-range tractor, the R 420. The AE range with its revolutionary architecture was unveiled, while Mack now became a wholly owned subsidiary. Also available was the V-MAC electronic engine management and control system.

1991 was a good year for V.I., as the AE was named Truck of the Year, and the FR1 GTX was Coach of the Year. The 256bhp Tracer, launched in 1991, was a favourite with professional operators of occasional and mixed transport. It had a flat floor throughout the length of the vehicle and a 2.2-m (86.6-in) roof height, a wide centre aisle and large glass windows. The engine fitted horizontally inside the wheelbase, freeing up space for luggage. A Tracer version – the Liberto – was intended for school bus applications.

A joint venture with Karosa was sealed in 1993, with Renault taking a majority holding in the firm three years later. A proposed merger with Volvo was announced in September 1993, only to be retracted in the December. The testing centre at La Valbonne (Ain) expanded in 1994, and the Agora bus range was launched the following year. The Agora was a low-floor bus with easy access for disabled passengers thanks to its floor height (320mm (13in) when empty). The range was composed of a standard 12-m (39-ft) bus, an 18-m (59-ft) articulated bus, a bare chassis or chassis equipped with a body structure. A natural gas-powered version, the Agora Natural Gas, wasn't far behind, and the Premium truck range appeared in 1996. Also launched in 1996, the Karosa-built 10-litre (610-cubic inch) 256bhp Recreo bus was specially designed for school bus operators.

It was a busy time with new ranges being launched en masse. In 1997, the Kerax trucks came out, along with the Iliade and Magnum Integral, while Mack's 12-litre (732-cubic inch) E7 engine became the engine adopted by

the Group's high-capacity ranges, while a joint venture was set up with ZF to develop gearboxes. The revolutionary Civis concept of light transport, developed in association with Matra, Alsthom and Michelin, using separate lanes was launched too. It was a motorised-wheel, electric traction technology, designed to develop clean, easy-access city vehicles: a sort of new-generation trolley bus.

In 1998 came another joint venture, this time with corporate giant Iveco Trucks, to market coaches and buses.

The Premium range was introduced in 1996 to cover two main areas – medium- and long-distance distribution – at the same time providing the driver with as many creative comforts as possible. This is a 1998 Premium 400 in the Alps.

Simultaneously, Renault V.I. bought a major stake in Heuliez Buses. Renault facilities involved in the joint company now included the Annonay plant and the R&D facilities at Vénissieux and St Priest, together with the Heuliez Bus subsidiary, and the Karosa company, located in Vysoke Myto, Czechoslovakia. On the Iveco side, the plants concerned were those at Valle Ufita and Turin, together with its Orlandi subsidiary and its majority holding in Altra, as well as the plants and R&D facilities at Barcelona and Mataro. Total volume was anticipated to be close to 4500 coaches and buses, and nearly 1500 body-ready chassis, and more than 1500 minibuses. With sales amounting to six billion French francs ($1.09 billion), it would be the second-largest truck manufacturer in the European market and a major player on the world stage for road passenger transport. With 1500 service centres in Europe, Renault V.I. provided a balanced service backup, with a network covering major highways and secondary roads. In addition, all these service centres used the same work methods and tools, based on its industrial and commercial experience.

TRUCK RANGES

Launched in 1990, the Magnum freight haulage range was based on the concept of a flat-floor cab independent from the mechanical components. Named Truck of the Year in 1991, Magnum trucks contained many technological innovations, including the new 12-litre (732-cubic inch) engine with electronic management, EBS braking system, Infomax and advances in comfort and safety. It got the name 'Magnum Intégral' in late 1997.

The Magnum range was intended for heavy-duty, long-distance haulage, while the Midliner range was specially adapted to distribution over short and medium distances. The Midliners covered the 6 to 15.7 tonnes GVW segment with two ranges: the S range from 6 to 9.5 tonnes GVW, and the M range from 10 to 15.7 tonnes GVW.

As urban and suburban distribution vehicles, the Messengers were mostly bought by small businesses, particularly in the building industry, and shop owners.

Introduced in 1996, the Premium range was developed to cover two particular areas in freight haulage: medium and long distance, and heavy

distribution. The Long Distance Premium was characterised by a high level of driver comfort and a reduced unladen weight, while the Premium Distribution family could be adapted to take a wide variety of equipment and bodies, including tankers, refuse collectors and tippers.

The Premium long-distance family included the 340 and 385 models and the more powerful 400. The 400bhp engine was based on the 11.1-litre (670-cubic inch) Renault MIDR 06.23.56. engine. Its power rating was increased in 1998 to 392hp. The tuning and electronic injection timing controls were reviewed and pistons cast in a new aluminium alloy, and the turbocharger was redesigned to give better pulling power.

The Kerax range that came out in 1997 was for construction site applications. The range-topping Kerax 400 was available in 4x2, 4x4, 6x4, 6x6, 8x4 and 8x8 versions, and its 400hp engine was also derived from the 11.1-litre (677-cubic inch) MIDR 06.23.56 unit. For mixed applications such as site approach, tankers and seasonal agricultural haulage, a rear air suspension was fitted to the 4x2 Kerax tractors. This system was composed of two air bags whose pressure was adjusted via an electronic levelling valve, so the suspension guaranteed that the chassis's position remained level. All 4x2 and 6x4 Kerax rigids could carry cranes with a capacity of up to 25t/m, and athermal glass prevented excessive heat inside the cab. Standard equipment included a sleeper cab and an air-suspended driver seat equipped with a seat belt. The cab had a four-point spring and shock absorber suspension set up.

SISU TRUCKS IN FRANCE

In 1998, Renault V.I. began marketing two new tractors in France, manufactured by the Finnish manufacturer Oy SISU Auto Ab. These vehicles were designed for heavy-duty applications such as timber haulage or tough digging sites. Renault and Sisu entered into a co-operation agreement in 1997,

RENAULT V.I.

Make: *Renault V.I.*
Model: *Magnum Intégal*
Type: *4x2, forward cab*
Engine: *12-litre (732-cubic inch) MIDR 06.24.65 six-cylinders 390–470bhp at 1900rpm, V-Mac control system*
Gearbox: *Renault B-18 P1370, single reduction rear axle*
Suspension:
 front axle: parabolic leaf springs, shock absorbers and anti-roll bar
 rear axle: pneumatic cushions, shock absorbers and anti-roll bar
Chassis: *parallel side frames with sheet steel cross-members, assembled with bolts and rivets*
Brakes: *EBS and disc front, drums rear*
GVW: *19-tonnes*
GCW: *40-tonnes*

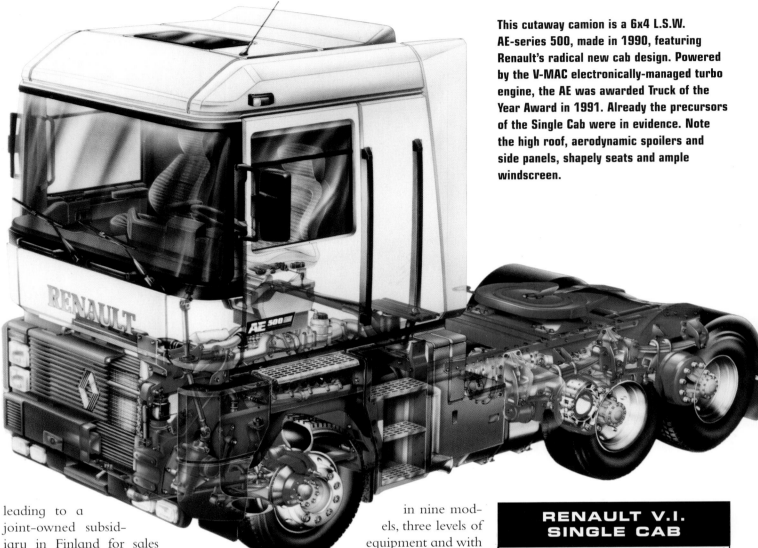

This cutaway camion is a 6x4 L.S.W. AE-series 500, made in 1990, featuring Renault's radical new cab design. Powered by the V-MAC electronically-managed turbo engine, the AE was awarded Truck of the Year Award in 1991. Already the precursors of the Single Cab were in evidence. Note the high roof, aerodynamic spoilers and side panels, shapely seats and ample windscreen.

leading to a joint-owned subsidiary in Finland for sales distribution and supply of components. The two tractor models available in France were the Sisu E12 M 470-19 T 4x2 (60 tonnes GCW) and the Sisu E12 M 470-35 T 6x4 (80-120 tonnes GCW). Both used the Renault 12-litre (732-cubic inch) MIDR 06.24.65. engine with a maximum power rating of 34gkW (470hp) at 1900rpm and maximum torque of 2200Nm (225m Kg) from 1100rpm to 1400rpm. The engine was equipped with the V-MAC electronic management and control system, and coupled to the Renault B-18 gearbox with double-plate clutch. Both Sisu models were fitted with the Premium Long Distance cab.

COACHES

The Iliade range of touring coaches was based on the tried and tested mechanical components and major body panels of the FR1. It was available

in nine models, three levels of equipment and with three Euro 2 engines, including a 380bhp version. All segments of the coach touring market were covered, including motorway scheduled line, day-long excursion, regional and national touring, medium-capacity touring, international line, hotel courtesy, as well as national and international grand touring. The Iliade coaches were built at the Annonay plant (Ardèche), starting off with anti-corrosion cataphoresis treatment and resin deposit in hollow box sections.

The dash was panoramic and ergonomic, providing an air-suspended seat and steering wheel that was adjustable in rake and height through a foot-operated air control. The hostess or courier position included a retractable reclining seat, heating and air conditioning unit, a map light, a locked glove compartment and a microphone.

RENAULT V.I. SINGLE CAB

Make: *Renault V.I.*
Model: *Single Cab*
Premium Long Distance Privilège
Designed for single occupant; flat floor; complete roof clearance; wide modern sofa, 441mm (17in) above floor; 350-litre storage capacity; potential to install regular passenger seat; left- and right-hand drive versions; climate control; refrigerator optional; althermal glass

The Agora bus range included a compressed natural gas (CNG) model, which was the result of work carried out since 1989, and 100 natural gas powered Agora buses went into service in 1998, earning the 'Golden Decibel' award, given each year in France by the National Council on Noise. An additional model running on liquefied petroleum gas (LPG) was in the pipeline, stemming from co-operation between Heuliez Bus and Daf.

EBS: ELECTRONIC BRAKING

All the Magnum Integral models were equipped with EBS, or Electronic Braking System, activated almost instantaneously when the pedal was pressed. The control circuits were pressurised some 500 milliseconds faster than in a conventional system, cutting reaction time and enabling the stopping distance to be shortened by 12m (40ft) from a speed of 90km/h (60mph).

Renault V.I.'s Infomax exclusive data collection and analysis software that monitored vehicle operation, and a hydraulic retarder, were available on all the models in the Magnum range.

EBS adjusts the braking effort to each wheel so that different road-adhesion conditions can be handled appropriately. By means of sensors located in the brake cylinders, Renault's V-MAC system calculates the pressure threshold throughout the entire braking action. The braking reaction of the EBS system is adjusted according to the pressure applied to the brake (moderate, firm,

and emergency). If the electronic system fails, a dual, pneumatic-control feature in the system components is activated instantaneously.

SPECIAL VEHICLES

The Master, Messenger, Midliner, Premium and Kerax ranges were all available to special order equipped as rescue and fire-fighting emergency vehicles. They could also be adapted for public utility and service applications. Premium was the optimum base for refuse-collection trucks (in particular the 6x2 version with rear steered axle), and also for sewage cleansing. The Midliner was adapted for street sweepers, sprayers and washers, and the range also included vehicles with basket hoists and snow-clearance equipment.

In 1998, Renault V.I.'s range of military vehicles included the B 80/110/ 120, which derived from the Messenger civilian range. This 4x2 or 4x4 small truck had a 1.7-tonne payload on a platform or in a van. The TRM 180-TRM 200 were derived from the Mid-liner 4x4 model. Based on the Kerax range, the 8x8 heavy truck was designed to haul the logistics of armed forces toward the combat zones. Its 26-tonne payload capability, its various bodies, its mobility in tough terrain, all made it well suited to the heavy supply missions of modern armies.

Renault V.I. began marketing the Finish make SISU in 1998. The E12 tractor was rated at 60-tonnes GCW and was powered by the 12-litre (732-cubic inch) MIDR 06.24.65 engine, and fitted with the Premium long-distance cab. It came in two wheelbases, as 4x2 and 6x6 variants.

MACK

It's an easy name to remember, so it's likely to be the truck that comes to mind when you think of a fabulous American rig. Mack's roots go back to the turn of the twentieth century, when five brothers founded the Mack Brothers Company in Brooklyn, New York. From a successful wagon-shop, they built their first motorised vehicle in 1901. It was a 1-ton New York sightseeing bus that could accommodate up to 20 passengers and was powered by a 24hp flat-four engine and, later, a 36hp straight-four unit built by the brothers themselves.

Their business did so well that in 1905 they relocated to Allentown, Pennsylvania, where production of the Manhattan bus and delivery trucks soon reached 50 vehicles a year. Demand for their vehicles, and the bus in particular, was widespread with customers as far away as Cuba. The first Mack trucks were 1.5 tons and 2 tons, followed by a 5-tonner powered by a 50hp Mack engine with an automatic starter, allied to their own constant-mesh selective gear transmission. Clearly the brothers had got the formula right first time, as these engines were good enough to stay in production until 1915.

The small capacity trucks were called the Mack Junior series, and were made in left-hand drive, whereas the bigger 5- and 7.5-tonners were Mack Seniors and came in right-hand drive. Until 1908, Mack's heavy trucks had been forward-control layout, but then trucks up to 5 tons became conventional bonneted designs. In 1910, the brothers adopted the Bulldog trademark, which is still in use. A new engine plant in New Jersey came on stream in 1911, when Mack's workforce totalled nearly 800, and some 600 trucks rolled off the production line.

Mack's B Series, introduced in 1953, was one of its most successful models. It was powered by the Thermodyne open chamber direct-injection diesel engine that came out the same year.

Expansion was inevitable, and that year Mack entered a partnership with the Saurer Motor Company, which built the Swiss Saurer trucks in the USA. The IMC holding company (International Motor Company) was backed by J.P. Morgan and Company, and sales of the two manufacturers were combined. In 1912, Hewitt trucks joined the IMC and while the three firms operated independently, their sales and marketing functions were a joint affair.

This corporate stuff was the end of the line for four of the Mack brothers, however, and although Willie Mack didn't retire until the 1920s, Gus and Joseph left the motor trade altogether. Willie Mack started up his own Mackbilt trucks in 1916, and Jack Mack went on to make the Maccar truck, which lasted until 1935.

The acquisition of Hewitt trucks brought with it the design expertise of

Edward R. Hewitt and Alfred F. Masury, and they were to have a lasting impact on Mack trucks. It was Hewitt who designed the Mack AB, built from 1914 until 1936, while Masury designed the Mack AC Bulldog, along with the Bulldog mascot that adorned Mack bonnets from 1932 onwards.

INTERNATIONAL MOTOR TRUCK CORPORATION

In 1913, the International Motor Truck Corporation was formed to counter rising competition and consolidate the business, and Hewitt trucks were dropped altogether. It was thought prudent to concentrate manufacturing efforts on the Mack AB and AC models. Effectively, the 30hp AB range replaced the Junior line, which lasted until 1916 as 1-, 1.5- and 2-tonners. Mack trucks with solid rubber tyres were limited to a top speed of 16mph

Mack trucks have always been impressive. This is the CH Series 6x2 tractor featuring 64-in (162-cm) Mid-Rise sleeper cab, popular with long-haul operators in the mid-1990s.

(10km/h). The four-cylinder AB brought with it the innovation of a worm-drive rear axle, relegating the old chain drive system, while the steering, transmission and axles were all built by Mack from 1915. After the First World War, during which over 4000 Mack trucks played their part behind the Allied lines, the worm-drive axles were superseded by Hotchkiss-type, double-reduction axles. The AC Mack came out in 1916 in 3.5-, 5- and 7.5-ton versions, and as four- and six-wheelers. It was built on a pressed steel chassis like the smaller models and was powered by a 75hp engine. Chain drive was standard fitting and lasted until the AC went out of production in 1938. Its radiator was mounted behind the engine against the front bulkhead, giving a sloping look to the bonnet. As well as protecting the radiator from stone damage, this rear location provided better access for engine and steering maintenance. A special fan was fitted to cool it, as clearly it wasn't sitting in the airstream.

After the war, Saurer was dropped from the range, and in 1922 the IMTC name was changed to Mack Trucks Inc. to avoid confusion with International Harvester. New models included an AB bus chassis and a fire appliance, while a Californian engineer constructed a refrigerated unit based on a Mack chassis.

The AB and AC used 60hp four-cylinder, side-valve engines, the crankcases of which featured inspection ports to check the condition of the main bearings. By 1921, Macks had electric starters, and lights were fitted on the AB model. Its frontal appearance changed in 1923 with the adoption of a taller, fin-and-tube radiator. In 1924, when the AB bus chassis was altered to a drop-frame layout, it also received pneumatic tyres – the only vehicle in the range to get them. Mack's first six-cylinder engine was the 120bhp AH, designed by Alfred Masury in 1923. It was superseded by the AJ, a smaller 100bhp long-stroke six-cylinder unit built in 1924 and fitted in an experimental six-wheel bus. The 97bhp AL six-cylinder unit made in 1926 was suitable for buses and fire engines made on the AC chassis.

Meanwhile, increasing demands from operators favoured the production of larger engines, and in 1926 the 150bhp unit appeared in the longer-bonneted AP model, a unit that could haul 7.5 tons at 30mph (48.3km/h). A six-wheeler version was capable of carrying 10 tons. In 1926, Mack's bus ranges included the AL and BK lines, powered by six-cylinder engines, and in 1934 the front-engined models were replaced with a new breed of streamlined vehicles with engines mounted transversely in the rear. Mack also built trolley buses between 1935 and 1943.

The short-lived, 1.5-ton BB model was produced from 1928 to 1932, and in 1930 the first light truck to be built since 1918 became available. This was the 1-ton BL, which was promptly christened the 'Baby Mack', which is what the old AB was known as. The AB, now with six cylinders, became known as the BG and endured until 1936. It had overtaken the AC in terms of sales with a total of 55,426 units delivered.

The manufacturing process was quite sophisticated, with one or two surprising touches, like the pressed, chrome-nickel steel-frame channels of the AC Bulldog, which were heat treated for extra durability. The cylinders were cast in pairs, and were heat treated, as were the cast-iron pistons. Crankshafts were case-hardened, while the radiator header tank was made of aluminium, as was the crankcase, timing-chain cover and transfer case. The front axle

was in drop-forged alloy in order to make it more resilient, and all these Mack specialities were patented.

Whereas the AC engine's cylinders were cast in pairs, the medium-duty AK model launched in 1927 used a 70hp mono-block unit with aluminium cylinder head. Subsequent modifications led to a thicker head casing that caused it to be dubbed the 'high hat'. After the AC model was fitted with a six-cylinder engine, the AK also got

Above: The CL Series was built to accommodate the most powerful engines, including the 500bhp E9 V8-diesel unit. It was available in a full range of configurations for heavy-duty on and off the road. It is seen here hauling tree trunks in the forests.

Left: The Mack Bulldog symbol was designed by Chief Engineer Alfred F. Masury, and it adorned the truck's bonnets from 1932 onwards. Here it stands sentinel outside one of Mack's six US plants, along with a CH Series truck with 74-in (188-cm) Millennium Sleeper.

one in 1931, to make it the AK-6. The AK looked similar to the AC model and featured shaft drive, four-speed transmission and a dual-reduction differential. Pneumatic tyres and four-wheel, vacuum-assisted brakes were standard from 1929. In 1931, its carrying capacity was raised from 5 tons to 8 tons. A tight turning circle meant the AK was popular with inner-city operators. Drivers liked the comfort and protection provided by its covered cab, with a one- or two-piece windscreen, and the rubber, shock-absorber cab supports. AK production reached a total of 2819.

The B Series long-distance, high-speed trucks came out in 1928. First was the BJ, which could haul 4 tons initially, and 8 tons by 1931. The angular-styled BB light delivery truck was next in the line in 1928, powered by the AB model's 57hp four-cylinder unit, and featuring a hypoid rear differential instead of the more usual worm-drive. The BB's appearance was gradually smoothed out over the following years, although the enclosed cabs were distinctly preferable to the open C-cab. The BK six-cylinder engine was adopted by both the AC and AP models in

1932, by which time Mack had introduced the Power Divider differential that drove both axles.

New Mack ranges in the early 1930s included the BC, which was simply a heavier version of the BB series with a 154-in (391-cm) or 172-in (437-cm) wheelbase and a larger 85bhp engine and dual-reduction rear axle. They were available with an open C-cab or an enclosed BB-style cab. The BF Series was introduced in 1932 as a fast highway truck with a 4-ton payload, powered by the same six-cylinder engine as the BG model with the same hypoid differential as the BB series. The latter was replaced by the BG model, which had two wheelbase sizes and the more powerful 70bhp six-cylinder engine and could carry 1.5 tons. This meant it was ideal for fast delivery work and it could be specified with a flat cargo deck, panel truck or other special body, including a truck tractor. Additions to the range

in 1932 included the BM, BQ and BX models. The BQ and BX were the heavy-duty versions of the B series, the 128bhp six-cylinder BQ 'highway freighter' being capable of carrying up to 8 tons on its dual-reduction rear axle. In reality, its maximum speed when fully laden was no more than 40mph (64km/h). The BX was powered by a 105bhp six-cylinder engine, and had vacuum-boosted brakes. It came with either shaft or chain drive. With shaft drive, its GVW rating was 36,000lbs, and with chain drive it was 40,000lbs. The BX was a dual-purpose vehicle, being suitable for long-distance haulage and also useful as a dump truck, when the chain drive was most likely to be specified. Its appearance was distinguished by door ventilators in

MACK MILLENIUM SLEEPER

Make: *Mack*
Model: *CH Series, E7-427 conventional*
Cab: *74-in (188-cm) Millennium Sleeper*
Options: *Seven sleeper box configurations*
Interior space: *340 cubic feet (9.6 cubic metres)*
Sleeper accommodation: *wide single*
Windows: *two-side, one front of roof*
Height: *8 ft (2.4 m)*
Depth: *74 in (188 cm)*
Facilities: *fridge, ventilation, storage*

the bonnet, and its front axle was set back to assist weight distribution. It was available with a C-cab for off-road construction site work, or with the enclosed cab as a long-distance vehicle.

SEMI-TRAILERS

Although truck tractors were built to tow trailers in the early 1920s, development of the articulated or semi-trailer was very slow simply because the railways were adept at carrying heavy loads over long distances. As road building increased and pneumatic tyres became more widely available, long-distance trucking became increasingly viable. Manufacturers built six-cylinder engines to increase hauling capability, along with special truck-tractor units, and Mack was among the first to do so.

The first Mack truck-tractors were built on modified AB and AC chassis, but by the 1930s, it was making semi-trailer tractors virtually right through the range. The cab-over-engine design was adopted for the 107bhp CH and 117bhp CJ models in 1933, rated at 5 and 6 tons respectively. To restrict the height of the engine, both models used updraft carburettors, and the flat-fronted Traffic model introduced in 1936 could have its engine removed via a sliding platform.

The Depression of the early 1930s hit Mack just as hard as other companies, and in 1934 a deal was made with Reo to give its light- and medium-duty trucks a face-lift and re-badge them as Mack Juniors. Accordingly, the new four-model Mack Junior range was launched in 1936, differing from Reo only in frontal grille treatment. They ranged in size from a 1-ton to 3-tonner, and apart from a forward-control cab-over version of the latter, they were conventional in layout. In 1937, the 2M Mack Junior came out as a re-badged Reo Speed Delivery truck. Like the Reo, it was available with a

four-cylinder or six-cylinder engine, and there were two wheelbase options. In this way a relatively small-volume manufacturer like Mack was able to operate on similar terms to the Big Three, who could call on other departments for componentry to offer a broad range of products. In fact, not that many Mack Junior delivery trucks were sold, but in 1936, overall sales picked up to just over 4000 for the first time since 1930.

Mack's ED Series light-duty trucks were produced until 1944 and powered by a Continental-made 67bhp L-head six-cylinder engine. They resembled the heavier-duty E series and were available with a 120.5-in (306-cm) wheelbase, or 136.5-in (346-cm) wheelbase in the case of the Special model, and overlapped with the Mack Juniors that Reo was building. These were quite basic vehicles, only ever made in very small volumes, and the standard ED model had no chrome plating. The bare chassis unit could be fitted with a variety of utility bodies, including a cab-over model, pickup or delivery truck. During the Second World War they were built as fire engines. The largest number was made in 1941, when 707 units were built.

A heavier EH model was introduced in 1936, using the six-cylinder engine found previously in the BG model, with hydraulic brakes, the archemoid steering mechanism and five- or 10-speed transmissions. Depending on specifica-

tion, the GVW was 18,000lb or 19,500lb, while smaller trucks in the E-series included the EE model, with 12,000lb GVW, and the EF model with 14,000lb GVW. Conventional bonneted models were all similar in appearance as they used the same one-piece windscreen cab, unlike the Mack Juniors, which had a two-piece screen. In 1937, four more models augmented the E Series, and the heavyweight F Series was introduced to replace the AC and AP models. The chain-drive F Series trucks included the FG and FJ models and used the C-cab. The FC6 was a special permit vehicle that was capable of hauling trailers with 50-ton loads, and the six-wheeler FCSW was used for pulling 30-ton trailers. From 1941

the FP model replaced the ER and ES models. Diesel power was on the increase, and as well as its own diesel engines, Mack trucks could be specified with Buda and Cummins units, while certain Mack engines used the same block for petrol and diesel fuel.

Identifiable by its frontal grille and bulldog mascot, the new cab-over E Series was available in six models ranging from the EEU and EHU to the EGU and EQU, all with varying engine sizes. Subsequent variations included the EQ cab-over truck and the ER model, which finally replaced the long-lived AB, which had been in production since 1914. The joint venture with Reo came to an end in 1938, bringing about the demise of the Mack

Junior range, and the next notable introduction was the heavy-duty L Series in 1940.

WAR EFFORT

Mack was predictably heavily involved in the war effort, and the US military ordered 368 EEU cab-over series and a further 80 EE dump trucks, while British and French forces ordered many hundreds of the EXBX tank transporters and the NR4 trucks from 1939 to 1940. Further requisitions of EH, EHT, EHU and EHUT trucks came from Great Britain, and in 1944 the US Army ordered 700 cab-over 4x4 NJU 6-ton, Traffic-type trucks. Somewhere in the region of 26,000 NO and NR trucks were built between 1940 and 1945, and the NO 6x6 was generally used as a tractor to haul the l55-mm Long Tom field guns. The Vultee naval torpedo bombers were made at the Mack plant at Allentown, and tank engines were made at the Brunswick, New Jersey, plant.

The lightweight E Series vehicles that had performed throughout the Second World War were discontinued in 1946, to be replaced by the CH and CJ cab-over models. Production of the entire E Series ended in 1950, in favour of the A Series models. But in deference to the demand for cab-over trucks, the EFU

reappeared a year later as the A2OU. The heavier L Series trucks were produced up to 1956, and the heaviest LV and LY models survived into the 1960s. They were usually powered by Mack's overhead-valve, six-cylinder Thermodyne engines, most frequently the 160bhp EN 510 unit allied to five- and 10-speed duplex transmissions. There were much bigger vehicles in the L Series, including the U, the LM and UT and LMT truck-tractor versions as well as a heavy, off-road dump truck identified as the LMSW. The six-wheel LRSW was somewhat larger still, equipped with Mack's Planidrive planetary-gear, final-drive system, which replaced the archaic chain-drive arrangement. The LTSW introduced in 1947 was a dedicated semi-trailer tractor, and it was modified especially for west coast use with a widespread use of weight-saving materials that

reduced its weight by a ton, which could be transferred to boost payload capability.

A special LRVSW off-highway version built in the 1950s had a cargo capacity of 34 tons, and Mack continued to build fire engines on the L Series chassis, like the Type 75 that was powered by the in-house ENFS1OA petrol engine. Mack fire engines were pretty prestigious vehicles, and it capitalised on the purchase of the fire appliance and equipment manufacturer Becks in 1956 to make more ladder carriers and articulated fire engines. They could be

Alongside Mack's conventional concrete carriers – the DM and RB Series vehicles – is this 1998 forward-control FDM Series model. This version has a rear-mounted engine and the mixer's forward-discharge chute is positioned over the cab for accurate deposits.

1953 B SERIES MACK

Make: *Mack*
Model: *B42*
Type: *4x2, conventional*
Engine: *Mack EN 401 Magnadyne*
Gearbox: *Duplex 5- and 10-speed planetary-gear, final-drive*
Suspension:
front and rear axles: leaf springs, shock absorbers
Chassis: *parallel side frames with steel cross-members*
Brakes: *drums*
GVW: *28,000lb*
Number produced to 1966:
127,786 (all B Series)

MACK VEHICLE RANGE 1998

In 1997, Mack's complete range consisted of the CH602, CH 603, CL 602, CL 603, CL 703, DM600X, DM600S, DM600SX, DMM6006S, DM6006EX, MR600P, MR600S, RB600S, RB600SX, RD600P, RD600S, RD600SX, RD600S, Western Contractor, RD800SX, CS200P, CS50P, CS300P, CS3ooT, MS200P, MS250P, MS300P and MS300T.

Available engines were the EM7-300 V-MAC, EM7-300, E3-190 and E3-220. GVW ratings ranged from 26,000lbs for the CS200P to a maximum of 103,000lbs for the RD800SX.

either completely open for easy access, or have closed cabs for protection against the elements.

GOLDEN JUBILEE

Mack's Golden Jubilee was celebrated in 1950, marked in practical terms by the launch of the four A Series medium trucks that replaced the E Series models. Bottom of the range was the A-20, rated at 17,000lbs GVW, going up to the A-5O, rated at 45,000lbs GVW. Three versions of the six-cylinder Magnadyne L-head engines were available, as well as the overhead-valve Thermodyne petrol engine and the END 510 diesel unit.

The B Series of medium trucks was derived from the M8 prototype of 1948, and was re-engineered for launch in 1953. There were numerous different models in the range, including the B-20, powered by the 290-cubic inch (4.75-litre) Magnadyne engine, the 21,000lb GVW B-30, and the B-30T truck tractor. The B-42 and B-425W six-wheel, semi-trailer tractor were most sought after, powered by the EN 401 Magnadyne engine with five- and 10-speed Duplex transmission. Successive B Series models included the B-53, B-72, B-73 and B-75, plus the B-70 and B-80 heavy trucks, which replaced the U and LM models, all of which were launched in 1956. Over a 13-year period, Mack built something in the region of 127,000 B Series trucks, most of which were cab-over layout. One of the most prominent was the 1953 H model, dubbed the Cherry Picker because of its high cab.

In 1958, the D Series was replaced by the N Series. Whereas the D Series cabs lifted up to provide access to the drive-train, the N Series were fitted with Budd-built cabs that hinged forward. The N range included the N-42, with 28,000lb GVW to the N-61 at 65,000lb GVW. The N Series was replaced in 1962 by the MB range, which coincided with production of Mack's END 864 V8 diesel engine that frequently powered the biggest trucks. In fact the majority of MB trucks ran with the Scania-Vabis-built 140bhp six-cylinder END 475 engine, although buyers could also specify the 190bhp

Chrysler hemi-head V8 petrol engine. Another sea change was taking place in the second half of the 1950s, and this was the swing to diesel fuel by commercial operators and the consequent shift in the manufacture of engines.

Mack brought out a line of short truck tractors in 1959 that were designated the G Series, and could be specified with a sleeper cab. They were available with Cummins or Mack diesel engines in the normally aspirated or turbocharged form. For some reason they didn't sell well, despite their modern styling and up-to-date engineering. The equally modern F Series that superseded them in 1962 was far more successful though, possibly because it had a sleeper cab as standard and was particularly compact.

The stop-gap C Series truck tractor was based on components sourced from the redundant B Series parts bin and sheet-metal pressings for its cab. But this vehicle too was replaced after only two years by the U Series, easily recognised by a curious offset to the right-hand side of the cab, intended to improve driver visibility.

Mack's west coast plant came on stream in 1966 at Hayward,

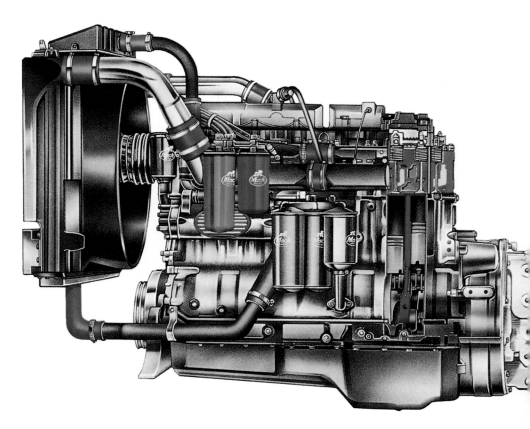

California, where a mix of RL conventional and FL cab-over trucks rolled off the production lines. The R Series consisted of the R-400, R-600 and R-700, powered by engines ranging from 140bhp to 255bhp. The Maxidyne diesel engine was also introduced in 1966, developing 206bhp to 237bhp between 1200rpm to a governed maximum of 2100rpm. A larger version of the Maxidyne engine built in 1970 produced 325bhp. Another muscle truck was created by combining the key elements of the R and U models, resulting in the DM model, an acronym for Dumper Mixer. All three models remained in production into the late 1990s, powered by either Cummins, Detroit Diesel, Mack or Scania engines. Caterpillar diesels were also available for the west coast conventional layout RL and RS models.

The cab-over Cruise-Liner truck tractor went into production in 1975, and there was a vast array of 31 different engine options, ranging from a 235bhp six-cylinder Mack unit to a 430bhp V8 Detroit Diesel. It was horses for courses, but sometimes the choice of engine didn't always appear logical. For instance, the HMM 8x6 front-discharge concrete-mixer truck used a relatively modest Maxidyne six-cylinder engine, but more appropriately, the colossal M Series, off-road, articulated bottom-dump trailer trucks with a capacity of up to 120 tons were fitted with 800bhp Detroit Diesel V16 engines.

The heavy-duty 6x4 DM Series was assembled at the Macungie, Pennsylvania, plant from 1985, while the 8x6 DMM 6006EX was made in Canada. Vehicles in the DM-series could be bought as a regular truck, dump truck, concrete mixer, refuse wagon or truck tractor for hauling low-bed trailers with up to 10 axles and 40 wheels. The DM800 used the 400bhp EM9-400 Mack V8 diesel coupled with Maxitorque 6F1R transmission, and the Cummins Formula 350 and Caterpillar 3208 and 3406 were also available. The most commonly used, heavy-duty transmission was the Fuller RTO-14613 14F IR allied to Mack 5W80 double-reduction rear axle. In situations where maximum weight per axle was restricted, DM Series trucks with five axles were occasionally used to pull a six-axle trailer rejoicing in the title of the Michigan Centipede.

RENAULT V.I. ACQUIRES MACK

Renault V.I. acquired a 20 per cent interest in Mack stock in 1979, and in 1990 it became a wholly owned subsidiary of the French conglomerate. Often that's the only way a small manufacturer can stay afloat. It didn't take long for the effects of Renault V.I.'s interest to be felt, especially when the Mack Midliner series was marketed in the USA, available in four wheelbases and a tractor version. To all intents they were simply rebadged Renault G models, powered by the turbocharged 175bhp Renault 175200P or the 210bhp 175300P six-cylinder diesel, linked to a Spicer 5052A SF IR all-synchromesh transmission in the case of the MS200P or a Renault transmission with the M5300 engines. Completing the essentially French specification was a Renault single-reduction, hypoid rear axle.

By the 1980s building fire engines had stopped being profitable, for Mack at least. European firms like Dennis and MAN were still managing well enough in the late 1990s. But in 1984, Mack stopped making fire appliances, although it went on supplying chassis to other specialist manufacturers.

The aerodynamic CH and CL Series trucks continued in production powered by various six-cylinder and V8 diesel engines including the 500bhp Mack E9 unit, coupled with triple countershaft overdrive. By 1995, most Mack trucks were equipped with electronic engine-management and control (VMAC). In 1996, Mack introduced its V-MAC II second-systems generation, electronic engine-control system, which consisted of a network of sensors and actuators working in conjunction with PC-compatible hardware and a software system linked to the Mack E7 12-litre (732-cubic inch) engine.

MACK E-TECH ENGINE

Make: *Mack E-Tech E7*
Type: *six-cylinder diesel*
Engine: *12-litre (732-cubic inch), 250-454bhp*
Gearbox: *Spicer 5052A SF IR all-synchromesh*
Engine management: *V-MAC electronic*
Transmission: *T-200 triple countershaft over-drive Mack dual-reduction bogie*

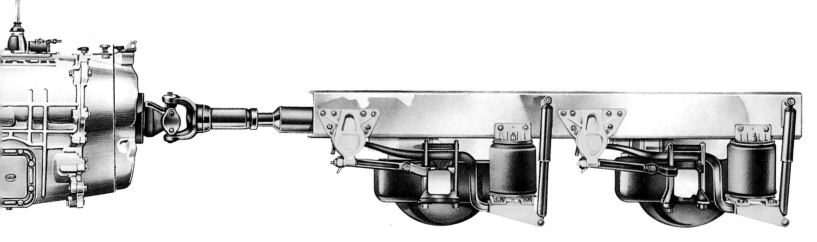

DODGE

In 1981, Renault V.I. bought out Dodge's European heavy truck operations, and since Dodge was a firm with a history virtually as long as that of Renault itself, it needs to be recounted in some detail. The Dodge Brothers sound like wild west bar-room brawlers, which apparently wasn't too wide of the mark. John and Horace Dodge got started in the motor business around 1902 by supplying transmissions to Ransom Eli Olds for his Oldsmobiles, and axles, engines and transmissions to Henry Ford. In 1914, they produced Dodge cars at their factory in Detroit, Michigan, and in 1916, the 24hp Dodge chassis was fitted with a light truck body. This was used extensively by the US Army as an ambulance in the First World War, and the civilian version was a screen-side business truck based on the Dodge car chassis and running gear.

Both of the Dodge brothers died in 1920 and their widows took over the company. Dodge momentarily slipped down to third place in US vehicle manufacturing tables and by 1924, Dodge had been sold off for a record $146 million. The new regime promptly acquired a controlling interest in Graham Trucks, which had a comprehensive model range, which became Dodge's truck division in 1925, complementing the Dodge half-ton and three-quarter-ton models.

Dodge's Series Four commercial range was introduced in 1926, when Dodge completely took over Graham's factory in Evansville and assembly plant in Stockton, California. Now Dodge trucks had fully enclosed cabs, and in 1927 Dodge began building a new panel truck on a 140-in (355-cm) wheelbase chassis. The same year, a new Continental-made 60hp L-head six-cylinder engine with seven main bearings was introduced for the Dodge 2-ton trucks.

Dodge now became a division of the Chrysler Corporation as Dillon and Read sold it for $170 million in 1927. Dodge had by now slipped to 13th place in the industry and by the mid-1930s Chrysler was also marketing DeSoto, Dodge and Fargo trucks in Canada.

In 1928, Dodge light trucks started with a half-ton model and continued to use the four-cylinder engine, while the heavier-duty models used six-cylinder engines with four-speed transmissions, spiral-bevel rear axles and hydraulic brakes all around. The formula was right and, by 1930, Dodge had recovered to fourth place, with sales amounting to 15,558 trucks. From 1933 to 1939, G80 series trucks were available with a 385-cubic inch (6.3-litres) straight-eight engine derived from the Chrysler Custom Imperial, coupled to a five-speed transmission. They were rated at 4 tons, and the lighter 2-ton and 3-ton trucks used the six-cylinder engines. However, the British subsidiary built Dodge G80 trucks with different specifications to the US versions.

By 1933, there was a complete range of commercial vehicles up to 4 tons. Price cuts and new styling helped see Dodge through the terrible slump of the Depression.

In a bid to rationalise the corporate look, the radiator grille and wing design were carried over from passenger cars to heavy trucks. An optional two-speed rear axle was available, and in 1937 the first forward-control Dodge truck was launched.

In 1938, a new $6 million plant at Warren, Michigan, came on stream and virtually all Dodge trucks were produced there. There were now four different six-cylinder engines, and the heaviest was the 3-ton RP 66 truck tractor used for pulling heavy trailers.

Dodge trucks were built at a number of plants outside the USA, notably Kew and Dunstable in the UK from 1927 and 1970 respectively, and by Barreiros in Madrid from 1963. Here is a Spanish-built K3820 P tractor hauling heavy plant in the UK.

As a way of marking its quarter century in 1939, the entire Dodge model line was redesigned, from the light-duty TC series to the big Airflow models. The VKD 60 was one of the heaviest models. For the first time, a standard diesel engine became available in two Dodge trucks, including the 3-ton truck tractors.

The onset of the Second World War brought with it a spate of military prototypes for defence and the British lend-lease supply. A great deal of the Canadian operation was placed on a war footing to produce Dodge and Fargo trucks. The VLA series was the first production Dodge truck to be built with a cab-over-engine design in truck-tractor form, and its specification included a comfortable sleeper cab and 95hp six-cylinder, seven-bearing diesel engine. By February 1942 production was entirely geared to the war effort, and the Canadian plant alone built 39,657 trucks that year. Between 1943 and 1945 Dodge built a staggering half a million military vehicles.

Post-war Dodge trucks were simply revived 1939 designs, apart from the Power Wagon, which was basically a military truck. Sales escalated rapidly, to the extent that 1947 was the best year ever for Dodge trucks. A new assembly plant for cars and trucks came on stream in San Leandro, California, coinciding with another wholesale restyling exercise in 1948, which saw the entire range revamped. A restyled, horizontal front grille distinguished all trucks, apart from the Power Wagon, which maintained a military appearance. With the onset of conflict in Korea, Dodge once again went into war production. The lightweight B-108 pickup was supplied in large numbers to the US Navy. Another popular military vehicle was the 6x4 M37, based on the three-quarter-ton chassis, with full air-braking system available.

Dodge's heavy-duty range received a new five-speed synchromesh transmission in 1950, and a completely new range superseded all existing models in 1951.

In 1954, a further stylistic update gave the B Series light trucks a single section curved windscreen. Engine-wise, Chrysler's 133bhp 241-cubic inch (3.9-litre) hemi-head V8 was now fitted in the 1.5-ton to 2.5-ton trucks, while the heavy-duty models, like the 3.5-ton V Series, in both conventional and cab-over format, were powered by a 153bhp 331-cubic inch (5.4-litre), hemi-head V8. By 1955, V8 engines were available throughout the entire truck range. A 12-volt electrical system was introduced throughout the range in 1955, and tubeless tyres made their first appearance.

For 1957, Dodge produced a new range of tandem trucks, powered by 201bhp or 232bhp V8 motors, but they were restyled the following year with the fashionable, four-headlight look.

With the renaissance of diesel engines, 228bhp turbocharged Cummins units became regular fittings fitted with twin-plate clutches and eight- or 10-speed transmission.

The light-duty trucks, which previously were not noted for their stylistic beauty, received a thorough facelift in 1961. Higher up the scale, the Series 700 was equipped with a 194bhp 361-cubic inch (5.9-litre) Power Giant V8. The following year Dodge introduced the Series 1000 three-axle, 5-ton truck in petrol or diesel format.

At the same time, Dodge built its first recreational vehicle on a bus chassis, and the 4x4 Power Wagon pickups now came with a six-passenger crew cab option. Another variant known as the Swamp Fox was fitted with massive Terra Tires and was probably the first factory built off-roader, from one of the Big Three at any rate. The largest Series 900 and 1000 were built as conventional or cab-over models with petrol or diesel options including V6 and V8 Cummins units. In 1964, the long-lived LN1000 and LNT1000 came out, and they endured for a full decade until 1975.

Around 1970, Dodge joined the heavy-duty, long-distance trucking fray with its LM-100 cab-over-engine tilt-cab. Engine options included the 318bhp Detroit Diesel V8 and 335bhp turbocharged Cummins V8 diesel. The 9-ton, 6x4 short-cab was called the Big Horn D-9500 and was principally sold as a diesel-powered, three-axle truck-tractor.

In 1974, the medium truck range was given a major facelift, but by the end of the following year, Dodge had discontinued its entire heavy-duty range. New federal legislation was blamed, but in actual fact, Dodge's heavy trucks were just not profitable. Three years later in 1977, the medium-duty trucks were also phased out.

Dodge increased production of its light pickup trucks, and by 1980 had begun importing Japanese-built light trucks. This was the segment that took the company through the following two decades. By 1993, the model line had a new look, and power plants included the V10 engine that Chrysler produced for its Viper sports car. In 1995, a high-performance V10 pickup truck was built by Dodge on a 2500 series 4x4 pickup platform. An all-aluminium 400bhp V10-powered Ram VTS prototype with six-speed Borg-Warner T-56 transmission made in 1995 was capable of 0-to-60mph (0-96.5km/h) in 5.9 seconds.

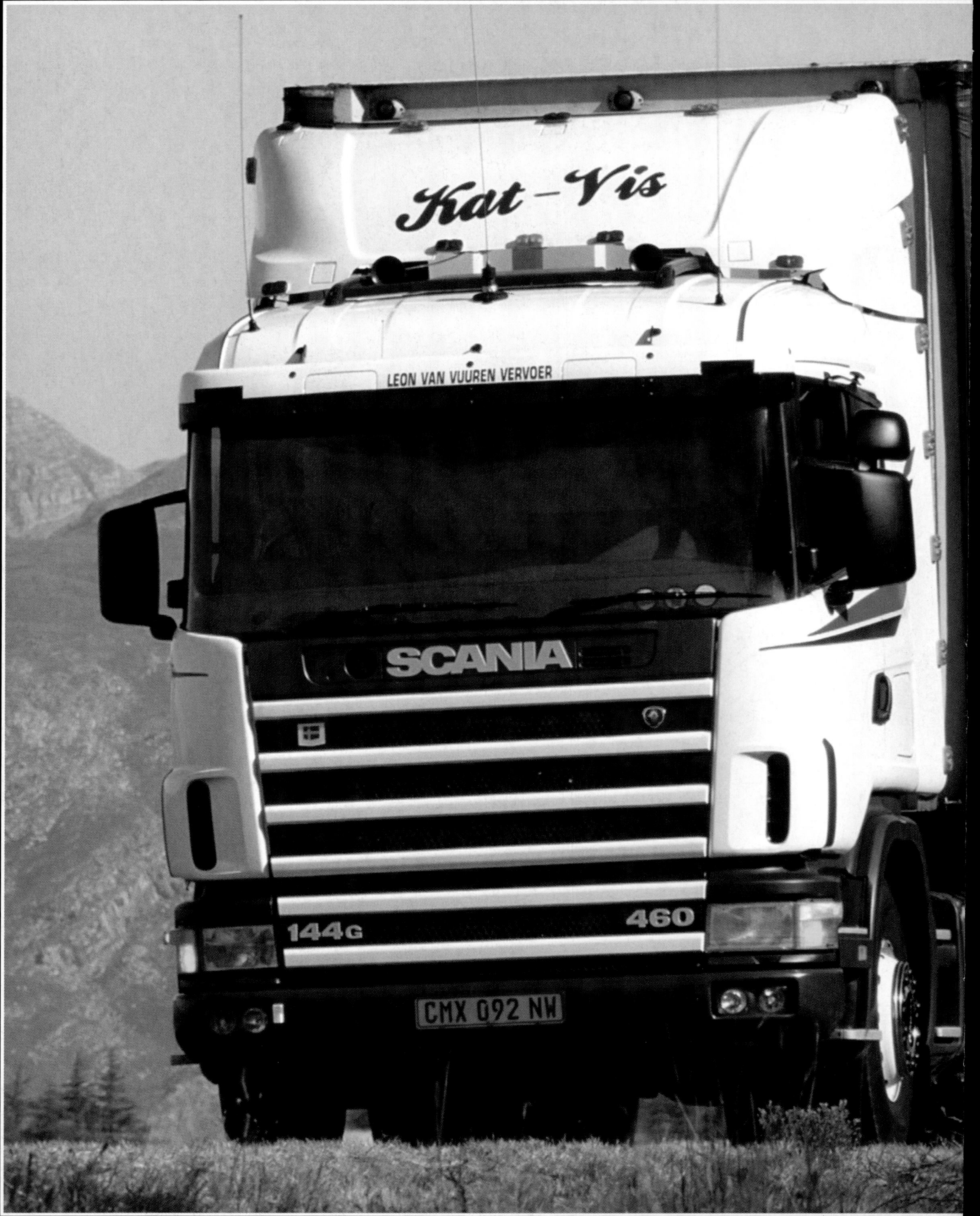

Kat-Vis
LEON VAN VUUREN VERVOER
SCANIA
144G
460
CMX 092 NW

SCANIA

By the last decade of the twentieth century, the Swedish Scania Company had become one of the world's leading truck and bus manufacturers. In fact, it was the fourth-largest heavy truck maker in the world and the third-largest in Europe, as well as being the fourth-largest bus producer in the world. Scania had production facilities in eight European and Latin American countries, including Sweden, Denmark, France, the Netherlands, Poland, Brazil, Argentina and Mexico. There were assembly plants in about a dozen more countries, employing a total workforce of some 23,800 employees worldwide.

Scania celebrated its centenary in 1991, and can trace its roots back to Vagnfabriks Aktiebolaget i Södertelge, founded in 1891 and known as Vagnfabriken for short. The town of Södertälje, 40km (25 miles) south of Stockholm, remained the headquarters of Scania with a third of all chassis assembled there, while bus manufacture was transferred to Katrineholm in 1967.

Conscious of its roots, the company began to buy back and restore some of its classic models to show in a museum that was opened in 1983, and the collection consisted of about 60 vehicles. It also included two railway carriages

Scania's R Class medium- to heavy-duty range was represented by this 6x4 R144 460, pictured in South Africa's Du Toitz mountains in 1998. Its 14-litre (854-cubic inch) engine provided plenty of power for on-road, long-distance haulage applications.

The 4-Series Class C chassis like this 260bhp 6x4 concrete mixer were designed for more arduous on- and off-road construction site duties. A variety of frames, power-units and cabs were available.

dating from 1900, representative of the original company's business, which was manufacturing railway rolling stock for the expanding Swedish railway system of the 1880s.

However, as the market for rolling stock became saturated as the development of the railways neared completion, the engineer Gustaf Erikson was asked to design Vagnfabriken's first car – and also the first Swedish car with an internal combustion engine – in 1897. In 1906, the name VABIS was coined, an acronym of the company title, but the cars weren't particularly successful. Meanwhile back in 1896, the English bicycle manufacturer Humber established a Swedish subsidiary, known as Svenska Aktiebolaget Humber & Co, at Malmö in the far south. This was taken over by Maskinfabriks Aktiebolaget Scania i Malmö in 1901, which began making cars.

A Scania motorcycle was displayed at the first Scandinavian motor show in Copenhagen in 1902, based around a 1.5hp Clement single-cylinder petrol engine. But whereas Vagnfabriken tried to make its own vehicles and engines, Scania copied foreign designs and sourced components from elsewhere. However, by 1905 it was building its own cars and trucks powered by its own engines. Typically, a Type A Scania comprised an 8hp 1.8-litre (110-cubic inch) two-cylinder engine, with a goods chest located behind the front seats. A 2-tonne Vabis of 1909 ran with a 2.7-litre (165-cubic inch) 15hp Type E2V two-cylinder engine, and was fitted with a rigid flatbed cargo deck. Demand outstripped production and in 1911, the two companies Vagnfabriken and Scania merged to become AB Scania-Vabis. Situated initially in Malmö, the head office was transferred to Södertälje in 1913, while truck production was concentrated in Malmö, and Södertälje was responsible for producing engines, cars and light delivery trucks. Scania's production records were largely destroyed when production was discontinued in Malmö and operations concentrated in Södertälje, but the first

Scania prototype truck was a 1.5-tonner powered by a 12hp two-cylinder engine, and was probably a modified version of a French model. The City of Stockholm Health Authority bought some 20 car-derived ambulances from Vagnfabriken from 1910.

EARLY BUS SERVICE

The Nordmark was probably the first Swedish-built bus in regular service, with a chassis built by Scania in Malmö, and an engine and body by Vabis in Södertälje. The seats were upholstered in rough elk hide to prevent the passengers from falling off due to bad road surfaces. The solid rubber tyres were continually splitting so the wheels were shod with iron. Nevertheless, they still had to be repaired after every journey. Its progress was so slow that missing the bus was not a problem. You simply had to run after it to catch up.

Another early commission came from the Royal Swedish Post Offices at Gothenburg and Stockholm in 1912 and 1913 for 25 post vans. These were built on the Type 2S chassis, powered by the 20hp 2.2-litre (134-cubic inch) Type G 42 four-cylinder engine and fitted with an elegant box-type body. Norrköping town council ordered a Scania-Vabis fire engine in 1912, which was in service until 1950, and two subsequent appliances were delivered to Helsingborg on the west coast. These were based on the Type DLa chassis, using the 60hp 8.5-litre (519-cubic inch) K1 four-cylinder engine and fitted with a 24-m (78-ft) ladder and water pump. A thriving export business developed with the neighbouring Scandinavian countries, as well as Russia and the Baltic nations. Subsidiaries were established in Copenhagen and Moss, Norway. A typical 1919 truck was the Type CLc, fitted with a fully enclosed cab and a flatbed that could accept 2000kg, and powered by a 2.8-litre (171-cubic inch) Type II engine developing 30hp.

It wasn't to be a smooth ride, however. Just 714 vehicles, including 427 buses, had been manufactured during the preceding decade, but they weren't sufficiently profitable and the company made a loss in six of those ten years. Output was roughly one vehicle a day from a workforce totalling four hundred. Plans to transform Scania-Vabis into a major European manufacturer after the First World War proved disastrous and the company went broke, mainly due to a proliferation of cheap war-surplus vehicles. Restructuring during the 1920s led to the cessation of car production in 1925, and the Malmö factory shut down in 1927.

Motoring in Sweden was not a problem in the mild summer months, apart from a lack of maintained road surfaces. Yet when the winter frosts wrought havoc with metalled roads, travel became much more difficult, and the horse-drawn sled was a more efficient means of transport. The largely

fresh-water Baltic Sea freezes over to the extent that you could walk to Finland if it weren't for the ferry channels that are kept open. The Swedish post office came up with a solution to winter motoring in the shape of a half-track bus with skis on the front axle for travelling in snow. The first such

motorised post bus ran between Lycksele and Tvärålund in 1923, and was based on the Type 3241 chassis and powered by a 36bhp 3.5-litre (214-cubic inch) Type IIa four-cylinder engine driving the rear wheels through a four-speed gearbox and a double-reduction rear axle. Scania-Vabis built

Below: This Type 3256 of 1928 was powered by a 4.2-litre (256-cubic inch) four-cylinder engine and fitted with a three-way hydraulic tipper body. This actual vehicle was restored in 1986 having spent 50 years on the bottom of Lake Fryken after falling through the ice.

Bottom: The Type LS23 was in production between 1947 and 1949, and used an 8.4 litre (513-cubic inch) six-cylinder diesel engine. The cab was by Brumunddal Mek, and could accommodate four, while the bogie-mounted cargo deck could carry a 6-tonne payload.

the chassis, which was fitted with a 12-seater Postens Verkstäder bus body at the Post Office workshops at Ulvsunda. The half-track concept was inspired by the Citroën Kegresse, and it also featured a heater, in which fresh air was heated by the exhaust system. The post bus was directly responsible for maintaining communications throughout the countryside in the Swedish winter. A new bus with progressive springing was introduced in 1923, and at the same time, the company was developing a new range of engines that soon gained a reputation for durability – reliability was crucial in remoter areas.

Drivetrains for trucks and buses were shared by now. The Swedish State Railway and a number of provincial bus services began buying Scania-Vabis buses, typical of which was the 14-seater Type 3243 Noblesse, which ran with a 75bhp 5.7-litre (348-cubic inch) six-cylinder OHV engine. In 1925, a new generation of conventional 2-tonne, medium-heavy trucks was launched, designated the Type 3251 and known as the Fast Truck. Powerplant was the 50bhp 4.2-litre (256-cubic inch) Type 1544 four-cylinder OHV engine, and a spacious fully enclosed, cab-fronted, rigid, flatbed platform. Early customers for the Fast Truck included the Södertälje brewery that ran a fleet of six of them. A tipper truck using the same cab and engine

was the Type 3256 of 1928, which had a slightly longer wheelbase. The Type 3244 produced the following year used the 85bhp 6.4-litre (390-cubic inch) six-cylinder engine and had a 3000kg payload capacity.

BULLDOG BREED

The Model 54 was a 24-seater bus, designated Type 8406 and built in 1928 with a rather dated-looking body by AB Arvika Vagnfabrik on a 5.25-m (17-ft 3-in) wheelbase, and powered by a 75bhp 5.7-litre (348-cubic inch) Type 1461 six-cylinder engine. During the 1930s, Scania-Vabis had a higher profile as a bus manufacturer than truck maker, with total output amounting to 1602 buses and 970 trucks. This was partly due to the introduction of the new forward-control 'Bulldog' bus, developed by technical director August Nilsson and launched in 1932. Designated Type 8307, this 36-seater model was powered by the 100bhp 6.4-litre (390-cubic inch) Type 1564 six-cylinder unit, and the modern coach body was built by Svenska Maskinverken. The engine was unusually

Most powerful of the L-Class trucks is the 14-litre (854-cubic inch) 460bhp model, running here with a CR19 cab featuring the regular air deflector. Correctly adjusted, these aerofoils can reduce wind resistance by as much as 40 per cent.

narrow and therefore ideal for the Bulldog, as it was located within the passenger compartment. The higher front axle weight placed greater stress on the steering, and the front-suspension geometry was completely recalibrated.

Forward-control buses began to appear after Stockholm Tramways imported a Leyland Tiger and the concept was copied first by Tidaholms Bruk and then Scania-Vabis. Between 1929 and 1935, all buses ordered by public transport operators in Stockholm were forward control. Scania won the manufacturing rights for the Twin Coach, a US model with a full-length body and an engine driving each rear wheel, and although it was never built in Sweden, it provided a certain amount of inspiration for Scania bus design.

Meanwhile, petrol engines started to be superseded in the 1930s, first by the Hesselman engine, which was built under licence and burned crude oil after it was started with petrol, and later by diesel engines. The Type 3352 conventional, medium-duty truck of 1934 was fitted with the 80bhp 7-litre (427-cubic inch) Type 1566 six-cylinder engine in Hesselman format.

The first true Scania-Vabis diesel was a pre-combustion-chamber unit introduced in 1936, and fitted in the Type 8422 Bulldog bus. The 120bhp 7.7-litre (470-cubic inch) six-cylinder diesel engine was designated Type 16641, and was the result of a licensing agreement with Magirus in Germany. As with the preceding generation of engines, it was essential that the width of the unit should not create a problem in the limited space available. Consequently, it was a compact, lightweight design, with weight-saving silumin used to make the pistons, intake manifold, engine covers and crankcase. Rubber engine mounts reduced noise and vibration, while the crankshaft and prop shaft were fitted with vibration dampers.

The new engine was also available in petrol and Hesselman versions, although all units could be adapted to burn the other fuels. Producer-gas engines began to come in as the

impending war threatened fuel supplies, although Swedish trucks were mostly petrol engined at the start of the Second World War, and completely dependent on imported fuel. Petrol rationing meant that long-haul trucks were given supplies only in exceptional cases.

The stage was set in the late 1930s for Scania's rise to prominence as a world-class truck-maker. The company's main shareholders were the Wallenberg family and in 1940, the young graduate engineer Carl-Beriel Nathhorst became Managing Director. He formulated guidelines for future expansion with an emphasis on heavy trucks and buses, and he initiated wide-ranging component standardisation, higher quality levels and an export drive. The war intervened, however, so this formula could not be implemented until 1945.

With the German occupation of Denmark and Norway, and the ensuing blockade of the Skagerrak in April 1940, imports of fuel to Sweden were halted and all long-haul traffic was diverted to the railways, while the horse and bicycle were the principal means of transport. Subsidised producer-gas (or coal-gas) engines became the chief power unit for motor vehicles. In 1938, an Örebro engineer called Axel Svedlund developed an all-Swedish unit that was fired with charcoal, and some 16,000 trucks were converted to producer-gas operation between April and November 1940. As petrol dried up completely, the number of gas-driven vehicles increased to 31,000 by 31 May 1941 and to over 90 per cent of the total truck population in 1942.

Although the Class G trucks are all-rounders, they really come into their own in heavy-duty applications over short distances such as construction sites or quarrying. Being loaded up here is a 12-litre (732-cubic inch) 400bhp 6x2 model.

By 1939, Scania-Vabis was manufacturing its four-, six- and eight-cylinder 'unitary' engines, designated the D400, D600 and D800, and these were converted to run on producer gas. In 1941, the company built a number of heavy-duty Type 33520 conventional, medium-duty trucks equipped with 10.3-litre (628-cubic inch) straight-eight engines designed to run on producer gas, petrol, diesel or light bentyl, which was another wartime fuel consisting of 75 per cent petrol and 25 per cent motor spirit.

The Swedish Defence Forces commissioned Scania-Vabis to build an armoured car in 1941 as an eleven-man personnel carrier. It was based on the 4x4 F11-01 truck chassis and fitted with an armour-plated body of reptilian aspect, and designated the SKP m/42. Production only began in late 1943, and 262 units were built during the next three years. It was used by the Swedish UN Forces in the Belgian Congo in 1960, and in the 1990s the majority

were still in service on the island of Gotland in the Baltic. They retain the original 115bhp 5.6-litre Type 402 four-cylinder engine, with four-speed non-synchromesh gearbox and two-

Ghosted cutaway of Scania's L-Class heavy-duty truck tractor, showing cab-over layout and 14-litre (854-cubic inch) V8 engine, drive train couplings and hub gear.

SCANIA L-CLASS

Make: *Scania*

Model: *53*

Type: *4x2, forward cab*

Engine: *Scania 14-litre (854-cubic inch) V8 turbodiesel*

Gearbox: *GRS 900 12-speed range-splitter*

Suspension:

front axle: parabolic leaf springs, shock absorbers and anti-roll bar

rear axle: air suspension, shock absorbers and anti-roll bar

Chassis F950 for two and three axle layout: *parallel side frames with sheet-steel cross-members, assembled with bolts and rivets*

Brakes: *discs with EBS, ABS*

speed auxiliary box. Scania was also commissioned by the Swedish military in 1943 to produce a self-propelled gun designated the Type SAV m/41. They were fully tracked armoured vehicles based on the m/41 tank chassis and armed with a 105-mm cannon, and had originally been ordered from a Czechoslovakian supplier. When Germany blocked the order, negotiations allowed Scania to make them under licence. So 220 SAV m/41s were built and they were only decommissioned in 1968.

Peacetime at Scania-Vabis in Södertälje meant not only the end of the producer-gas era but also of petrol-fuelled engines. Not only was diesel fuel cheaper, consumption was lower, engine torque higher and engine life longer. A crucial factor, too, was the use of the Bosch injection pump. Even in late 1944, a new series of conventional, twin-axle L10 diesel trucks was in production, equipped with the new 90bhp four-cylinder D402 pre-combustion engine, a four-speed gearbox and servo-assisted brakes. The 2L10 was introduced as an 8.5-tonne, medium-duty truck in November 1946, and uprated to 9 tonnes with new front springs and stronger auxiliary rear springs. From 1948 onwards, an auxiliary gearbox doubled the number of ratios. The L10 was the first Scania-Vabis truck to have the steering wheel on the left in anticipation of future export requirements. The radiator was now fronted by a protective grille. The Swedish trucking industry was still hamstrung until 1947 by a dearth of decent tyres, and until then journeys were restricted to just 40km (25 miles).

For 1948, Scania-Vabis introduced an 11,425kg GVW medium-duty truck designated the Type LS23, based on a 5-m (16-ft) conventional chassis and powered by a D604 six-cylinder diesel unit. It had a large, four-man cab made by Brumunddal Mek, and a payload capacity of 6000kg. In total, 280 units of the LS20 range were built until 1949, but they tended to remain in service for at least 20 years. Updates included a longer platform, cab heater and additional instrumentation.

The anticipated export drive gathered pace in the 1950s. Over a thousand vehicles were exported in 1952, and the vehicles spearheading the foreign sales were the new 40 and 60 Series trucks that came out in 1949. Typical of these was the Type L65, fitted with the new direct-injection 135bhp 8.4-litre (513-cubic inch) straight-six diesel engine, linked from 1951 to a five-speed synchromesh gearbox. A total of 3939 L60 and 1124 L560 Series models were built up to 1954.

In 1953, the company won its tender to make 200 diesel buses for Stockholm Tramways. The Scania-Vabis Metropol was the product of a joint venture with US manufacturer Mack that gave Scania-Vabis sole manufacturing rights for the Mack C50 in Europe and worldwide sales rights outside the USA. Thus the 48-seater Metropol was a regular sight on the streets of Stockholm. The 11.3-litre (690-cubic inch) eight-cylinder D821 engine was mounted transversely at the rear, with Spicer two-stage, fully automatic hydraulic transmission. The engine was accessed through a large hatch at the back. The factory-built body was mounted on a steel chassis, with double-entry door system, power steering and heater. The passenger doors were opened and closed by sensors under the door-well steps. The Metropol's American origins meant that it was over-large for Stockholm's city centre and, although 200 units were made, it was phased out when Sweden went over to driving on the right in 1967.

DRABANT CONVENTIONAL

The next evolutionary step in the medium-heavy truck sector was the L51 Drabant conventional, which came out in 1953 and lasted until 1959, during which time over 9000 units were assembled. The L51's four-cylinder Scania-Vabis diesel produced 100bhp, and GVW was rated at between 10 and 11.5 tonnes. Like its six-cylinder counterpart, the L71 Regent, the Drabant was fitted with a new five-speed synchromesh gearbox with an optional two-speed auxiliary box. The L51 also played a major part in the company's exports, selling strongly in the Netherlands, Norway and Belgium. The L71 Regent was built for heavy, long-haul, construction-site and timber-haulage applications, frequently traversing Sweden across east–west and north–south routes. The Regent was available with air brakes and power steering and could be equipped with ancillaries such as cranes, hoists and tipper bodies. The new gearbox also had a 25bhp power take-off. In all, over

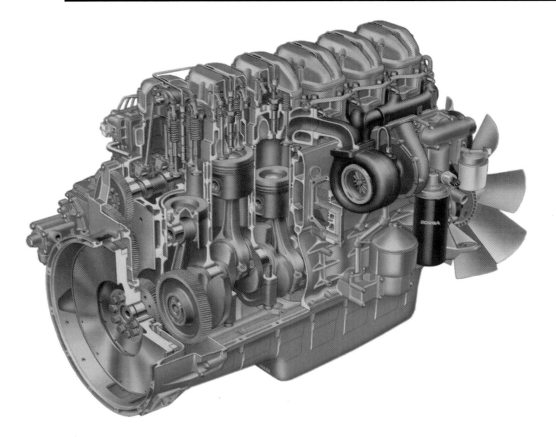

it remained in production until 1980. The LT75 was built in twin-axle and three-axle format, with an auxiliary axle and a double-drive bogie also available. GVW ratings were from 12.6 to 22 tonnes. It was powered by a new, 165bhp direct-injection six-cylinder DS10 diesel unit, and five- or 10-speed transmission with an auxiliary box and, from 1961, by Scania-Vabis's first turbocharged truck engine with an output of 205bhp. The customers could specify any cab they liked, and most were made by AB Be-Ge Karosserifabrik in the little Baltic seaport of Oskarshamn. The cab was fitted by Scania-Vabis, and was a European 'first' in that it was built as an integral unit consisting of cab, bonnet and wings, and supported on rubber mountings. It incorporated a new bonnet design by Björn Karlström, replacing the butterfly-wing type, and was known as the 'alligator' bonnet because it opened straight upwards. Another novel feature was the grouping of the instruments around the driver, rather than in the centre of the dashboard.

SCANIA IN-LINE 6

Cylinders: *6*
Size: *12-litre (732-cubic inch) turbo diesel*
Power output: *360bhp and 400bhp*

7700 L7ls and LS7ls were built between 1954 and 1958.

Two new bus models appeared in the mid-1950s. The first of these was the one-man, operated BF73, in which the D635 six-cylinder diesel unit was mounted ahead of the front axle. It was based on a low-slung chassis with outriggers to locate the 40-seater body, made by Svenska Karosseri Verkstäderna. It was more of a country bus than an urban bus, and was the company's first front-engined bus to have power steering. The next public transport vehicle was the C75 Capitol, which was basically a shortened version of the Metropol, created in response to complaints about the size of the bigger bus. GVW was 14 tonnes, and the 34-seater body was made in house. The Capitol was subsequently equipped with air suspension all round instead of leaf-springs, and was powered by the new 165bhp 10.2-litre (622-cubic inch) Scania-Vabis six-cylinder D10 engine allied to an automatic three-speed hydraulic gearbox. A total of 429 Capitol buses were built, some were rebuilt in 1967 for driving on the right and 135 chassis were shipped to Argentina, where they were fitted out as long-distance buses.

A truck of Scania's that proved to be the most enduring was the heavy-duty, conventional LT75 series. Launched in 1958 and evolving as the LT76, LT110 and LT111,

SCANIA V8

Cylinders: *eight V*
Size: *14-litre (854-cubic inch) turbo diesel*
Power output: *460bhp and 530bhp*

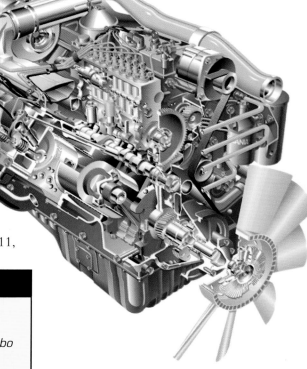

The earlier type of brake pedal, which needed a high leg action, was replaced by one at the same level as the accelerator, making operation of the air brakes more comfortable. Cab safety regulations, including crash tests using a one-tonne pendulum weight, were introduced in Sweden in 1961. The impact tests were carried out first by Scania, then by the National Testing Institute for Agricultural Machinery at Alnarp, near Uppsala.

For 1963, the standard and turbocharged engines of the LT76 were uprated to 190bhp and 260bhp respectively, while GVWs were also increased and a dual-circuit braking system was adopted. Power steering became standard in 1967. More significantly, the main and auxiliary gearboxes were combined in 1964, creating a ten-speed unit that was 50kg lighter and more space efficient. From 1966, Scania-Vabis provided its own cab, which was similar in appearance to the Be-Ge version but made entirely of steel. It was based on the L36's, and was also available in extended rest cab and sleeper versions.

CAB-OVER TIME

In the early 1960s most European countries limited vehicle lengths to 15m (50ft) for semi-trailer rigs and 18m (60ft) for truck and trailer combinations, to the enormous benefit of rail freight. But as trucks became more numerous and more powerful, the scales began to tip more towards road transport. It was at this point that Scania-Vabis came out with its forward-control, cab-over LB76 model, prompted by the incentive of selling in markets where length mattered, and a cab-over truck providing maximum cargo space within a limited overall length was an attractive proposition. The company branched out into Europe in 1964, when it opened an assembly plant for the LB76 at Zwolle in the Netherlands, and by 1966 the model was being successfully marketed in the UK.

A bigger and more powerful straight six-cylinder engine, the 190bhp D11, powered the LB76, and from 1966 the 240bhp supercharged DS11 six-cylinder diesel units were also used. Other standard features included differential locking, air brakes and a synchromesh gearbox. Somewhat later, the handbrake lever and pneumatic brake servo were replaced by a small lever located on the instrument panel that operated the parking brake by means of a pneumatic valve. Like the conventional L76, the LB76 was also available in twin-axle and three-axle versions, rated at 16.5 and 22 tonnes GVW. The engine was uprated to 260bhp in 1967, as engineers moved towards turbocharging. The LB76 remained in production until 1968, with 2575 units built in total.

The new 50-seater CF65 bus was introduced in 1959, and in most respects the chassis was based on the five-year old BF73. This chassis, however, was lower, lighter and welded to the body frame that qualified as a monocoque construction of sorts. The outer panels were of aluminium or glass-

SCANIA POWERTRAIN

Engine: *Scania 11–12-litre (677–732-cubic inch) straight six*
Gearbox: *GRS900R 12-speed range splitter with Scania Retarder*
Crawler gears: *2*
Rear axle: *R780*

fibre-reinforced plastic for complicated shapes. In 1963, an 11-litre (671-cubic inch) engine was fitted and the designation was changed to CF66. The model was superseded in 1966 by the CF76 city bus. All 910 units built remained in Sweden, apart from a single vehicle that was exported to Iceland.

The 80-seater CR76 stayed in production until 1971, and it was notable for its low floor, lengthy overhangs front and rear, and side-impact members that helped support the body. The 190bhp D11 six-cylinder engine was set up for minimum exhaust emissions, and drove through an automatic two-stage ZF hydromedia gearbox.

Possibly the last light-duty truck produced by Scania, the 12-tonne conventional L50 was introduced in 1968, along with the larger L80 and L110 models. From this point, the Vabis name was dropped from the logo, and the trucks were just badged as Scanias. This coincided with the merger with Saab to form Saab-Scania AB, and Scania also manufactured Saab petrol engines until 1990. The L50 was used for a variety of tasks, including construction site work, gravel haulage, quarrying, as a milk tanker, or simply with a flatbed deck for carrying pallets. By the time the L50 was discontinued in 1975, 4183 units had been built, and 2578 of these were exported.

As fashions changed in cab shapes to ever more practical, flat-faceted, cab-over designs that conserved space and provided easy access, a new model appeared in 1968 with a cab designed by Lionel Sherrow. It was the LB110, which superseded the LB76, and despite its boxy appearance it was hailed as an ergonomic advance. There was also a choice of standard or sleeper cab. The LB110 specification extended to power steering, air brakes and servo-assisted clutch and, subsequently, an air-conditioning system. The new design included a large front hatch for access to the engine for checking fluid levels, while the complete cab tilted forward for major servicing. It was powered by the 260bhp 11-litre (677-cubic inch) DS11 engine allied to a ten-speed gearbox.

One advantage of the CR19 cab is that the passenger seat can be moved completely out of the way – either forward against the dashboard or back against the wall. It comes with a double-jointed backrest, heating and suspension.

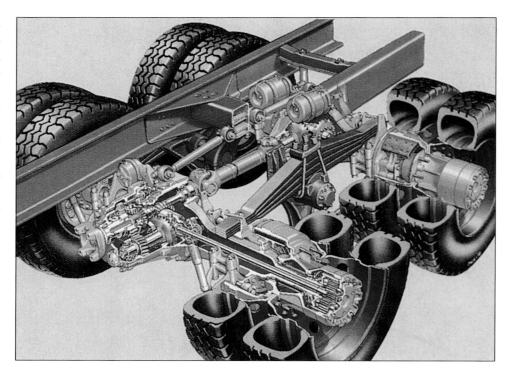

SCANIA TAKES THE LEAD

The Type DS14 direct-injection turbocharged diesel engine that made its debut at Frankfurt in 1969, and was fitted in the new LB140 range of Super trucks, brought Scania to the top of the European manufacturers' performance charts. The 14.2-litre (866-cubic inch) V8 engine belted out 350bhp, which was a serious increase over the 260hp rating of the 11-litre (671-cubic inch) straight-six unit. GVW rating was up to 22.5 tonnes, which made the LBS cabover model particularly attractive to continental hauliers, Germany in particular. Scania had developed turbocharging in the 1950s, and its system of forced induction now became standard, along with gear-driven oil pump, brake compressor, coolant pump, injection pump and power-steering pump. The LB140 was fitted with the same forward-control tilt cab as the LB110.

Military vehicles are built to last, and the heavy-duty LA82 Anteater, also designated the Ltgb by the Swedish Defence Forces, was introduced in 1960 and, with appropriate updating, was expected to remain in active service well into the 21st century. Hardly a thing of beauty, this big conventional had a GVW of 16 tonnes and was powered by the 220bhp DS10 six-

The RBP730+ RP730 bogie has the combined advantages of a relatively light weight and hub reduction, and is found in all but the heaviest of applications where its 100-tonne capacity comes into its own.

cylinder engine, coupled with a 10-speed transmission, and was capable of hauling 5 tonnes of cargo as well as towing a howitzer weighing 10 tonnes. There was also provision for a troop-carrying shelter on the forward end of the cargo deck, with a machine gun mounted on top of the driver's cab. It was a 6x6 configuration, and with diff-locks and power steering it was ideal for off-roading in uncharted countryside. Some 300 of the original run of 440 Anteaters were adapted by the military in the mid-1980s for bridge building in remote areas, with the designation Brotgb 9572A MT.

Talking of obscure designations, another army vehicle developed specially for the Swedish Defence Force in the late 1960s was the SBA/SBAT111, evolving from the Scania 4x4 LBA110 and 6x4 LBAT110 prototypes. This ungainly pair went into service in 1975, but their appearance belied their superb off-roading abilities on the most difficult terrain imaginable. They were built under a peculiarly speculative contract, in which the price paid for each unit depended on its running costs. If these were low, the price of the truck would be higher, but if they proved expensive to maintain, Scania would loose out. However, the capabilities of the vehicles more than ensured Scania's profit.

The trucks had vast ground clearance and were built to negotiate a 6-in-10 gradient and traverse a 4-in-10 side-slope fully laden. Both versions were powered by the 11-litre (671-cubic inch) D11 engine allied to a six-speed automatic gearbox, and in 300bhp turbo format for the three-axle SBAT111 model. The twin-axle SBM11 had a load capacity of 4.5 tonnes and generally pulled a 6-tonne trailer, while the SBAT111 could haul a 12-tonne trailer. The cargo deck was mounted so as to remain level at all times, and the principal function of both vehicles was as artillery transport.

The final incarnation of the L75 model appeared in 1974, designated the L111, which actually wasn't so very different in appearance from the LS71 Regent of 1954. Not much radical new styling here, then. But under the skin, things had moved on. The heavy-duty conventional ushered in a major technical innovation in the form of a 10-speed gearbox with five gear-lever positions. The cab interior was improved ergonomically, and a modern spring-brake, chamber-type handbrake was fitted, operated by a small lever on the dashboard. The L111 was powered by the 296bhp DS11 turbo engine and output rose to 305bhp in 1977, and customers were also offered the option of a 305hp unit. Meanwhile, the gearboxes were developed and strengthened. Built at Scania's Swedish, Dutch, Brazilian and Argentinean factories, the L111 was discontinued in 1982, with some

This G-Series 6x2 rigid hauls a drawbar trailer, both loaded to capacity with timber in the Scandinavian forests, which are one of its natural habitats. Note the battery of spotlights mounted on an additional front bumper bar – winters are long and dark in Sweden.

SCANIA C-CLASS

Model range: *medium- to heavy-duty and special applications*
Cabs: *CP14, XCR14, CT14, CP19, CR19, CP19L*
Engines: *9 litre (549 cubic inch), 11 litre (671 cubic inch), 12 litre (732 cubic inch), 14 litre (854 cubic inch)*
Power: *260bhp, 310bhp, 340bhp, 360bhp, 400bhp, 460bhp, 530bhp*
Gearboxes: *8–12-speed*
Configurations: *4x2, 4x4, 6x4, 6x6, 8x4, 8x6*

30,000 units made, most numerous of which were the three axle 6x2 LS version. The twin-axle L model and three-axle LT with double-drive bogie were rare in Sweden.

Somewhat more up-to-date in appearance was the LS140, another heavy duty conventional, introduced in 1972, and powered by the 350bhp 14-litre (854-cubic inch) V8 that brought the LBS140 cab-over to prominence. The LS140 was popular with timber hauliers who traditionally preferred trucks with bonnets, owing to the psychological boost of having all that metal out in front on an icy road. They were also widely used for construction site and heavy-haulage work, and as truck tractors. The broad sloping bonnet was integral with the front

wings and for the first time was made of glass-reinforced plastic (GRP). The complete unit tilted forward to access the engine and front axle. Internally, the cab was advanced for a workhorse like the LS140, containing much of the interior comfort of the cab-over LBS140. Its front axle was rated at seven tonnes, giving a GVW of 23 tonnes, which was 500kg more than the cab-over model. A 17-tonne bogie fitted in 1973 lifted the GVW to 24 tonnes and in 1975, a tandem-drive truck-tractor version, designated the LT145, was introduced to cope with the most demanding tasks such as hauling excavators on a low-bed semi-trailer.

What was most notable about the CR145 bus that appeared in 1971 was its engine. Installed transversely at the

rear was the normally aspirated version of the turbocharged 14.2-litre (866-cubic inch) V8, which developed 260bhp, and that was quite something for a humble bus. The Scania-Bussar body was constructed in a different way from normal, consisting of separate front and rear sections attached to a conventional chassis. The CR145 functioned as an inter-city tourist coach and went out of production when the non-turbo V8 engine was discontinued in 1978.

DOUBLE-DECKER

Scania's only double-decker bus was the result of a joint venture with British coachbuilders Metro-Cammel Weymann Ltd, an enterprise considered daring in a market dominated by Leyland in the late 1960s and early 1970s. The operation bore fruit with eighteen single-deckers produced in 1971 with Metro bodies and Scania running gear, designated BR110. What was notable was the combination of monocoque body, low floor, powerful

An interesting version of the CP28 and CP31 cabs is this crew cab, seen here on a P94 DB4x2 fire engine operating in Auckland, New Zealand in 1998.

engine, automatic gearbox and air-suspension system. The double-decker version was designated the BR111 DH, and launched in 1973 as the Metropolitan. However, a variety of insurmountable problems, including corrosion of the bodies and disagreement over marketing, led to the end of the affair in 1978. Production totalled 133 BR111 single-deckers and 663 BR111 DH double-deckers.

As traffic density increased in Sweden's cities, trucks were subjected to length limitations and other restrictions. Paradoxically, people still expected fast, reliable distribution of goods. The LBFS111 was a compact cab-over truck with a high payload, Scania's first four-axle model. Having two rear axles and twin-steered front axles provides much improved mobility in urban traffic, and the extra rear axle means the payload can be increased without having to lengthen the vehicle.

A completely new truck series with designations ending in 2 was introduced in 1980, starting with the conventional T82, T112 and T142. Standardisation of components was the key, and by utilising a restricted selection of chassis, powertrains and cabs, the range could be varied to suit the most diverse trans-

port applications. The T-range was split into three chassis classes of medium, heavy and extra-heavy, with GVW ratings from 16 to 36 tonnes.

The 11-litre (671-cubic inch) K112 and 8-litre (488-cubic inch) K82 buses launched in 1982 went on to become Scania's best-selling bus chassis and in 1984, the K82 was succeeded by the K92, powered by the new 9-litre (549-cubic inch) engine. The long-distance K112 was available with the charge-cooled 11-litre (671-cubic inch) unit developing 333bhp. A new generation of chassis known as the 3-Series appeared in 1988, and the K92 and K112 now became the K93 and K113. The Nielson-made body was mounted on a chassis consisting of front and rear subframes, providing capacious baggage space between the axles. Air suspension permitted the bus to be lowered for ease of entry or raised for increased ground clearance when boarding a ferry, for example. Computed-Aided Gear-changing (CAG) eliminated mechanical linkages between the driver's station and the gearbox and the throttle linkage was replaced by the latest 'drive-by-wire' system.

SCANIA G-CLASS

Make: *Scania*
Model: *G-Class*
Type: *4x2 to 8x6, cab-over or conventional*
Engine: *Scania 12-litre (732-cubic inch) six or 14-litre (854-cubic inch) V8*
Gearbox: *Scania GRS 890 and Scania GRS 900 12-speed*
Suspension:
front axle: parabolic leaf springs, shock absorbers and anti-roll bar
rear axle: pneumatic cushions, shock absorbers, anti-roll bar and heavy-duty, hub-reduction bogie
Chassis: *parallel side frames with sheet-steel cross-members, assembled with bolts and rivets*
Brakes: *discs with ABS, EBS*
GTW: *150 tonne*

A variation on the regular bus theme was the articulated bus, popular in a number of European cities, and back in 1978, Scania-Bussar developed a prototype in collaboration with Schenk of Germany and Belgian coachbuilders, Jonckheere. The main hurdle to overcome was the prospect of jack-knifing on icy roads, a problem solved by electronic traction control.

The 4x2 R143 ML medium- to heavy-duty model was powered by the 450bhp DSC14 turbodiesel V8 engine and a new 10-speed gearbox with cruise-control standard, and was partly responsible for the company's 3 Series scooping the European Truck of the Year award in 1989.

When it was launched in 1988, the light- to medium-duty G Series was nicknamed the Geisha and was used primarily as a delivery truck. The G prefix referred to the lowest cab height,

and in order to maximise the cargo space, the turbo, cab rear suspension and other ancillaries were both located further forward. The 4x2 cab-over G93 ML was generally powered by the 210bhp 8.5-litre (519-cubic inch) six-cylinder DS9 engine, available with turbo or both turbo and charge-cooler, and automatic and manual transmissions. GVW rating was 16 tonnes.

The 3 Series line was discontinued in 1996, superseded in 1997 by the new 4 Series trucks, which were available in four classes – L, D, C and G – each designed for a specific application. Class L trucks were on-road, long-distance, heavy-haulage vehicles. Class D cab-over trucks were designed for short distances as a two-axle or three-axle truck or as a tractor with light or articulated trailer, powered by 9-litre (549-cubic inch) engines producing 220bhp, 260bhp or 310bhp. Class C

This T-cab is a recent addition to Scania's line up, being a cab-forward – somewhere between a conventional and cab-over lay-out. Here is a T114 GB 6x4 tipper at work in a quarry in Sweden in 1998.

trucks were medium- to heavy-duty, cab-over, construction site vehicles, fitted with concrete mixers or tipper platforms and two, three or four axles. Both conventional and cab-over Class G models were built to handle train weights of up to 150 tonnes and high axle loads, powered by any engine in the range from 220bhp to 530bhp, coupled with eight or 12 forward ratios plus crawler gears.

In 1997, output from the Södertälje factory rose to 30,000 units, and by the turn of the century, Scania was represented in about 100 countries worldwide, through 1000 distribution points and 1500 service workshops.

VOLVO

The Volvo name is Latin for 'I roll', and was originally a reference to ball bearings. The company was founded by Assar Gabrielsson, and Gustaf Larson.

The two men met up and elected to start their own automotive business over a crayfish dinner at Stockholm's Sturehof restaurant in 1924. The scheme was that all the main components would be of their own design, but produced under contract by outside suppliers.

The first Volvo trucks consisted of a couple of small light delivery vehicles for the company's own use, made in 1927 and based on the open-top car chassis.

While Volvo cars are abundant today, it was clear from the outset that a motor manufacturer in Sweden could not survive by building cars alone. Volvo production was sustained, indeed dominated, by heavy trucks until the late 1940s.

The Model 1 truck proved to be more popular than the first Volvo car, with which it shared its engine, despite the fact that most operators were critical of its lack of power. The wider tracked 'Truck Model 2' appeared late in 1928, followed by a six-cylinder version known as 'Truck Model 3' in the spring of 1929.

The company ethos was to build Swedish vehicles, however, so instead of going straight to a foreign engine manufacturer, Volvo subcontracted Pentaverken in Skövde who based the construction on the side-valve DA engine. The DB unit was first in a series of in-line, side-valve six-cylinder petrol engines that would see the company through to the late 1950s.

In appearance, the new LV60 trucks were similar to their predecessors, though with longer and more rounded bonnets. The standard cab was also similar to the original Åtvidaberg cab, although in practice most chassis were delivered without cabs.

Volvo's FH range was available in a wide range of cab types and trim levels, including this sleeper with roof-mounted air-deflector. By 1999 it was Volvo's best-selling model – ever.

Production of the LV60 and LV64 carried on until 1932, a year which saw the introduction of the 65bhp type EB engine. In order to achieve higher payloads, an additional axle was fitted behind the driven axle. This new 'bogie' version was designated the LF 'Long Frame', and it went into production in 1931. Although the LV64LF was designed as a truck chassis, it was more generally used as a bus.

Until 1930, Volvo had stuck to making small trucks, leaving the heavy-duty market to Scania-Vabis. It was decided at this point to make a proper truck out of dedicated components rather than car-derived parts. They settled on a 4097cc (250-cubic in) 75bhp overhead-valve six-cylinder engine, coupled to a four-speed gearbox with double-reduction final drive. The new trucks were designated the LV66 series and the LV68 series, with chassis variants equipped for different wheelbases and GVWs. Modern steel wheel rims and hydraulic brakes were also fitted.

While MAN and Mercedes-Benz were fitting more economical diesel engines, Volvo sought a compromise, and the solution was supplied by Gustaf Larson's engineer friend, Jonas Hesselman. Hesselman's hybrid unit was based on a type DC petrol engine, adapted to run on relatively inexpensive heavy fuel oil. All three Swedish truck makers utilised Hesselman engines as options during the 1930s, and Volvo fitted it from 1933 to 1947, by which time its first diesel was ready. The Hesselman ran best when revved hard, although combustion efficiency was poor and emissions high.

LIGHT-DUTY TRUCKS

Model changes came thick and fast during the 1930s, and by 1932, Volvo began to develop more modern light-duty trucks, designated the LV71, the LV73 and its long-wheelbase variant, the LV74. The LV71 was very popular and sold well – 1267 units in 1932, and it was Volvo's main export model for a while, representing 75 per cent of all trucks exported. The company's first shot at a forward control or cab-over engine model was unveiled at the 1933 Amsterdam Motor Show. This was based on the chassis and running gear of the LV74, and was known as the LV75. Its practical advantage was a lower loading of the front axle and greater cargo space, achieved by locating the steering gear further forward and repositioning the driver alongside the engine. Roughly 300 were built up to 1935, and most of these were buses.

When Tidaholm shut down in 1933, Scania-Vabis and Volvo shared the pickings of the Swedish truck market, although in fact the difference in annual output was large. Scania-Vabis made several hundred heavy-truck chassis and Volvo built around 4000 light- and medium-duty vehicles. However, in 1937 Volvo sought to encroach on Scania territory by introducing a new series of heavy trucks. They were the short wheelbase LV180 and the long wheelbase LV290, based on a 4.5-tonne chassis and powered by either a 4.4-litre (268-cubic inch) or 6.7-litre (409-cubic inch) engine in petrol or Hesselman heavy fuel oil format. The LV290's long bonnet, which projected ahead of the front wheels gained it the appellation 'Long-nose' and, in twin-axle configuration, it was certainly the biggest Volvo truck to date. The majority of the Tidaholm's key staff joined Scania-Vabis when it closed down, but, crucially, Chief Engineer Gotthard Österberg was hired by Volvo. His ex-Tidaholm design was probably the basis for the 120bhp 6.7-litre (409-cubic inch) engine that powered the new, heavy LV290 series. This engine, or at least its dimensions, endured for no less than five decades. Its bore and stroke of 104.8mm x 130mm (4in x 5in) would

Volvo's truck Model 1 was superseded in 1928 by Model 2, which had a wider track, and Model 3, powered by a six-cylinder engine.

become enshrined Volvo specifications, cropping up in the TD71F of 1985. Volvo fitted versions of the Spicer gearbox in all heavy trucks until its own F3 unit appeared in 1941.

A new model line was introduced in 1938, consisting of light and medium-heavy trucks. Their principal styling characteristic was a pointed radiator grille, with fully flared and rounded mudguards, and the rather obvious nickname was 'Sharp-Nose'. At the lightest end of the range were the LV101 taxis, light vans and pick-up trucks, though later on the distinctive look was applied to a medium-duty truck. As with the Carioca car three years earlier, there were strong hints of American design influence, and from the front the sharp-nose looked like a contemporary car.

SHARP-NOSE

The Sharp-Nose LV161 was the smallest truck that Volvo ever made, and it was fitted with the 3.6-litre (220-cubic inch) side-valve EC engine that produced 86bhp. Despite a family resemblance throughout the range, relatively few components were shared in common by the different models. Introduced in 1943, the Sharp-Nose LV103 was a truck-tractor, built at the request of the Swedish Defence Forces, for use with a single-axle semi-trailer. Due to the wartime fuel shortages, they were fitted with LPG-fuelled ECG engines and performance was not brilliant. The original Sharp-Nose LV101 was discontinued in 1945, and the LV110 remained in production for a further year, although the intermediate Sharp-Nose LV102 lasted into the 1950s. Nothing dates so much as a fashionable look, and by this time these vehicles were showing their age. They were succeeded by the L340 series.

Another pre-war model line was the 'Round-Nose' medium-duty range, identified as the LV120 series. At this stage in its history, Volvo was still concerned with mechanical specifications, and its only corporate involvement in the styling of the vehicles was in the shape of the bonnet. The design and construction of the cab was specified by

the purchaser, who had the cab made by any one of the independent body-builders that proliferated at the time. Until 1938, all Volvo trucks bore a strong resemblance to the company's contemporary cars, but the Round-Nose was the first Volvo truck to have its own exclusive styling. That it made its debut on the eve of the Second World War in autumn 1939 was potentially both disastrous and fortuitous, because although the civilian truck market was on the point of collapse, the Swedish Military was not. But since the Round-Nose remained in production for some 15 years, it became a familiar item after the war ended.

Sweden may have been neutral, but as war clouds loomed in 1939, Volvo took steps to guard against the inevitable petrol shortage by manufacturing an alternative power source for its vehicles. These were called producer-gas units (otherwise known as coal-gas generators) and Volvo was able to corner the market simply by offering them ahead of anyone else, and they proved very popular in both civilian and military applications from cars to heavy trucks.

STUCK IN NEUTRAL

By 1939, Volvo was already a regular supplier of modified trucks and cars to the Swedish Defence Forces. But the first real advance into military hardware came with the TVB that could be used as a gun tractor, which went into

The LV290 came out in 1937, and its long bonnet earned it the nickname 'Long-Nose'. It was Volvo's first attempt at gaining some of Scania's monopoly of the Swedish heavy-duty market.

production in 1940. It wasn't all-wheel drive, but excellent rear-axle articulation gave it superb, off-road mobility. The subsequent TVC version was the first all-wheel drive Volvo, and it was a forward-control vehicle rather like a 101 Land Rover in appearance, except for its twin rear-axle layout. It was powered by the dry-sump FBT engine. But despite its all-wheel drive, it proved in practice to be less efficient than the TVB, mainly because of its high front-axle load. Far from being abandoned, the TVC was fitted with a larger cab and 10.6-litre (647-cubic inch) Volvo D96 diesel engine and remained in service with the Swedish Coastal Artillery Service until the 1980s.

Meanwhile, back in the war, Volvo acquired a licence from digger manufacturers Landsverk to build an armoured car that was identical at each end, and could be driven rapidly in either direction. It was equipped with a 20-mm cannon and was known as Armoured Car m/40. A more serious piece of kit was the Tank m/42, powered by the colossal A8B 22.6-litre (1379-cubic inch) V8 engine, with Volvo and Landsverk's development costs paid for by the Defence Forces.

Volvo's first regular, all-wheel drive truck was the m/42V, based on the 1939 LV130 Round-Nose model powered by a 5.6-litre (342-cubic inch) 105bhp engine. Models were designated the TLV141 and TLV142, and introduced in 1944. They were normally used as light- to medium-duty trucks, but the weirdest-looking version was the KP armoured cross-country vehicle, which resembled a flattened armadillo and was built by both Volvo and Scania-Vabis. The KP went on to see service with the UN. Another all-wheel drive personnel carrier was the more conventional-looking, light-duty TPV, fitted with an adapted 1938 PV801 taxi body and based on mechanical components sourced from the Sharp-Nose parts bins, including an 86bhp type EC side-valve engine with four-speed gearbox, supplemented by Volvo-designed drive-splitter. The TPV remained in service with the Swedish Defence Forces until the 1960s.

Volvo's own diesel engine was completed just before the war. The company was a latecomer in the diesel stakes because co-founder Gustaf Larson and his friend Jonas Hesselman simply did not rate the diesel engine. Not until 1937 did they give the go-ahead to design one: the first direct-injection diesel engine was the 9.6-litre

(586-cubic inch) VDF unit, fitted in the L395 Titan truck in 1950.

By now, the proceeds from truck sales, and the LV150 in particular, enabled Volvo to press ahead with expansion of its car range, centred around the new PV444. It was a unit-construction body (the bodyshell doubled as the chassis), a concept new to Volvo, but the PV445 used a separate chassis suitable for use as a van and estate car. The company built its own stylish Duett model in direct competition with the independent coachbuilders. The PV445 was superseded by the P210 in 1960, and this was the final flowering of the car-derived truck platform.

The production of the new L340 medium- to heavy-duty truck began in 1950, lasting until 1956. It was a conventional bonneted design with rounded contours, and was normally used as an urban delivery truck with a rigid platform or as a brewery truck, fitted with racks for holding barrels.

Back in the big league once again, the Titan L395 launched in 1951 became the replacement for the long-running Long-Nose LV290C2 in the heaviest class. It was the largest and most powerful Volvo truck ever built, and it was the first Volvo vehicle to be formally named in a national name-the-truck competition. Other trucks followed, called the Viking, Brage,

VOLVO FL6

Make: *Volvo*
Model: *FL626*
Type: *6x4, cab-over*
Engine: *Volvo in-line six-cylinder supercharged 250bhp*
Gearbox: *Volvo 9-speed synchromesh*
Suspension:
  front axle: parabolic leaf springs, shock absorbers and anti-roll bar
  rear axle: two-spring, parabolic bogie, shock absorbers, anti-roll bar, optional height control
Chassis: *parallel side frames with sheet-steel cross-members*
Brakes: *Z-cam drums, ABS optional*
GVW: *26 tonnes*

Starke, Raske, Snabbe and Trygge, but the L395 Titan remained Volvo's heavy-duty vehicle until it was succeeded by the similar-looking L495 Titan, produced from 1959 to 1965. Its conventional design endured in the N88 made between 1965 and 1973, even though every mechanical part was different. The Titan's hydraulic brakes were replaced in 1956 by compressed air

brakes, which made hauling trailers a reality. It generally saw service as a long-distance truck or in the form of a semi-trailer tractor, as a low loader, timber carrier or fuel tanker. In 1954, the 185bhp Titan Turbo was available as an alternative to the normally aspirated 150bhp version. Even though both petrol and diesel were relatively cheap and the Swedish kilometre tax on diesel

fuel was yet to come about, Volvo experimented with turbo diesels as a way to increase engine ratings without resorting to new designs. Its first turbocharged diesel engine was the TD96AS unit of 1954, and by 1961 when the 4.7-litre (287-cubic inch) engine also became available in a turbo version, all Volvo diesels were offered with a turbo as an option. The first

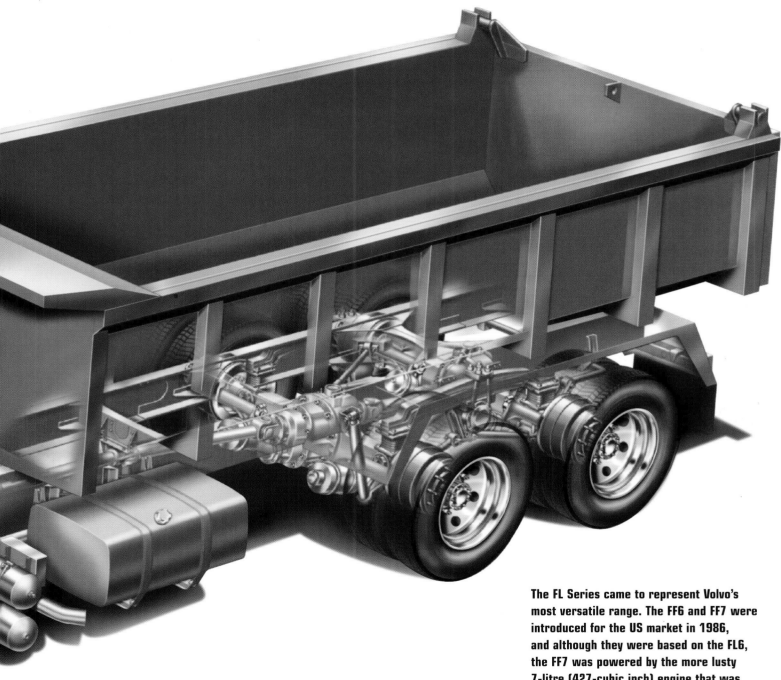

The FL Series came to represent Volvo's most versatile range. The FF6 and FF7 were introduced for the US market in 1986, and although they were based on the FL6, the FF7 was powered by the more lusty 7-litre (427-cubic inch) engine that was unavailable in Europe at the time. The FL626 pictured here as a 6x4 rigid was principally used on construction sites.

model to get a turbo as standard issue was the F89 of 1970, the last normally aspirated model was produced in 1980.

The Brage and Starke sold well in northern Europe and were used as all-purpose models, from light delivery work to construction site operations. They were supplied complete with a steel cab made by the Nyström Cab Company of Umeå in northern Sweden and remained in the Volvo range until 1965.

While most conventional Volvo trucks were fitted with an Åtvidaberg cab at the works, the new cab-over Snabbe and Trygge light-duty vans and trucks were fitted with Volvo's own design – or rather that of noted engineer Helmer Pettersson. The new units were made in steel at the Olofström body shop, and were rather upright with rounded corners and wraparound windscreen. While the chassis was traditional Volvo, (but arched over the rear axle to lower the platform height), the cab design was

unlike anything they'd previously made. The Snabbe power-plant was designated the B36AV, a 3.6-litre (220-cubic inch) overhead-valve petrol engine producing 120bhp at 4000rpm, which made it a relatively fast vehicle especially when unladen. The L420 Snabbe was in production from 1956 to 1975 as the F82S, and the more powerful Trygge L430 from 1957 to 1975 as the F83S. Diesel options were available from 1964 and 1965 respectively. The Trygge also had a sturdier chassis and rear suspension, and it was made in larger numbers than the Snabbe.

Volvo introduced another medium-heavy, cab-over model in 1962, this time with tilt facility, known as the L4751 Raske TIPTOP. Two years later it was followed by the L4851 Viking TIPTOP, based on chassis components from the conventional Raske and Viking models. The introduction of the tilting cab transformed the job of servicing the cab-over truck into a

The FL12 was introduced in 1995 and was an obvious choice for long-haul transport duties requiring a GVW of up to 40 tonnes. Choice of transmissions included manual, Geartronic and Powertronic options.

more simple operation than on a conventional vehicle. It was developed with Nyströms, which was soon to become part of Volvo as its cab-manufacturing plant. The Raske TIPTOP was fitted with a 120bhp turbocharged engine as standard. Both vehicles were designed as all-purpose trucks for light deliveries, construction site and utility work, operating anywhere that the shorter, cab-over layout was advantageous, and they included concrete mixers, fire tenders and ski-lift carriers.

Volvo attempted unsuccessfully to break into the lucrative US market in 1958, but it hadn't appreciated how different the northern European trucking requirements were from those in the USA, where distances were vast and specification regulations different. To have another shot at cracking the US market, a cab-over prototype was developed for the US market in 1964, using components from the L495 Titan, including the turbo engine. It was known as the L4951 Titan TIPTOP, and it certainly looked the part. The cab contained the most up-to-date design and safety concepts and the whole unit was mounted on rubber pads which, together with the sprung seats, minimised road vibration and enhanced driver comfort. The Titan TIPTOP's successor, the F88 went on to be hugely successful.

ALL SYSTEMS GO

In 1965, Volvo put into practice its modernisation scheme, known as System 8, because eight major components – engine, gearbox, final drive, chassis, steering, brakes, suspension and cab – were all scheduled for attention in the Master Plan, which culminated in the setting up of the Truck Division in 1969. Exterior changes to the vehicles were limited to new badges, and in all cases, the cabs and front ends were virtually unchanged.

It was the need to replace the Titan model that brought about the System 8 product-renewal programme, because some components dated back to the LV290 series built from 1937 to 1951. All models contained the number 8 in their designation, and the forward-control F88 became the mainstay of the 88 series. This opened up many overseas markets for Volvo, while the introduction of completely new engines was the most important innovation in the 88 Series. The 9.6-litre (586-cubic inch) engine proved to be ideal for the new heavy truck, while a 12-litre (732-cubic inch) unit was developed for the F89 introduced in 1970. All transmissions were developed and manufactured by Volvo, and progressive springing was introduced to enable the suspension to adapt to differences in load.

The 290bhp F88-290 was designed exclusively for the British market and produced alongside the standard model that ran the popular 260bhp TD100A

unit. The F89 of 1970 had its engine mounted at such an angle that the truck could not be built in right-hand drive, which was lucky, since Sweden had only just switched to driving on the left. So the more powerful F88-290 was required for the right-hand drive UK market.

The F88 surfaced in a different guise in 1974, when Volvo and the small Dutch truck maker Terberg made an agreement in which the Benschop-based firm would assemble two new models, one of which was based around the cab, engine and gearbox of the F88. This was designated the F1350, and the other one, the SF1350, was based on the same components as the N10, using Terberg's own chassis and suspension parts. Terberg's specialities included heavy-duty truck tractors and transporters for desert use, and ultra-narrow, refuse-collection vehicles. Having previously relied on Daf and Mercedes-Benz as component sources, Terberg turned more and more towards Volvo, and a further joint agreement was made with Volvo in 1996 to set up Special Transport Vehicle B.V. to make refuse vehicles out of Volvo components.

Back at the Frankfurt Show in 1969, the F88 was shown with a transmission splitter added to its R60 gearbox, doubling the number of ratios to 16. The driver had only to pre-select the high or low setting as appropriate, and the

actual shift was performed simply by pressing and releasing the clutch pedal.

The F89 that came out in 1970 was intended to compete with the heaviest European long-haul trucks as well as its homegrown competition. It used the 330bhp TD120A engine and was available in a single-axle drive configuration or with a tandem-drive, three-axle bogie. As well as being a heavy-duty, long-distance vehicle, it was used as an emergency fire tender, and a Swiss variant was the narrow-wing CH230. In total, over 21,000 units were built, and the F89 remained in production until 1978.

The new N-range of conventional, heavy-duty trucks that came out in 1973 was fitted with the powerful 12-litre (732-cubic inch) engine. In actual fact, it was probably more of a short-conventional range, since the truck bonnet was not as long as traditional-looking predecessors like the N86, but it had the advantage of a better load distribution on the front axle, which in turn made for greater carrying capacity. The complete front section was

One of Eddie Stobart's 1999 fleet, an FH12, featuring a full-side-opening trailer, which is a Stobart innovation. This rig is fully insulated and has a 23-tonne capacity, enough for 26 pallet loads, and can be used for ambient or chilled food distribution.

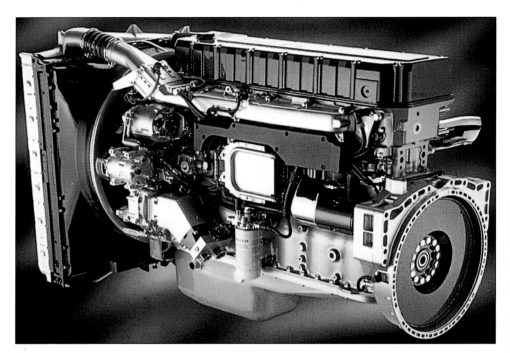

FH models were powered by new DC12C 12-litre (732-cubic inch) 16-litre (976-cubic inch) engines. The latter was first shown in 1987 in the FH16, equipped with four valves per cylinder and, later on, an electronic fuel-injection system.

VOLVO FH12 GLOBETROTTER

Make: *Volvo*
Model: *FH12 Globetrotter*
Type: *4x2, cab-over*
Engine: *Volve DC12C in-line six-cylinder, 380bhp-460bhp*
Gearbox: *Volvo VT 12-speed, two crawler gears*
Suspension:
  front axle: air absorbers and anti-roll bar
  rear axle: air as standard, optional parabolic leaf springs, shock absorbers and anti-roll bar
Chassis: *parallel side frames with sheet-steel cross-members*
Brakes: *Z-cam drums, engine brakes and ABS standard*

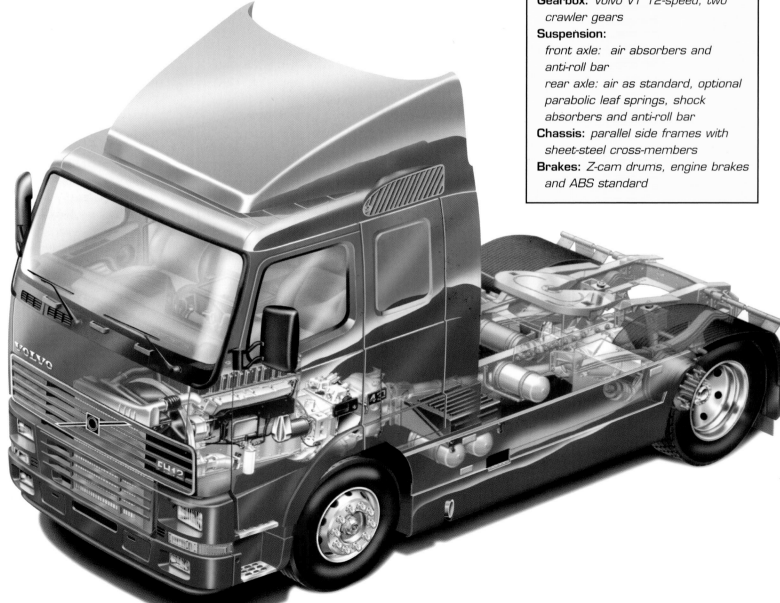

made of glass-fibre as a weight saving measure, and could be tilted forward for servicing the engine. They were based on new, steel-chassis units, with a new and stronger rear-axle arrangement known as the T-ride bogie, which appeared on the N10 and N12 in 1975. This was installed to ensure robustness in off-roading situations. These N Series models were designed for heavy haulage (often in developing countries), freight transport, construction site work, concrete and timber carriage.

Most powerful of the N Series was the N12 Intercooler, introduced in 1982 and fitted a year later with the new TD121 engine when it was exported all over the world. From 1986, all conventional trucks with 10-litre (610-cubic inch) and 12-litre (732-cubic inch) engines were available with the TD101 Intercooler engine. A completely new generation of gearboxes was introduced in 1986, and the N7 was discontinued that year, as it was becoming overshadowed by the cab-over, medium-duty FL7 model.

JOINT VENTURE
In order to market its light- and medium-duty trucks effectively outside Sweden, Volvo needed a credible, service back-up network, and this was achieved by entering into a joint venture with four other manufacturers. The so-called 'Club of Four' was formed in 1971, and consisted of Volvo, Magirus Deutz, DAF and Saviem. The partners were to develop, buy in, or manufacture the common components for a new range of 4x2 light- and medium-heavy duty models, co-ordinated from a Paris headquarters and in Volvo's case, manufactured at its Oostakker plant near Ghent in Belgium. Volvo's 'Club of Four' models were the F4 in three sizes, and the far more numerous F6, which came in six different versions. They were in production from 1975 to 1986. Although the general appearance was uniform, Volvo's offerings differed from the other three makes in respect of cab reinforcement, and it emerged that chassis components, engines, gearboxes, final drives, cab frames and interior fittings.

In sales terms the FH Series was a worldwide success, even in markets like Brazil, where conventional truck models were traditionally more popular than cab-overs. The most powerful variant was the FH12, whose output was increased to 460bhp in 1998.

The first of the 1980s generation of modern, heavy-duty trucks were the cab-over F10 and F12, introduced in Autumn 1977. They incorporated much of the development work that had been carried out on the new N-types, especially in the chassis and powertrain components. A special lightweight chassis was developed for short, twin-axle tractors, made of high-strength steel, with aluminium fuel tanks to save weight and increase carrying capacity in restricted continental markets. The new cab was supported by coil springs at both the front and rear, and for the first time a European truck was equipped with an air-conditioning

and climate-control system incorporating a dust filter. Volvo's first Intercooler model, the 230bhp TD70F unit, was the most popular engine option in the range. The F6S was designed and built at Oostakker, and used almost exclusively as delivery truck, while the F7 was used for site work, using four-axle, tandem-drive versions and long-haul deliveries. It was nominated for the Truck of the Year award in 1979. Over 35,000 units were built, with more than 9700 of the F6S.

In the wake of the expansion of the long-distance trucking business in the early 1970s, Volvo came up with a new and palatial cab design. It was known as the Globetrotter and was basically an F12 cab with full, standing headroom and luxurious interior, aimed at providing drivers with a more comfortable working environment. It was unveiled at Frankfurt in September 1979, and the Globetrotter name soon identified the

F12 truck as well as the new cab unit. Refinements included fridges and self-catering facilities, which were a boon for long-haul truckers obliged to use routes to and from the Middle East, where there was a dearth of hotels.

Volvo announced further innovations to its heaviest F-type models in 1987, including new drivetrain for the existing F10 and F12. A major event of the year was the launch of a new flagship, the F16 – designed to compete with the most powerful trucks built by Volvo's main competitors. A new 24-valve six-cylinder engine with turbocharger and intercooler powered its driving through a new 12-speed gearbox. Being relatively long, the engine limited the choice of cab to two layouts, the long sleeper version and the Globetrotter. The F16 was a natural choice, especially for long-haul operations and timber-haulage duties, as well as in undulating landscapes, where power resources and efficient engine braking came into their own.

Volvo's trump card was played in December 1980, when the once-great US marque, White Motor Corporation, went into liquidation and was offered for sale. Volvo stepped in and bought much of the company's assets for $75 million, including the White and Autocar names, the product range and three plants. These were the assembly lines at New River Valley and Ogden, and the cab works in Orrville. Now it

This 8x4 heavy duty FM12 is powered by the 420bhp version of the 12-litre (732-cubic inch) D12 six-cylinder unit, and is at home in off-road, construction site environments. The FM cab was designed for this sort of role, providing easy access and driver comfort.

had the springboard it really needed to take off in the USA, and the updated product range provided a solid foundation for Volvo to revitalise the image of White and Autocar. Serious money was invested in improving vehicle quality and reinforcing the dealer network.

Meanwhile, another major sea change was afoot. In 1986, Volvo and General Motors agreed to merge their North American heavy truck divisions, thus establishing a stronger, joint-dealer network and developing more competitive products. In October 1987, the old Autocar name was revived and used to designate the first completely new American Volvo truck. It was fitted with an aluminium cab as a weight-saving scheme, in line with an Autocar tradition that had long been neglected. The White GMC Autocar, or Volvo Autocar as it became known, was a success in sales terms, although built in small numbers because of its role as a rugged site vehicle in remoter locations like Michigan or Canada.

In 1989, the Volvo NL10 and NL12 were introduced to replace the N10 and

N12. They were impressive looking conventional models, reminiscent not only of their solid-looking predecessors but also of the American White GMC Aero models, a result of the need for minimum drag at medium and high speeds.

Volvo began to make use of its foothold in the USA by manufacturing its vehicles there. While the FE6 and FE7 were built in Belgium, the new FF42 and FF64 were produced at the Volvo GM plant at New River Valley. Only the cab and certain powertrain components were supplied from Sweden, rather than Belgium, so the FF42 and FF64 were based almost entirely on US-made components. The standard engine was a 200bhp 6.6-litre (403-cubic inch) Caterpillar 3116, although a Volvo TD73 could be specified.

Future trends were indicated by the introduction of three-axle versions of the FL6, which, in conjunction with advanced engine technology, meant smaller trucks would be able to undertake heavier duties. However, by the late 1990s the FH 'Globetrotter' heavy-duty series had become Volvo's most successful truck ever. The FH was available as a rigid platform, truck-trailer rig, a semi-trailer tractor for heavy distribution or long-haul work, or a construction site vehicle. FH models were powered by a new 12-litre (732-cubic inch) engine and a 16-litre (976-cubic inch) unit. The latter was first shown in 1987 in the FH16, equipped with four valves per cylinder and, later on, electronic fuel injection. The new 12-litre (732-cubic inch) in-line six with four valves per cylinder and an overhead camshaft was known as the D12A, and fitted in the Volvo FH12 truck and the American White GMC/Volvo trucks. Further development work saw torque levels increase in 1996 and, in 1998, the maximum output of the most powerful FH12 variant was increased to 460bhp. This was equipped with the new VEB system – or Volvo Engine Brake – which could slow the vehicle dramatically.

In sales terms, the FH series was a worldwide success, even in markets

VOLVO FM SERIES

Make: *Volvo*
Model: *FM12*
Type: *6x4/8x4 heavy-duty, construction site rigid*
Engine: *D12 12-litre (732-cubic inch) six-cylinder turbocharged, intercooled, 340, 380, 420bhp*
Gearbox: *Volvo VT2014, 6-speed Powertronic*
Suspension: *conventional leaf springs*
Chassis: *high, construction-type ladder frame*
Brakes: *Z-cam drums with ABS, exhaust brake standard, optional engine brake*
GVW: *26 tonnes*

like Brazil where conventional truck models were traditionally more popular.

The next model to be launched by Volvo was the VN, in 1996. It was the direct equivalent of the FH, but developed specifically for the US market and effectively replaced the Fl0, F12 and F16. One reason why many US makes are conventional while European models tend to be cab-over designs is because European regulations specify a maximum overall vehicle length, whereas the American rules specify the length of the load compartment, excluding the cab and bonnet. The VNs therefore were conventional in the most unfettered way, housing a virtual mobile home in the rear of the cab. While all FH trucks were powered by Volvo engines, and some VNs were fitted with the Volvo DM2 unit, most used Caterpillar, Cummins or Detroit Diesels, which accounted for the overtly generous bonnet dimensions. The 2230/VN was used almost exclusively as a semi-trailer truck-tractor with three axles, of which the rear couple were driven.

Perhaps surprisingly, most of the development work on the VN was carried out in Gothenburg, in parallel with the FH project, although much of the VN design work was done in Greensboro, using contemporary CAD/CAM and IT systems. Like the FH, the VN underwent pre-launch testing in the laboratory, on Swedish and US test tracks, and on ordinary roads. The VN was available with a choice of

four cabs, including the luxurious Volvo 770, with double bed, TV, video, refrigerator, clothes cubicle, plus full-height standing room.

Another variant was the Australian NH model, which was a hybrid based on the FH12 chassis fitted with the VN cab. It was seen as more of an allrounder than the VN, and was built in Volvo's Brisbane plant.

In 1998, Volvo launched another heavy-duty, cab-over model, the FMseries, intended for local and regional transport duties, as well as construction site work. The design was based on the successful FH model, and the FM7, FM10 and FM12 were launched in late summer 1998, bridging the gap between the FLC and FL6 light distribution trucks and the FH12 and FH16

long-haul models. Accordingly, the cab was mounted lower than the FH, and its standard equipment was comparable. Three basic cab variants ranged from a short, day cab and a long, sleeper cab to the Globetrotter version that could accommodate two bunks. This arrangement wasn't available with the tall XL cab as it wasn't designed for long-haul work over very long distances. Its air suspension meant it could be programmed to halt at different loading heights. The FM was available with three engine sizes in several different output classes, in 7.3-, 9.6-, and 460bhp 12-litre (732-cubic inch) format. Two-, three- and four-axle variants with one or more driving axles were available for construction site work, coupled with Volvo's fully automatic Powertronic transmission. The new VT2014 gearbox was designed for the FM12, and, finally, the propeller shafts were lubrication free and the FM could be equipped with central lubrication. Its scheduled service interval was 75,000km (46,600 miles), and an onboard diagnostic system monitored engine condition.

Volvo's US-built, streamlined VN conventional range was introduced in 1996, followed a year later by the Brisbane-built NH Series. The interior of the cab has all modern creature comforts and is the closest thing to a trucker's mobile home.

WHITE

Many firms that became well known in the automotive world started life in some other light industrial context. White Trucks was no exception, as the founder Thomas H. White began by making sewing machines in Orange, Massachusetts in 1859. Having relocated to Cleveland, Ohio in 1866, the production line was extended to include bicycles and roller skates. In 1900, his four sons, Thomas II, Rollin, Walter and Windsor, built their first steam-engined vehicle and pretty soon they were making three vehicles a week.

By 1906, White was offering several body styles, including fire engines, buses, mail trucks and military ambulances for the US Government, the heaviest of which were of 3-ton capacity. Annual production of passenger and commercial vehicles was up to 1500 units per year by 1906 and the White Company was formed to produce motor vehicles while the founder left to concentrate on his sewing machine business.

White's first petrol-engined vehicles appeared in 1909, equipped with French Delahaye engines. The same year White introduced its so-called Domestic Express, which was a particular form of light delivery vehicle popular with owner-operators, with a lightweight body stiffened on the outside and a hinged tail board.

The commercial model line-up was expanded to include the three-quarter-ton GBE vehicle, the 3-ton GTA and the 5-ton TC model, which was powered by a larger, four-cylinder engine and dual-chain drive. All light-duty models were fitted with pneumatic tyres and used shaft drive, while the two heaviest models used hard rubber tyres and chain drive. A typical purchase was the acquisition in 1912 of eight White buses by the Chicago Motor Transport Company, while a milestone of a different kind was an 826-mile (1329-km) crossing of Alaska in 1913 by the US Army Corps of Engineers in a three-quarter-ton White truck in 22 days.

White's 3000 model came out in 1949 and is seen here in fuel tanker mode. During the following decade it became the best-selling cab-over model in the USA. The engine was located to the rear of the cab and the floor was completely flat. It was also available with an integral sleeper.

On the mechanical front, a shift from right-hand drive to left-hand drive came about in 1914 for all White trucks. Only the 5-ton model had this layout until then, and one of White's notable products that year was a 5-ton, steel-wheel, log truck powered by the new 60bhp six-cylinder engine. In 1915, White came out with a bus built on a 1.5-ton chassis that received much acclaim for bearing more resemblance to a limousine than the street car that was still the norm. Its interior was upholstered in black leather with cork carpet on the floor.

REORGANISATION PROVES PROFITABLE

A reorganisation that took place in 1916 led to the company being renamed as the White Motor Company with $16 million capital, soon increased to $25 million, an increase that implies its burgeoning prosperity. At this point, some 800 White trucks were owned by dry goods and department stores in the USA, Canada and England, while the US Army bought no less than 18,000 1- and 3-ton White trucks for use during the First World War. By contrast, White also built open-sided, sightseeing buses for the Yellowstone National Park in 1917, based on the 20-45 TDB truck chassis and these, logically, were designated the YP-type. By 1918, White buses were in use with the municipal transit system of San Francisco, and similar vehicles were bought the following year in Ohio. White vehicles and taxis also made up much of the fleet run by the Californian Star Auto Stage Association and the Motor Transit Company of Los Angeles, although by 1918 White had virtually stopped production of passenger cars.

As chain drive was abandoned in 1919, White's heavy-duty, 3-ton and 5-ton chassis were fitted with double-reduction, two-piece shaft drive, and brakes were improved. The engines now had removable cylinder heads and the cast, vertical-tube-type radiators also had removable heads.

The new company president, Walter White, announced an operating profit

of $3,486,000 on sales of $51,998,000 for 1920. However, the 1921 recession brought a loss of $2,346,000 on sales totalling $30,320,000, which serves to indicate the dramatic, if not catastrophic financial implications of the economic downturn.

The new Model 50 was introduced late in 1921, based on the 20-45 chassis, and the four-cylinder GN engine that powered it later evolved into the GR and GRB engines. Typical of White's output at the time was the four-cylinder Model 45-D power-dump truck. White's bus chassis also used the Model 45 engine, with dual or single rear wheels shod with pneumatic tyres. A 50bhp engine powered the Model 50 chassis, and in bus format it could carry 25 passengers.

By the middle of the decade, White was producing a variety of commercial vehicles, including the three-quarter-ton Model 15, powered by a 22bhp four-cylinder GK engine and the 2-ton

Between 1951 and 1977, Freightliner's cab-over models were marketed by White – hence the joint names on the badge. This is a 1972 WF-8164, which preceded the more imposing Powerliner of 1973, which could run with 600bhp Cummins NTC600 power-plant.

Model 20 that ran with the same engine, while the Model 45 had a 50bhp engine.

The new Model 54 bus was unveiled at the American Electric Railway Association annual convention in 1926. It was also known as the Six, since it was powered by a 100bhp six-cylinder overhead-valve engine with seven main-bearings, and its sophisticated specification also included air brakes as standard. This model was also available in a four-cylinder version. A new dump truck known as the Model 52-D was also introduced in 1926, with an auxiliary transmission and gear-type hoist. The Model 51 was rated at 2.5-tons and the Model 40A at 3.5-tons. That

same year White brought out its new 2-ton Model 56, powered by a side-valve, mono-bloc, four-cylinder unit with a removable cylinder head, a centrifugal water pump and four forward gears. In 1927, White introduced the Model 57 and a 1.25-ton truck chassis, while a couple of light-duty delivery vans came out a year later, identified as the De Luxe Package Car and the Town Car Deluxe. These were based on 1- and 1.25-ton chassis and aimed at prestige buyers, with smart, two-tone paint finish and a pair of side-mounted spare wheels and special upholstery.

The carrying capacity of White buses was improved with the Model 54-A of 1928. This was achieved simply by relocating the dashboard over the rear of the engine, which was also shifted further forwards over the front axle, and in so doing the capacity was increased from 29 to 38 passengers without major chassis changes. Two additional bus models were the long wheelbase Model 65 and the intermediate Model

In the mid-1960s White, Diamond T and Reo were using the plastic Royalex cab with steel underframe for conventionals, with aluminium units for cab-over models. Typically, conditions were cramped, due to short bumper-to-back-of-cab dimensions, a legacy of overall vehicle length restrictions.

65A. Another variant in the bus range that never made it into production was an experimental hybrid built in 1927. It was powered by a regular, six-cylinder engine, which was interchangeable with two General Electric motors, driving the rear wheels.

Between 1927 and 1929, the company expanded its chassis model line from 12 to 17 models. Taking into account the weight legislation newly introduced in 22 states, White announced its Model 58, which had a GVW of 22,000lb. It was available as a dump-truck, flatbed stake platform or with van body, and was identified by a tall, narrow, aluminium radiator and round-top mudguards. White's new

heavy-duty truck ranges included the 16-ton GVW 620/640 series powered by 100bhp overhead-valve six-cylinder engines with full air brakes on all wheels on the range-topping models. White was also producing articulated semi-truck tractors such as the 12-ton Model 64T, and the US Army bought the first 6x4 model employing Timken worm-drive transmission.

In 1929, White acquired Indiana trucks, followed by a merger with Studebaker, which had itself acquired Pierce-Arrow. Indiana trucks was one of the few US makes to pioneer the use of diesel engines, while White continued to use only petrol engines throughout the 1930s, except for a few export models that were fitted with Cummins diesel units. Pierce Arrow trucks were assembled for a short time at White's plant at Cleveland, but Studebaker was obliged to relinquish its connection with Pierce-Arrow and White.

These were tough times, and White sold only 2138 vehicles in 1932. One positive event that year was the unveiling of a new 143bhp 505-cubic inch (8.3-litre) flat-twelve engine, with dry-sump lubrication and a pair of down-draught carburettors. These units were destined to be fitted in big-100-passenger capacity buses and located centrally beneath the floor. The following year, an even larger 811-cubic inch (13.3-litre) version of this engine was built for the so-called streetcar type bus, which had a wood-and-steel composite body. It was very well equipped mechanically, and incorporated power steering, power clutch and power brakes, twin starter motors and four- or five-speed, helical-gear transmission. But due to the inordinately high fuel consumption of the flat-twelve motor, the model was discontinued after four years. Meanwhile, a stylish, long-distance version, with a raised rear compartment fronted by a second windscreen, was developed for operators like the Washington Motor Coach System. More mundane buses were sold in considerable numbers to city-based transit operations in Boston, Cleveland and Los Angeles, among others.

The 700 Series trucks were restyled in 1934 with V-pattern radiators, and all vehicles over 3-tons capacity were equipped with an overhead-valve six-cylinder engine. The 12-cylinder unit was reserved for the truck known as the Model 53. The redesign was entrusted to the celebrated stylist Alexis de Sakhnoffsky, whose streamlined cabs for White's conventional trucks lasted for two decades.

The cab-over Model 731 came out in 1935, and by 1937, White's catalogue listed 48 different truck models, ranging from the three-quarter-ton Model 700P to the big, 10-ton Models 623X, 722A and cab-over 731H. Power

output was 148bhp for the Model 700K that used the White 250 engine, and up to 226bhp for the heavier units, which included 16-ton GVW dual-axle 6x4 trucks. A smaller version of the 706 was the Model 704, which served as a platform for school buses fitted with body shells made by Bender. A new range of streamlined forward control buses came out, replacing the earlier conventional models. Meanwhile, a new range of light-duty delivery van known as the Merchandor appeared in 1938, using an under-floor engine layout. This range was followed a year later by the unitary construction White Horse light-duty delivery model, which had a 2-ton capacity and, peculiarly, it was powered by a rear-mounted, detachable, air-cooled 40bhp four-cylinder Franklin engine, allied to three-speed

transmission and coil rear suspension. Considering this unusual configuration, they proved amazingly popular, with about 2000 being sold in the first year of production. They were made from 1939 to 1942, and again for a brief post-war period.

In 1939, with the outbreak of war imminent, White began building Cummins-powered 6x6 trucks for the US Army, and, up to 1945, 20,000 units of the Indiana-designed M3A1 scout cars were made. White also built 4000 half-tracks, powered by the side-valve six-cylinder engine, as well as large numbers of 4x4 truck tractors, 6x4 and 6x6 trucks powered by Cummins diesels or Hercules six-cylinder petrol engines.

After the war, White gained some useful business from civil authorities anxious to revamp ageing transit systems, and a

During the 1950s, tough restrictions were imposed on overall vehicle lengths and train weights, and White's WC22PLTD conventional was introduced in response to the new US regulations. It had shorter bumper-to-back-of-cab dimensions and a considerably lighter chassis.

large number of buses were produced accordingly. From 1948, White went back to truck building and introduced the cab-over Super Power 3000 Series, which had tilt-cabs, two-speed rear axles and five-speed transmissions.

TAKE-OVER TIME

Big news in 1951 was White's acquisition of Sterling Trucks and the merger with Freightliner. Their subsequent products were badged as Sterling-White and White-Freightliner. Two years later, White took over Autocar, a company that dated back to 1897, when it was founded by Louis and John Clark in Pittsburgh, Pennsylvania. At the turn of the century Autocar moved to Ardmore, Pennsylvania, and from 1908 it produced many thousands of trucks there until the White take-over in 1953. It was a decade in which acquisitions of famous makes came fast and furious,. Reo Motors was taken over in 1957, and the following year Diamond T also came under White's control, even though both carried on for ten years as individual makes.

Reo was founded in 1904 by Ransom Eli Olds of Oldsmobile fame and its most celebrated model of the 1920s and 1930s was the Speed Wagon – so you thought that was a rock band? – and after the White take-over, the Reo D-600 and D-700 series were offered in six models. The new E Series used Cummins diesel engines, ranging from 180bhp to 262bhp, and the cab-over

Under White's ownership, Reo's 1962 range included the conventional E500 Gold Comet with 96-in (244-cm) BBC dimension, powered by 180bhp to 262bhp 854-cubic inch (14-litre) turbocharged Cummins, Detroit Diesel or Perkins engines.

Reo AC with LPG-fuelled engine was quite successful. In 1961, Reo produced a tilt-cab highway tractor that used simple, flat sheet metal on the cab in order to minimise tooling costs, and by the following year, Reo offered eight truck models, eight highway tractors and four tandem-axle trucks, in both cab-over tilt-cab and conventional format, and in no less than 43 different configurations. There were 14 diesel engine options from Cummins, Detroit Diesel and Perkins. Reo also made the Model 29X5, a 7.5-ton 6x6 military truck also known as the Type Fl, which was identical to one built by Federal. A new swing-open bonnet was available in 1966, and Reo was still building a wide range of 6x4, 6x6 and 8x6 chassis. By this time, Diamond T and Reo specifications overlapped to such an extent that White consolidated both makes under the name Diamond-Reo in May 1967.

DIAMOND T

No truck book would be complete without at least a word or two on Diamond T, justifiably canonised since its demise as a classic marque. Founded in 1911 by C.A. Tilt, Diamond T produced a selection of trucks covering all

duties until 1951, when it dropped the light models altogether and just offered trucks from 3-ton capacity upwards. These included Models 660, 720, 722, 920, 921, 921 R, 950 and 951, the largest of which were powered by 300bhp Cummins NHRBS or 280bhp Buda 6DA5844 diesel engines. Like other truck makers, Diamond T adopted International's new comfort cab, featuring a curved windscreen and concave instrument panel, and these cabs were used sporadically until 1960. Diamond T's 1953 tilting cab-over Model 723C received the National Design Award, which was the first time an industrial product had been thus honoured. Its chief attributes were a counterbalance system that tilted the cab, and a stylistically noteworthy dip in the bottom of the side window ventilators, which was copied by a number of other trucks for many years. The same cab was also fitted by Hendrickson and International until the early 1970s. Diamond T's output rose steadily during the 1950s with volumes of approximately 3000 to 5000 units produced a year. In 1954, an agreement was made with International for joint component production, including the assembly of certain International models by Diamond T. During this decade, Diamond T also built 5-ton 6x6 trucks for the US military, powered by a 224bhp Continental R6602 engine with synchromesh transmission and six-wheel drive. The specification also included power steering and waterproofed electrical, induction and exhaust systems for driving through deep water.

Just prior to its acquisition by White, Diamond T introduced the Model 831, powered by a 239bhp Hall-Scott 590 engine that could also run in a modified form on LPG. The tilt-cab Model 911C was powered by the 300bhp Cummins diesel engine. In 1959, Diamond T trucks could be supplied with a wide choice of power units, including one four-cylinder engine, 14 six-cylinder motors and two eight-cylinder units.

In 1960, the Diamond T manufacturing plant was moved to the Reo factory at Lansing, Michigan, and two new V8 models were available, designated by horsepower as DT8-207 and DT8-235. Now, both Reo and Diamond T's conventional models used White's wider D cab with a wraparound split windscreen, and also White's other conventional R cab that had a rounded roof line and one-piece curved windscreen, as fitted on the big Model D-5000. A glass-fibre tilt-cab was standard on Models 534CG, 634CG and 734CG, while five six-cylinder and two V8 petrol engines were available, as well as four six-cylinder Cummins diesels, and one each of GM's four-cylinder and six-cylinder diesel engines.

For 1963, Diamond T introduced three new diesel models based on the R-cab, called the P2000D, P3000D, plus the tilt-cab truck-tractor Model 533CG, which used the glass-fibre cab. By 1965, the engine options included the Perkins 6-354 six-cylinder diesel, and this was the year that Diamond T launched the 1000 Series heavy-duty trucks. These included the 4x2 Model 1044 FL and the 6x2 Model 1046FL, with Caterpillar, Cummins and Detroit Diesel power units, ranging from 218bhp to 335bhp. The range expanded in 1966 to include the 1090 Series, built as the 1094 two-axle or 1096 three-axle versions. Aluminium cabs and Royalex plastic wings and bonnets could also be specified, and in 1967 a new plastic tilt cab was shared with White and Reo, known variously as the Trend HF3000 and the White 1200. In 1966, Diamond T's production stood at 4000 units, and the last Diamond T rolled off the line at the end of the model year. Diamond T's total output during its 56 years of manufacturing was a quarter of a million trucks.

Diamond-Reo continued building essentially the same trucks as previously, offering 30 models of the combined marques under a combined badge. They made three-axle 6x4 and 8x6 conventional articulated trucks, along with the more common 4x2 conventional truck-tractors. Two models used White cabs, and diesel engines up to 435bhp as well as seven petrol engines from 130bhp to 250bhp. In 1968, the cab-over model line included the CF59 compact, which used a White cab, and the 24,000-lb GVW Trend line, which was available in four models and was fitted with the plastic Royalex cab with steel under-structure. For 1968, the overall model line included conventional trucks designated C-90, C-101 and C-114, while cab-over models were

In the mid- to late-1950s, light truck styling mirrored car design to a certain extent, as demonstrated by GMC's model 370 of 1957. The national obsession with jet fighters and space rockets was reflected in the extravagant frontal treatment of bumper and radiator grille.

designated CO-50, CO-78, CF-55, (cab forward) CF-68 and CF-83 series. A 73-seater, school-bus chassis with a 225-in (571-cm) wheelbase was also available. In 1969, the CF-83 Series was fitted with a fibreglass cab, and a heavier, all-steel cab as an option. The Trend series could be specified with Cummins V6-140 engine, while the Cummins NHCT-270 custom torque unit was available with the C-90, C-114, CO-50 and CO-78. Transmissions included the Spicer 8552A or Fuller T-905J. The so-called 'Cleanaire' LPG engines were developed in 1970 to run on propane fuel, and the 8-250 V8 petrol engine joined the options list. While Gold Comet petrol engines continued to be available, diesel power gradually took over. However, White disposed of Diamond-Reo in 1971, but in the mid-1990s the firm was still producing around 150 class 8 trucks a year.

Meanwhile, back on the White production line, White's cab-over models were redesigned for 1959 with entirely different cabs that had split windscreens and twin headlights, like the Model 5464TD. By using aluminium extensively throughout its cab construction, White reduced overall unladen weight by perhaps as much as a ton. White continued to build school-bus chassis in 1960, powered either by the standard White OA-110 engine or the optional GA-130 unit. A 335bhp Cummins diesel was offered in the 6x4 cab-over Turnpike Cruiser model of 1960, and transmissions for the 5000 Series could be either Clark, Fuller or Spicer. Special 3000 Series models included 6x2 twin-steer trucks, fitted with automatic transmissions for airfield duties, while the heavy-duty Construktor 6x4 model was used for off-road and concrete mixer work.

Until the 1970s, US regulations governing overall vehicle length were in direct conflict with the need to transport long containers, and this resulted in the development of extremely short cabs to maximise the capacity of the semi-trailer. A good example of this was the White 5000, which measured only 50in (127cm) from front to back – the

bumber-to-back-of-cab (BBC) dimension. But legislation in most states altered around this period to restrict only the length of the load space, and this encouraged the production of conventional trucks with long bonnets and ample accommodation for the driver.

WESTERN STAR

Another of White's subsidiaries was Western Star, and this Division produced trucks for the western state markets at Ogden, Utah, and Kelowna, Canada. The Ogden plant was subsequently shut, but Western Star continued to build only diesel-powered conventional 6x4 and 6x6 trucks and truck tractors at its Canadian headquarters, merging with the UK truck-maker ERF in 1996.

Automotive companies have always struggled for appropriate nomenclature for their products. White pushed the boundaries of the lexicon to the limit with its Road Xpeditor 2 in the early 1970s. This low-tilt, cab-over model evolved from the Compact, and was powered by Caterpillar and Cummins six-cylinder diesel engines. The Road Commander cab-over truck-tractors were available in 4x2 or 6x4 configurations, with engines up to 450bhp and a wide choice of transmissions. The Road Boss conventional trucks had tilting glass-fibre bonnets and were available with power steering and Allison automatic transmissions. By 1975, the Construktor range was built by White's Autocar Division, which, along with output from Diamond-Reo, Freightliner and White's own models, amounted to 30,000 units. And yet, the company lost $50 million that year. As a sign of the times, White broke off its marketing deal with Freightliner in 1977, although Freightliner continued to be a subsidiary, and Diamond Reo was sold in 1977. Meanwhile, there was apparently still some mileage left in badge engineering Autocar trucks, and as the licensing agreement with Western Star continued, the three makes were advertised together under a new combined logo.

More significantly, the new factory at New River Valley, Virginia, came on

stream and superseded the Cleveland plant. But all was not well, and by 1981 White became effectively bankrupt. By the end of the year, Volvo stepped in and bought White for $51 million. The company's name was changed to Volvo White Truck Corporation, and the majority of White's 10,000 workforce kept their jobs. Two years on, Western Star became independent when Volvo White ended their sales and licensing agreement.

THE GMC MERGER

Next phase in the complicated tangle that forms the ancestry of modern day Volvo was the merger between Volvo and GMC announced in December 1986. No truck book would be complete without at least a glance at what was once the largest truck maker in the world. Founded by William Durant in 1911, the General Motors Truck Company started production in Pontiac, Michigan, and the first GMC truck was shown at the New York Auto Show in 1912.

William Durant also formed the Chevrolet Company with Louis Chevrolet, and by means of corporate leverage he managed to regain control of GM in 1916. Within a year, GMC trucks were being manufactured for the war effort, and the company produced approximately 21,000 vehicles, in the shape of light and medium trucks, ambulances, fire engines, ammunition and infantry transport. GMC's post-war production extended to farm tractors via the Sampson Tractor Division, and refrigerated transport had its beginnings in its Frigidaire Division. In 1925, GMC bought a controlling interest in Yellow Cab, which made Yellow Trucks and Yellow Coaches for GMC, from rental pioneer John Hertz.

From 1929, larger 89bhp Buick-based six-cylinder engines powered heavier GMC trucks, and in 1931, GMC took over development of the Buick engine, a unit that endured until 1960. In 1931, GMC began offering heavy-duty trucks of up to 15 tons capacity, while Chevrolet built lighter trucks in large numbers.

In 1935, GMC and Chevrolet trucks were restyled according to the general trend, with streamlined cabs and hydrovac brakes for the medium-range models, and full air brakes on top-of-the-range models. Synchromesh gearboxes were fitted and diesel engines were also used for the first time in GMC models. They were developed by General Motors and called Detroit Diesels, and were of three- or four-cylinder configuration.

At the start of the Second World War, GM's Opel Division was promptly nationalised by the Nazis in Germany, while in the USA, GMC responded by gearing up for the war effort. Probably the most prolific was the 104bhp 6x6 Army Workhorse 2.5-tonner, of which more than 500,000 units were made.

By 1950, GMC listed 20 improved models, including conventional and cab-over layouts, with seven new models for the year and capacity ratings from a half-ton to 20-tons. GMC built its 100,000th truck for the year – a 650 Diesel – in December 1950.

For 1955, GMC made major styling changes and introduced two V8

engines, while in 1957, air-suspension was tentatively introduced in the heavier trucks. This allowed the vehicle height to remain the same, regardless of payload, permitting the use of a fifth wheel and the trailer floor to be three inches lower, effectively adding 70 cubic feet in a 35-ft trailer. In 1979, the largest GMC truck was the Astro 95 cab-over model, which was virtually identical to the Chevrolet Titan, and the conventional General model was essentially the same truck as the 80,000 GVW Chevrolet Bison. By 1982, the heavy-duty, cab-over Astro 95 truck-tractors all had turbocharged, after-cooled engines, as well as more aerodynamic designs that included a patented, adjustable, roof-mounted air deflector, called the Dragfoiler, which matched the cab to various trailer heights.

The merger between Volvo White and GM officially took place in January 1988, creating problems for dealer selection, as well as putting the new company in third place in the medium and heavy truck sales tables. Prior to the merger, GM had fallen back to eighth place in 1987 behind Navistar,

Freightliner, Mack, Kenworth, Ford, Peterbilt and Volvo White. A new 530 series was announced for 1990, by which time 410bhp Volvo engines had begun to find their way into White-GMC heavy trucks. The earlier, adjustable air deflectors had given way to the Tall Integral Sleeper on White-GMC conventional trucks, in which the aerodynamic cab top was designed into the overall package, permitting an 8-ft 6-in ceiling. All former Autocar and White-GMC models became Volvos in July 1995, and the alliance with GM came to an end in 1997.

When it comes to truck brands, corporate business is ruthless, unless there are marketing expedients in retaining or reviving once-great names. Thus, when Volvo dropped the Autocar and White names in 1996, these two classic marques disappeared.

The merger with White revitalised GM and it began to penetrate the medium-duty market with its C7 Hot Shot models. However, the marriage was anulled in 1997. The trucks shown here are the 7500 series conventional and cab-over of 1999.

PICTURE CREDITS

Mack Trucks, Inc: 6-7, 129, 131, 134 (both), 135, 136-137
Quadrant: 9, 25, 54, 70-71, 88-89, 90, 114-115, 116(t), 154-155, 160, 163, 164
TRH Pictures: 10-11, 12, 24, 26, 46, 47, 49, 66, 80, 81, 116 (b), 121, 138, 156, 157, 166, 167, 171
John Tipler: 14, 44-45, 51, 53, 54-55
ERF Ltd: 15, 19, 38-39, 40, 41, 42
MAN Truck & Bus UK Ltd: 16, 91 (both)
Eddie Stobart Ltd: 17, 93, 161
Mercedes-Benz (United Kingdom) Ltd: 22-23, 27, 30, 32
Mike Schram: 37, 43, 48, 58-59, 64-65, 68, 69, 102, 165, 168, 169, 170, 173
Sterling Trucks: 56, 57
Bryan Jarvis: 60, 63, 83
Hino Motors Ltd: 61, 62
IVECO: 72, 73, 74, 75, 76, 77, 78, 79, 82
Oshkosh Truck Corporation: 94-95, 96, 96-97, 98, 98-99
Kenworth Truck Company: 100-101, 103
Peterbilt Motors Co: 106, 107
DAF Trucks: 110, 111, 112-113, 113
DAF Museum: 114
Paccar Inc: 117
Renault V.I: 118-119, 120, 122, 123, 127, 128, 130-131
Fondation de L'Automobile Marius Berliet – Lyon – France: 126
Scania CV AB: 140-141, 142, 143 (both), 144, 145, 148 (both), 149, 150 (both), 151, 152, 153
Volvo Truck and Bus Limited: 162 (t)

ARTWORK CREDITS

Julian Baker: 12-13, 18-19, 20, 34-35, 36, 50, 52, 84-85, 86-87, 92-93, 104-105, 108, 125
Mike Fuller: 28-29 (all), 31, 33, 67, 109, 132-133, 146, 158-159, 162 (b)